Mystery and Promise

A Theology of Revelation

John F. Haught

A Michael Glazier Book
THE LITURGICAL PRESS
Collegeville, Minnesota

NEW THEOLOGY STUDIES
General Editor: Peter C. Phan
*

Editorial Consultants:
Monika Hellwig
Robert Imbelli
Robert Schreiter
*

Volume 2: Mystery and Promise

A Michael Glazier Book published by The Liturgical Press

Cover design by David Manahan, O.S.B.

1   2   3   4   5   6   7   8   9

Library of Congress Cataloging-in-Publication Data

Haught, John F.
    Mystery and promise : a theology of revelation / John F. Haught.
        p.   cm. — (New theology studies ; v. 2)
    "A Michael Glazier book."
    Includes bibliographical references.
    ISBN 0-8146-5792-3
    1. Revelation. 2. Mystery. 3. God—Promises. I. Title.
II. Series.
BT127.2.H35   1993
231.7'4—dc20
                                         92-46908
                                            CIP

Contents

To Paul and Martin

Editor's Preface

This series entitled *New Theology Studies,* composed of eight volumes, is an attempt to answer the need felt by professors and students alike for scholarly yet readable books dealing with certain Catholic beliefs traditionally associated with dogmatic theology. The volumes treat of fundamental theology (revelation, the nature and method of theology, the credibility of the Christian faith), trinitarian theology, christology, ecclesiology, anthropology, and eschatology.

There has been, of course, no lack of books, published singly or in series, both in this continent and elsewhere, which are concerned with these central truths of Christianity. Nevertheless, there is room, we believe, for yet another series of texts on systematic theology, not because these offer entirely novel insights into the aforementioned teachings, but because it is incumbent upon Christians of every age to reflect upon their faith in light of their cultural and religious experiences and to articulate their understanding in terms accessible to their contemporaries.

Theology is traditionally described as faith in search of understanding, *fides quaerens intellectum.* The faith to which the contributors to this series are committed is the Christian faith as lived and taught by the (Roman) Catholic Church. It is, however, a faith that is ecumenically sensitive, open to ways of living and thinking practiced by other Christian communities and other religions. The understanding which the series seeks to foster goes beyond an accumulation of information, however interesting, on the Christian past to retrieve and renew, by means of the analogical imagination, the Christian Tradition embodied in its various classics. In this way, it is hoped, one can understand afresh both the meaning and the truth of the Christian beliefs and their multiple interconnections. Lastly, the contributors are convinced that theology is a never-ending quest for insights into faith, a *cogitatio fidei.* Its ultimate purpose is not to provide definite and definitive answers to every conceivable problem posed by faith, but to gain an understanding, which will always be imperfect and fragmentary, of its subject, God the incomprehensible Mystery. Thus, theology remains an essentially unfinished business, to be taken up over and again in light of and in confrontation with the challenges found in every age. And our age is no exception, when, to cite only two examples, massive poverty and injustice structured into the present economic order, and the unprecedented meeting of religious faiths in new contexts of dialogue, have impelled theologians to reconceptualize the Christian faith in radical terms.

Contrary to some recent series of textbooks, *New Theology Studies* does not intend to advocate and advance a uniform or even unified viewpoint. Contributors are left free to present their own understanding and approach to the subject matter assigned to them. They are only requested to treat their themes in an integrating manner by situating them in the context of Tradition (highlighting their biblical, patristic, medieval, and modern developments), by expounding their theological meaning and function in light of current pronouncements of the Magisterium, by exploring their implications for Christian living, and by indicating possible different contemporary conceptualizations of these doctrines. The goal is to achieve some measure of comprehensiveness and balance by taking into account all the important issues of the subject matter under discussion and at the same time exhibit some thematic unity by means of a consistent method and a unifying perspective.

The eight volumes are intended primarily as resource books, "launching and landing bases," for upper-division theology courses in Catholic colleges and seminaries, but it is hoped that they will be useful also to people—priests, permanent deacons, religious, and educated laity, inside and outside of the Roman Catholic communion—interested in understanding the Christian faith in contemporary cultural and ecclesial contexts. We hope that these volumes will make a contribution, however modest, to the intellectual and spiritual life of the Christian Church as it prepares to enter its third millennium.

Peter C. Phan
The Catholic University of America

PART ONE

1

The Gift of an Image

Christian faith is a response to the "revelation" of a divine mystery. It is the obedient embracing of a promise by God given to the world first through Israel and then through Jesus Christ and the Church. The word "revelation" is derived from the Latin word *revelare* (literally, to remove a veil). And although we must avoid basing a theology of revelation on the etymology of this term, we may at least say that in some sense "revelation" entails a disclosure. It is the "word" of God, the communication of a promising and saving mystery. In the final analysis, the substance of the revelatory word of promise is the gift of God's own self to the world.

In traditional Catholic systematic theology, revelation is generally understood as the *locutio Dei,* the "speech of God." Although to Augustine it implied a divine "illumination" of our souls, it has usually meant God's passing on to us propositional truths to which we would otherwise have no access. A standard traditional definition of revelation is "the communication of those truths which are necessary and profitable for human salvation . . . in the form of ideas."[1] Alternatively, revelation has been defined typically as "direct discourse and instruction on the part of God." It is "an act by which God exhibits to the created mind his judgments in their formal expression, in internal or external words."[2]

To many believers, such definitions are still sufficient. But for some time now, Christian theologians have questioned the adequacy of this rather "propositional" understanding of revelation. In contemporary the-

---

[1] From P. Schanz's *Apologie des Christentums* (1905), quoted by Werner Bulst, *Revelation,* trans. by Bruce Vawter (New York: Sheed & Ward, 1965) 18.

[2] B. Goebel, *Katholische Apologetik* (1930), as quoted by Bulst, 18.

ology, both Catholic and Protestant, the concept of revelation has come to refer more radically to the gift of God's own self to the world. Although even the First Vatican Council stated that it has pleased God to reveal *himself* and the eternal decrees of his will to the human race (Denz. 1785),[3] the Protestant theologian Paul Althaus is quite correct in pointing out that Catholic theology of the past has had an overly intellectualized and depersonalized notion of revelation.[4] Today, this situation has dramatically changed. A new reading of the Bible, the Church Fathers and other theological sources, and perhaps especially the documents of the Second Vatican Council have been moving Catholic theology toward a new consensus about the nature of revelation. More and more theologians propose that the content of revelation is fundamentally the very reality of the divine self. In this book, we shall explore some of the implications of this development in the theology of revelation.

In the Bible, God's self-revelation comes in the form of *promise*.[5] Although the formal theological notion of revelation is not the subject of explicit discussion in the Scriptures, it is substantively present in the many shapes that God's promise takes in the biblical stories. One specific type of revelatory promise, that of Jesus' post-Easter appearances to his disciples, is the foundation of Christian faith and hope.[6] Christians believe that a special "promissory" revelation from God lies at the origin of their common faith. Promissory events in its history have summoned the Christian community, the Church, into being. The revelation of a great promise is what gives the people of God their sense of origin, identity, and future destiny. And for all who place their trust in it, this revelation illuminates reality in an ever new and surprising way.

Christianity, however, is not the only religious tradition based on a sense of revelation. Indeed, in a broad sense at least, most religions may be interpreted as responses to the revelatory disclosure of a sacred mystery. Any Christian reflection on the idea of revelation, such as we shall undertake in this book, now has to be situated in a context shaped by our growing appreciation of the plurality of religious revelations. However distinct Christian revelation may appear to be, it is still linked to the long human

[3]Bulst, 23.

[4]Bulst, however, thinks that Althaus' observations are unjustified (22).

[5]From the perspective of biblical theology it was especially Gerhard von Rad who brought this theme of revelation as promise to the front. *Old Testament Theology*, 2 vols., trans. by D. M. G. Stalker (New York: Harper & Row, 1962–65). But it has been especially Jürgen Moltmann who has made it a central theme in contemporary systematic theology. *Theology of Hope*, trans. by James W. Leitch (New York: Harper & Row, 1967).

[6]Moltmann, *Theology of Hope*, 139–229.

search for meaning and mystery upon which our earliest human ancestors embarked as long ago as the Old Stone Age. We cannot leave out of our considerations the broader religious context from which Christianity historically emerged and within which it now has to understand itself. In order to appreciate any possible uniqueness of a Christian revelation we must seek to locate it within the context of the wider world of religion.

The Problem of Revelation

However, we cannot ignore the fact that the very possibility of *any* kind of religious revelation has been seriously challenged by modern thought. While we shall be concerned in this book primarily with the *nature* of revelation, we must also honestly acknowledge that today there is much doubt about whether what we call "revelation" has actually happened and if the notion has anything to do with reality. In former ages, divine revelations were seemingly commonplace. Even the dreams of ordinary people were interpreted as messages from the gods. Shamans, seers, prophets, ecstatics, and other mediators of the "other world" abounded. Cultures devoid of a sense of revelatory phenomena were rare indeed. But the assumption that nature, history, and human consciousness can be abruptly perforated by sacral manifestations from a realm beyond the ordinary has been rejected by modern skepticism. Even though popular culture is still open to supernormal appearances from the "beyond," many sincere seekers of truth now scoff at the very idea of revelation. That a sacred or mysterious realm of alternative reality can intervene in and startlingly illuminate our profane or secular experience seems unbelievable to many. And that we should base our lives on the alleged authority of any such apparently extraneous intrusions, rather than on empirically and publicly testable experience available to all, often seems preposterous.

The following quotation from Paul Davies, a well-known contemporary scientist and writer, illustrates the negative light in which the idea of revelation is often perceived today:

> The scientist and theologian approach the deep questions of existence from utterly different starting points. Science is based on careful observation and experiment. . . .
>
> In contrast, religion is founded on revelation and received wisdom. Religious dogma that claims to contain an unalterable Truth can hardly be modified to fit changing ideas. The true believer must stand by his faith whatever the apparent evidence against it. This 'Truth' is said to be communicated directly to the believer, rather than through the filtering and refining process of collective investigation. The trouble about

revealed 'Truth' is that it is liable to be wrong, and even if it is right other people require a good reason to share the recipients' belief.[7]

Even if Davies' position is an enormous caricature, it shows clearly that in the arena of public and, especially, academic discourse we can no longer take the idea of revelation for granted. Revelation has become a problematic notion even to some theologians. Indeed, academic theologians have at times proposed that we drop it altogether. It seems to them, no less than to scientific thinkers, to be magical and superstitious. Stanley Hauerwas, a widely respected contemporary theologian, writes: "The very idea that the Bible is revealed . . . is a claim that creates more trouble than it is worth."[8] And Ronald Thiemann, who disagrees, nevertheless observes that Hauerwas' statement

> captures well a growing consensus among contemporary theologians. . . . Despite the prominence of doctrines of revelation in nearly every modern theology written prior to 1960, very little clarity has emerged regarding the possibility and nature of human knowledge of God. Indeed, most discussions of revelation have created complex conceptual and epistemological tangles that are difficult to understand and nearly impossible to unravel. A sense of revelation-weariness has settled over the discipline and most theologians have happily moved to other topics of inquiry.[9]

Both Hauerwas and Thiemann are speaking, though with differing convictions, out of a Protestant context. Catholic theology (as well as most Protestant theology), on the other hand, has not experienced the same degree of disillusionment with the notion of revelation. In fact, it has kept the theme very much at the forefront of its systematic theology. One of the documents of the Second Vatican Council, *Dei Verbum,* was devoted especially to the topic of revelation, and it has encouraged theologians to deepen and broaden their interpretations of it.

But is this persistence in affirming the importance of revelation theology perhaps another sign of Catholic theology's not yet having caught up with the times? Is it a signal of its unwillingness to adhere to current academic standards? Whatever answer one may give, we may at least acknowledge that Catholic theology cannot afford to ignore the problems that have given rise to the disaffection with revelation theology in much contemporary secular and Christian thought. For Catholic thinkers also

[7]Paul Davies, *God and the New Physics* (New York: Simon & Schuster, 1983) 6.

[8]As quoted by Ronald Thiemann, *Revelation and Theology* (Notre Dame: University of Notre Dame Press, 1985) 1.

[9]Ibid.

dwell within the same general intellectual and cultural world out of which Hauerwas and Thiemann are writing. And so, if their theology is to speak to our present situation, it must show that it is aware of the problematic character of the idea of revelation. And it must undertake some response to the ways of thought that make the notion of revelation seem implausible or pointless to other contemporary theologians. In the past whenever Catholic theology failed to take into account the issues raised by current intellectual developments (such as the rise of science, the Enlightenment and historical criticism) it began to lag behind the times and thereby lost a great opportunity for growth. It then became irrelevant to many cultured individuals. The same may happen to its theology of revelation unless it addresses the ideas that provoke even some present-day theologians to dismiss it as an obsolete notion.

What are these ideas that lead some theologians to question the very possibility of revelation? Although there are many, they all come to a head in the general mood of suspicion, fostered by our universities, that symbolic or metaphoric expression, the primal language of faith, is incapable of putting us in touch with a transcendent world. Modernity has given birth to the widespread conviction that religious symbolism cannot truly reveal or disclose anything other than our own secret wishes and desires. And now in some of its so-called postmodern variants, contemporary thought portrays symbols, and all of language for that matter, as a completely self-referential play of discourse devoid of any transparency to transcendent reality. Rationalism and scientism (belief in the epistemological supremacy of reason and especially of scientific method) produced the conjecture, in some quarters at least, that the symbolic/mythic/poetic/narrative modes of expression employed by all the religions are perhaps nothing more than our own subjective projections or constructs, and not representations of an independent sacral reality.

Such skepticism forces us to ask whether any sort of revelation can withstand the scrutiny of "enlightened" consciousness. And now another kind of suspicion has been superimposed upon rationalism and scientism. It suggests that all religion is little more than a covering up of childish desires or oppressive ideology. Karl Marx, Friedrich Nietzsche, and Sigmund Freud, to name the most prominent representatives of this suspicion, all taught that religion, including the idea of revelation, is an expression of weakness, wishful thinking, or resentment.[10]

As we move forward in our study of revelation we shall keep the fact of modern skepticism in mind. For the moment, though, it is sufficient to observe how deeply it has influenced contemporary theology, leading

---

[10]See Paul Ricoeur, *The Philosophy of Paul Ricoeur*. Ed. by Charles Reagan and David Stewart (Boston: Beacon Press, 1978) 213-22.

at times to utter embarrassment about the idea of revelation. Modernity has brought forth much that is good and true. To repudiate it entirely would be to dismiss a great deal that our religious traditions themselves would fully endorse. But modernity, like other periods of history, is ambiguous. In addition to its humanizing and liberating developments it has also produced some beliefs that themselves may now need to be critically examined.

Among these modern beliefs is the suspicious attitude in which symbolic expression is now held by philosophy, psychology, sociology, anthropology, literary criticism, and theology. Much of this suspicion of symbols is very helpful, for it brings to our attention the childishness, escapism, resentfulness, and oppressiveness that have at times become attached to religious consciousness. What Paul Ricoeur calls the "hermeneutics of suspicion" needs to become a component of all our theologizing today.[11] However, suspicion has always been an essential aspect of authentic religion. The religious motif of silence (the apophatic aspect of religions) has had the precise purpose of discouraging us from clinging to our religious symbols in so possessive a way that they no longer disclose the mystery of reality. Thomas Merton once wrote that our ideas of God usually tell us more about ourselves than about God.[12] He and others who are sensitive to the apophatic side of religion see the role of silence in religious worship as an admission of the inadequacy of any of our religious images. But today the theme of silence and suspicion has been wrested from the religious matrix out of which it originally appeared in human history. It has turned back, vengefully at times, upon the whole world of religion with an almost nihilistic repudiation of the revelatory power of symbols. Isolated from its sacramental nursery, the "way of silence" has now become the "way of suspicion" iconoclastically declaiming the revelatory possibilities of *all* symbolic expression.

Contemporary theology has not been untouched by this suspicion. And if it is to be faithful to the silent or apophatic aspects of humanity's cumulative religious wisdom, it must appropriate aspects of suspicion as part of its method. However, as long as we go to the extreme of doubting altogether the disclosive power of symbols we shall not be able to construct viable theologies of revelation. For symbols remain the primary medium of revelation. If they are constantly being debunked, then the idea of revelation is indeed in serious trouble. Therefore, a theology of revelation has to be concerned with the question whether religious symbols are only our imaginative human constructions, as theologian Gordon Kaufmann as-

[11]Ibid.

[12]Likewise the thirteenth-century mystic, Meister Eckhart, is said to have prayed: "God deliver me from God."

serts,[13] or whether they can be taken as interruptive, revelatory mediators of a mystery of being and new life that lies beyond our own power to penetrate.

In Chapter 11 we shall return explicitly to a discussion of how we may address the doubt that has arisen regarding the likelihood of revelation. But throughout our entire inquiry we shall keep an eye on its problematic character. If we are to construct a plausible theology of revelation for our time we cannot ignore the reasons why many intellectuals and even some theologians now question its very possibility. But first we must attempt to formulate the nature and meaning of revelation. We cannot make a case for its possible truthfulness until we have attained some clarity as to what it is we are talking about. This will be the primary task of the following chapters.

The Cosmic Setting Of Revelation Theology

Theology is now required, both by the sacramental emphasis of our religious traditions and also by our growing environmental crisis, to bring the cosmos back into the theological picture, and perhaps even to give it primacy over history, as the fundamental context for a theology of revelation. Thomas Berry has even proposed that we must now look at the universe, within whose unfolding our human and religious histories are only a very recent chapter, as the "primary revelation."[14] And Jürgen Moltmann, likewise, has pressed the case for situating the historical dimension of revelation within the more encompassing notions of creation and cosmos.[15]

We live in an age of science, astrophysics, evolutionary biology, and information. These cumulatively have given us an entirely new picture, or story, of the universe, and we are obliged to treat the notion of revelation in terms that relate it to these developments. The perennial human questions concerning what this universe is all about are being raised in a new and striking way today. Does cosmic evolution have any direction

---

[13]See Gordon Kaufmann, *An Essay on Theological Method* (Missoula: Scholars Press, 1975).

[14]See Thomas Berry, *The Dream of the Earth* (San Francisco: Sierra Club Books, 1988) 120. See also the articles by and about Thomas Berry collected in *Cross Currents* XXXVII, Nos. 2 & 3 (1988) 178–239. Also see Anne Lonergan and Caroline Richards, ed., *Thomas Berry and the New Cosmology* (Mystic, Conn.: Twenty-third Publications, 1987). For a popular introduction to some of Berry's ideas see Brian Swimme, *The Universe is a Green Dragon* (Santa Fe: Bear & Co., Inc, 1986.)

[15]Jürgen Moltmann, *God in Creation*, trans. by Margaret Kohl (San Francisco: Harper & Row, 1985).

to it? How does our species fit into the evolutionary picture? How are we to understand our own existence now that it has become clearer than ever that we too are part of an evolving world? What sense can we make of the apparent randomness, struggle, and impersonal natural selection that seem to be the main ingredients of evolution? Why did the universe take fifteen billion years to bring forth conscious beings here on earth? What sense can we possibly make of the immense size of the universe, in which so far we have no evidence that other intelligent life exists? And what if intelligent or spiritual life does exist elsewhere? Then what is the meaning of Israel's election or of the redemptive significance of Jesus of Nazareth with respect to these hypothetical cosmological conjectures?

Scientifically informed people are asking such questions today, and their inquiries should not remain off-limits to our theologies of revelation. Working along with science, theology is obliged at least to attempt some response to them from the point of view of whatever intelligibility is discerned by faith in revelation. From the beginning, Christians have been called upon to give an account of their faith in terms of contemporary modes of thought (for example, 1 Peter 3:15). Questions about the universe and our place in it enchant more and more people today, but revelation theology remains pretty much mute with respect to them. Yet if our theologies of revelation cannot respond—in some fashion at least—to the big questions of our time, then they will quite rightly be ignored by contemporary culture.

Of course, revelation cannot and should not be made to address any of the questions that science is in principle capable of answering by itself. This, as we shall see, would be a desperate misuse of the concept of revelation, which is not in the business of handing out otherwise accessible information about the world. But if we fail to relate revelation to the most interesting, and especially the ultimate or "limit" questions that arise out of the scientifically informed inquiries of many people today, it will eventually become a lost notion for all of us. Hence, with all due respect to the autonomy of science, we must seek to situate revelation in terms of the important cosmological issues of today. We must not allow the content of faith and theology to intrude into the sphere of scientific investigation. But we may certainly relate their substance to the scientific understanding of the cosmos. In fact, we shall even argue that revelatory knowledge not only does not contradict or interfere with scientific knowledge, but that it actually promotes the autonomous pursuit of science along with other disciplines.

The content of revelation must speak to our deepest questions about the universe. Among these questions today are those raised by our global environmental situation. What relevance might revelation have to the new flurry of issues raised by the environmental crisis? Does revelation have anything substantive to offer us as we rethink our relationship to nature? For many sensitive people this is the most urgent question of all today, and they often look in vain to theology for some assistance. The perceived environmental ineptitude of theology and religious education is accentuated now by the many accusations, often well-founded, that "revealed" religions are themselves partly responsible for promoting ideals of cosmic homelessness that have set us adrift from, and made us indifferent to, nature. A theology of revelation must now pay special attention to such observations as these. As we shall see, revelation cannot be construed in such a way as to provide a specific environmental policy (any more than we can expect it to offer us a definitive social or economic program). Revelation does not work that way. However, if it has a truly worthwhile content, we may at least look to it for some illumination about the fundamental nature of the universe, as well as for some vision of the natural world and our relation to it that would provide good reasons why we should care for it at all.

Without entering into the intricacies of scientific discussion itself, the present book's reflections on the meaning of revelation will presuppose the framework of the new cosmology that has been emerging for some time now out of contemporary physics, astrophysics, and biology. We shall take for granted the evolutionary character of the cosmos as well as other discoveries of modern science. If our theology is to be taken seriously by scientists and other intellectuals, it is imperative that we frame our theories of revelation in terms that reflect our living in the universe as it is described and understood by the best of contemporary science.

For the past century, the idea of revelation has usually been tied closely to the notions of history or existential subjectivity, seldom to cosmology. But in its primal expressions, revelation was always linked in some way to nature, usually without its devotees being self-conscious about it. The revelations of all the religions have a sacramental character, in that they come to expression in terms of correlative views of the cosmos. Recognizing, quite correctly, that we today cannot *literally* accept the original cosmological clothing of biblical and other religions, recent theology has gone to the extreme of "de-cosmologizing" revelation altogether. This uprooting of revelation from any cosmic setting whatsoever is disastrous for our theologies. For it ends up leaving the universe, and that eventually means us too (since we belong to nature more than it belongs to us), out of the theological picture.

For example, in order to salvage the "core" of Christian faith for the scientifically informed, Rudolf Bultmann argued that revelation has to do primarily with God's address to the hidden subjectivity and inner freedom of each person. His theology gives the impression that nature, considered independently of us humans, is in no significant way revelatory of God. God acts in the world, of course, but primarily through the medium of our privately transformed selfhood. Bultmann's existentialist theology with its penetrating portrayal of theological method and hermeneutics (the art of interpretation) was an important breakthrough in theology, and there is no need here to be excessively critical of the work of this brilliant theologian. We are all indebted to him. Nevertheless, we must question the theological legitimacy of his tying the idea of revelation so closely to human freedom, or for that matter to human history, without connecting it also to an updated view of nature. Perhaps Bultmann himself was not in a position to make such a connection, but now the resources are available for us to re-cosmologize Christian revelation. We shall sketch the outlines of such a task in Chapter 8.

History and the Self

Although in one sense cosmology provides a more encompassing framework than history for a theology of revelation, the conscious awareness of a revelation of God comes into the universe through individual selves embedded in human society and its history. In the prophetic religions, the revelation of God's promise came first to Abraham and to Israel. Out of this promise, a sense of reality as history arose. For that reason, our theology has become accustomed to thinking of revelation in terms of God's interventions in human history. Therefore, the notion of a cosmic revelation has been subordinated and even suppressed. While revelation holds that God created the world, the theme of creation has been subordinated to that of the history of a redemption that takes place in order to set right what happened as the result of the so-called Fall. An important trend in recent theology is now asking whether the emphasis on our fallenness and sinfulness has made us focus so intensely on the history of redemption that we have forgotten the foundational doctrine of creation and, along with it, the need for attention to the fundamental goodness and beauty of the cosmos.[16]

However, it is no longer necessary for us to keep the themes of cosmology and redemptive history apart. For now we are coming to see more clearly than ever before that the universe itself is an enormously adventurous and revelatory *story*. Because of its own historical character we may now link nature more explicitly to the story of revelation. Science itself is providing solid reasons for our envisaging the cosmos as historical. And in doing so, it challenges us to bring the theme of historical revelation into deeper synthesis with cosmology.

[16]See especially Matthew Fox, *Original Blessing* (Santa Fe, New Mexico: Bear & Co.).

Finally, a theology of revelation will be of little interest to us if it fails to address the individual's personal search for significance. The surprising and even shocking content of revelation must address us in our solitary existence, at those levels of our being that the categories of history and cosmology cannot adequately cover. Even though revelation is offered to the entire universe, at the human level of cosmic emergence it is obviously in the transformation of our own personal lives that it is most vividly experienced. Contemporary theology has rightly emphasized the need to de-privatize revelation, to display its power in socio-political transformation. We shall highlight this feature of revelation theology in our discussions of church (Chapter 7) and history (Chapter 9). However, the very notion of revelation would never have arisen were it not for the fact that its substance is experienced intimately and palpably by especially sensitive individuals. Because awareness of revelation is always mediated to a people by way of individual experience, in the case of Christianity by Jesus' intimate experience of God as "abba," a study of it must examine in some detail what happens to the *self* as it is shaped by faith in revelation. This will be our topic in Chapter 10.

An examination of the meaning of revelation for the individual self, however, looks simultaneously to the themes of mystery, cosmology, and history. For as individuals we are not isolated from the network of spiritual, historical, and cosmic relationships that shape our personal existence. Even in the depths of our aloneness we are still a unique synthesis of sacred, natural, and social occurrences. Thus the question of the meaning of our individual lives is interwoven with those concerning the meaning of mystery, cosmos, and history. A theology of revelation must constantly keep this ecology in mind.

Theological Method

If theology is to produce appropriate results, it must follow a method. And like any other discipline, it needs to become self-conscious about its method. As Rudolf Bultmann puts it, method is nothing other than a way of putting questions.[17] Being methodical means being careful and critical about the kinds of questions we address to the sources of our theology. This is also the basic principle of "hermeneutics," the process of interpreting texts.

Theology is a hermeneutical process in that it constantly seeks to address questions to and interpret classic texts that traditionally shape a

[17]Rudolf Bultmann, *Jesus Christ and Mythology* (New York: Charles Scribner's Sons) 49–50.

religious tradition.[18] A theology of revelation has to look to those classic texts, persons, symbols, and events in which the divine promise is embodied. For Christian theology these sources include especially the Bible, but also the deposit of interpretations of revelation known as tradition. In a critical fashion, theology sets up a kind of conversation between our situation and the revelatory texts. It has to be very conscientious about the kinds of questions it addresses to the classic sources, for it is quite possible to ask the wrong questions and thus miss the real substance of the significant texts.

Theology must avoid reducing these sources to what responds only to our carelessly formed interrogations. It also has to strive to maintain a posture of attending in openness to the texts in order to catch their challenging "otherness." Nevertheless, the first step in any theological formulation of the meaning of the classic sources *for us* is that of critically clarifying the questions that arise out of our own situation.[19] The situation in which we exist may be pictured as a series of four concentric circles going from more encompassing to less: mystery, cosmos, history, and the self. Our method is the venerable one of *correlating* the questions arising from an analysis of our experience within each circle with the answers that revelation appears to offer to these questions. Obviously, our formal understanding of these four circles that make up our situation will already have been shaped to a great extent by a history and tradition influenced by the classic texts and events associated with the biblical revelation. Thus our theological method is bound to be somewhat circular and "impure." None of us are so untouched by the biblical stories of God's self-disclosure that our understandings of mystery, nature, history, and self are innocent of the interpretations provided of them by the impact of biblical faith and doctrinal traditions on our culture and language. And yet there is always such a wide margin of unintelligibility in our present experience of these four circles that a fresh conversation with illuminative texts and sources, in this case those of biblical faith, is always in order. Thus a method of correlating our sincerest questions with the classic

---

[18]David Tracy states, "What we mean in naming certain texts, events, images, rituals, symbols and persons "classics" is that here we recognize nothing less than the disclosure of reality we cannot but name truth. . . ." In these classics, he goes on to say, we find a "disclosure of reality in a moment that must be called one of 'recognition' which surprises, provokes, challenges, shocks and eventually transforms us; an experience that upsets conventional opinions and expands the sense of the possible; indeed a realized experience of that which is essential, that which endures." *The Analogical Imagination* (New York: Crossroad, 1981) 108.

[19]See Paul Tillich, *Systematic Theology* Vol. I (Chicago: University of Chicago Press, 1951) 8, 30-31, 34, 59-66; and David Tracy, *Blessed Rage for Order* (New York: Seabury, 1975) 45ff.

sources of revelation seems to be the most fruitful way to approach theology.[20]

The Gift of An Image

What do we discern in the classic sources of revelation? H. Richard Niebuhr suggests that these sources offer to faith, among many other rich elements, the gift of an *image* that makes intelligible what would otherwise remain unintelligible: "By revelation in our history we mean . . . that special occasion which provides us with an image by means of which all occasions of personal and common life become intelligible."[21] In the surrender of faith we allow ourselves and our consciousness to be shaped by a set of revelatory images and stories. Revelation is comparable to the surprising appearance in science of imaginative models that, all in a flash, illuminate the world of nature and tie together previously unexplained enigmas in a fresh way. The best of such models also promise further discovery and richer syntheses in the future. An imaginative breakthrough in science has the extraordinary capacity to bring previously unreachable aspects of nature abruptly within the explanatory ambit of a single integrating picture or model. Newton's theory of gravity is one such example. More recently, Einstein's theory of relativity, Max Planck's discovery of the quantum, and other developments in contemporary physics have gathered together widely diverse natural occurrences into tighter unity and surprising coherence that leads to even further discovery. Science now looks forward to an elegantly simple formula capable of illuminating the in-

[20]This is true in spite of the critiques of the correlation method made by Karl Barth and more recently in the nuanced discussion by the so-called "Yale school" of interpretation. See George A. Lindbeck, *The Nature of Doctrine* (Philadelphia: The Westminster Press, 1984); also, in a Catholic context, Francis Schüssler Fiorenza, *Foundational Theology* (New York: Crossroad, 1985) 276–84. Any theology that strives to be relevant to our situation practices a method of correlation, whether it is aware of it or not. If it is not attempting in some way to be relevant (without being reductionistic) then it will not arouse the interest of any potential readers.

[21]H. Richard Niebuhr, *The Meaning of Revelation* (New York: The Macmillan Co., 1960) 80. Niebuhr writes that through the image given in revelation "a pattern of dramatic unity becomes apparent with the aid of which the heart can understand what has happened, is happening and will happen to selves and their community" (80). We shall suggest that the revelatory image illuminates not only history and human community, but also, because of our inextricable connection with it, the cosmos in its entirety. As long as we leave the cosmos out of our theologies of revelation we display an exclusivity that in the end impoverishes our sense of God's revelatory vision for the world.

credible diversity of physical manifestations observable in the cosmos in an even more integral and intelligible fashion.[22]

Analogously, revelation, if it is to catch our attention, would also have to provide an image, or a set of images, that can respond to the confusions arising out of the four circles in which our lives are embedded. We rightly expect it also to provide a new coherence and openness to further insight. Indeed there is little point in our making reference to revelation unless it brings with it an unexpected power to make reality more intelligible and our lives more meaningful.[23] In this book we shall be asking whether the central revelatory image given in Christian faith can bring fresh intelligibility to our experience of mystery, cosmos, history, and personal existence. As in the case of science we shall also examine the capacity of this revelatory image to lead us indefinitely deeper in our explorations of the four-circled world. One major criterion of revelation's authenticity will be its heuristic power, that is, its capacity to bring the now unintelligible, forgotten, and even absurd aspects of our experience into the framework of a continually expanding and deepening intelligibility.

But is there in fact any *centrally* revelatory image presented to us by the classic Christian sources that might function as such an illuminating, integrating, and heuristic principle of meaning? The chapters that follow will argue, each in its own way, that there is indeed such an image. Much contemporary theological reflection has begun to focus, perhaps with more clarity than ever before, on what it discerns to be a startlingly interruptive, but remarkably healing and integrating image embedded in the sources of revelation, but not often sufficiently highlighted. This is the image of the humility of God made manifest in Jesus. The biblically based portrait of an all-powerful yet self-abandoning divine mystery is now emerging more decisively than ever out of our present-day theological reflection on the roots of Christian faith. Informed by contemporary experience of the apparent eclipse of mystery, by the sorrow and oppression in much social existence, by the horrors of genocide, and by the modern threat of meaninglessness to the individual's existence, we now seem to be noticing more explicitly than ever before the image of God's self-emptying, or *kenosis,* that has always been present in Christian tradition.[24] We now behold more

[22]Stephen Hawking, *A Brief History of Time,* (New York: Bantam Books, 1988) 155-69.

[23]See Niebuhr, 69.

[24]See, for example, the studies by Donald G. Dawe, *The Form of a Servant* (Philadelphia: The Westminster Press, 1963); Lucien J. Richard, O.M.I., *A Kenotic Christology* (Lanham, Md.: University Press of America, 1982); Jürgen Moltmann, *The Crucified God,* trans. by R.A. Wilson and John Bowden (New York: Harper & Row, 1974); and Hans Urs Von Balthasar, *Mysterium Paschale,* trans. by Aidan Nichols, O.P. (Edinburgh: T & T Clark, 1990).

clearly in the passion and crucifixion of Jesus the illuminating and healing image of a vulnerable, suffering God who, out of love for the world, renounces any claims to coercive omnipotence and gives the divine selfhood over to the world in an act of absolute self-abandonment.

Dietrich Bonhoeffer's reflections from prison that only a "weak" God can be of help today were a powerful stimulus to this contemporary theological re-imaging of God. Much theology now speaks provocatively of the powerlessness of God. Perhaps though, with Edward Schillebeeckx, it is more appropriate for us to speak of the "defenselessness" or vulnerability of God rather than of weakness or powerlessness. We need not deny that God is powerful in order to emphasize the divine humility. Experience teaches us, Schillebeeckx says, that those who make themselves vulnerable are actually capable of powerfully disarming evil. God remains powerful, but power—the capacity to influence reality or bring about significant effects—is redefined through the divine decision to remain defenseless in the face of our own human use of power in order to oppress:

> The divine omnipotence does not know the destructive facets of the human exercising of power, but in this world becomes 'defenceless' and vulnerable. It shows itself as power of love which challenges, gives life and frees human beings, at least those who hold themselves open to this offer. But at the same time that means that God does not retaliate against this human refusal.[25]

Theological reflection on the image of divine defenselessness (which is not the same as powerlessness) can help us make new sense of our otherwise confused and even desperate experience of the enigmas accompanying the four circles of our lives.

The image of a self-emptying, fully relational God seems to lie at the very heart of Christian revelation. It is the underlying dynamism of the doctrine of the Trinity which Karl Barth held to be the central and distinguishing content of Christian revelation.[26] And the self-emptying of God is now also seen to lie at the foundation of the world's creation as well. In the words of theologian Jürgen Moltmann:

> God 'withdraws himself from himself to himself' in order to make creation possible. His creative activity outwards is preceded by this humble divine self-restriction. In this sense God's self-humiliation does not begin merely with creation, inasmuch as God commits himself to this world:

[25]Edward Schillebeeckx, *Church: The Human Story of God,* trans. by John Bowden (New York: Crossroad, 1990) 90.

[26]See Eberhard Jüngel, *The Doctrine of the Trinity: God's Being is in Becoming,* trans. by Scottish Academic Press Ltd. (Grand Rapids: Eerdmann Press, 1976).

it begins beforehand, and is the presupposition that makes creation possible. God's creative love is grounded in his humble, self-humiliating love. This self-restricting love is the beginning of that self-emptying of God which Philippians 2 sees as the divine mystery of the Messiah. Even in order to create heaven and earth, God emptied himself of all his all-plenishing omnipotence, and as Creator took upon himself the form of a servant.[27]

What does this image of a self-humbling God mean in terms of each of the four circles that make up our situation? In faith's response to its kenotic image of God there lies a surprising way of bringing new meaning to our normally confused sense of mystery, to our puzzlement about evolution and other recent discoveries about the physical universe, to our perplexity at the broken state of social existence, and finally to our own individual longings and sufferings. The realms of mystery, nature, history, and personal existence can take on deeper coherence and significance as we view them in the light of the vulnerability of God.

At the same time, a persistent reflection on this central image may be able to explain, to some extent at least, why Christian theology has arrived at so many dead-ends in its ruminations about mystery, creation, suffering, and human freedom. Theology's failure to take seriously this most shocking and yet so simple of revelatory images (a revelation so startling and surprising that we are immediately compelled to doubt that we could ever have thought it up all by ourselves) leads only toward further perplexities and incoherences in our experience of each of the four circles. The refusal of much traditional theology to place the kenotic image of God at its center has led to impossible tangles in its attempts to interpret the world and human experience. On the other hand, the hypothesis of the self-emptying God who lovingly renounces any claims to domineering omnipotence has enormous explanatory potential in our attempts to interpret things.

Our reflections will focus especially on the potentially illuminating capacity of this kenotic image of God. We shall not lose sight of other aspects of revelation, but we shall constantly seek to relate them to the theme of divine suffering love that comes to fullest expression in the image of the crucified man, Jesus. Especially the theme of God's word and promise, but also those of exodus, redemption, covenant, justice, wisdom, of the Logos made flesh, of the Spirit poured out on the face of creation, of the compassion, paternity and maternity of God, and especially the Trinitarian character of God—all of the indispensable elements in a Christian theology—communicate their depth only when they are united with the

[27]Moltmann, *God in Creation,* 88.

theme of divine self-abnegation which, at least to Christian faith, comes to its most explicit expression in the life, death, and resurrection of Jesus.[28]

We shall seek to emphasize as sharply as possible just how interruptive of "normality" is the picture of the incarnate God who suffers along with creation. This image is shocking, even almost blasphemous, when examined from the point of view of our ordinary standards of rationality, or of what we usually think should qualify as ultimate reality, or omnipotence or as the foundation of our being. Because it is so arresting of the ordinary, it justifiably bears the name "revelation." While it breaks apart our pedestrian interpretations of mystery, universe, history, and existence, the idea of a self-emptying absolute can paradoxically bring an unprecedented intelligibility to our experience of these four interwoven realms. Retrospectively it can help us understand why, in the absence of faith in a suffering God, we experience so many unsolvable puzzles and blind alleys in our exploration of the world and our efforts at self-awareness.

The history of the idea of revelation in Christian theology is long and complex, and it is not the purpose of a systematic theology of revelation simply to reiterate this chronicle. In any case, able historical studies have already set forth the story of revelation theology, and they require no duplication here.[29] A contemporary theology of revelation must inevitably be somewhat selective and synthetic with respect to the themes it wishes to highlight and correlate with our most urgent questions. But the image of the God who suffers, the Absolute who through "defenselessness" manifests its power, seems to sum up, even if it does not exhaust, the substance of the Christian interpretation of the mystery that enfolds us. And so it is upon this image (and along with it the theme of revelation as promise) that we shall focus in the following chapters.

A systematic theology has to do more than just retell the biblical stories. Nor should it simply repeat doctrines from the past in their customary formulations. If it is really to speak to people in their actual lives, it must continually search for new ways of presenting the insights of traditional faith. This is the only way it can be loyal to the tradition it represents. It is the judgment of the present author that the doctrines and theologies surrounding the idea of revelation, in the linguistic and conceptual shape that they have come down to us, are now in need of drastic refashioning. This is in no way to suggest that they be discarded. Rather, they must

---

[28]We will not be able to develop in this book how the kenotic image of God also has potential for illuminating interreligious conversations, especially those taking place between Christianity and Buddhism. See, however, John B. Cobb, Jr. and Christopher Ives, editors, *The Emptying God* (Maryknoll: Orbis Books, 1990).

[29]See especially Avery Dulles, *Revelation Theology: A History* (New York: Herder and Herder, 1969) and *Models of Revelation* (New York: Doubleday, 1983).

be reinterpreted. In their customary crystallizations they do not always address our contemporaries at those points of anxiety or inquiry where people need the most assistance and illumination. In at least some of their traditional formulations, theologies of revelation are often strange-sounding, if not entirely alien to the ways in which people today actually live and think. This is especially true of the intellectuals for whom many traditional theological formulations of revelation have been deeply un-satisfying.

For such sincere inquirers we need to restate the meaning of revelation in a way that does not place unnecessary or impossible demands on them. With Bultmann we must seek the place where revelation challenges us and even disturbs us, but we should avoid all false stumbling blocks to faith.[30] This means first of all that a certain economy of expression is essential in our theology today. Without being reductionistic, we need to come directly to the point about the substance of revelation. We must avoid excessively elaborate descriptions of traditional theological disputes. It is too much to ask, even of the most enlightened readers of theology, that they become acquainted with two thousand years of terminological and doctrinal controversy as a condition for being introduced to the substance of their faith. A fuller understanding of revelation may eventually require such historical knowledge, but it is the task of systematic theology, as distinct from historical theology, to sift out of the traditional material what strikes it as the content most suitably challenging, as well as Good News, for our time and for our present readers. This means that systematic theology will always have a provisional, selective, and somewhat speculative character. It will also suffer considerably from the limitations of the particular theologian.

In this book, our focus is on the image of the self-humbling mystery to which even the word "God" itself may no longer always seem to be fully adequate. Because the concept of God has been associated in the minds of many with a reality that is anything but self-effacing or humbly relational, it has become a problematic term itself. At times we are tempted to abandon it, but as Paul Tillich has reminded us, it is really irreplaceable. We cannot let go of it. However, we can come to a better and more biblical understanding of it. And the quest for such understanding is one of the tasks of a theology of revelation. In his study of the doctrine of kenosis, Donald Dawe writes:

> Basic to Christian faith is the belief in the divine self-emptying or condescension in Christ for the redemption of men. According to Christian

[30]Rudolf Bultmann, *Jesus Christ and Mythology* (New York: Charles Scribner's Sons, 1958) 36.

faith, God in his creation and redemption of the world accepted the limitations of finitude upon his own person. In the words of the New Testament, God had "emptied himself, taking the form of a servant." God accepted the limitations of human life, its suffering and death, but in doing this, he had not ceased being God. God the Creator had chosen to live as a creature. God, who in his eternity stood forever beyond the limitations of human life, had fully accepted these limitations. The Creator had come under the power of his creation. This the Christian faith has declared in various ways from its beginning.

But Dawe adds a sobering comment:

> The audacity of this belief in the divine kenosis has often been lost by long familiarity with it. The familiar phrases "he emptied himself [heauton ekenosen], taking the form of a servant," and "though he was rich, yet for your sake he became poor" have come to seem commonplace. Yet this belief in the divine self-emptying epitomizes the radically new message of Christian faith about God and his relation to man.[31]

The image of a God who renounces omnipotence enters into our consciousness with such unexpectedness that we cannot help but see it as a revelation. It is a radical deconstruction of what we anticipate the absolute to be. Our normal powers of reason and even our religious imagination could hardly have conjured it up. In the words of St. Paul, it is "foolishness" when viewed through the eyes of conventional wisdom (1 Cor 1:25). There is an otherness or reversal inherent in this revelatory image that completely confounds and surpasses our more superficial expectations. But by breaking through our projections, it awakens in us new hope and new life. John Macquarrie writes:

> That God should come into history, that he should come in humility, helplessness and poverty—this contradicted everything—this contradicted everything that people had believed about the gods. It was the end of the power of deities, the Marduks, the Jupiters . . . yes, and even of Yahweh, to the extent that he had been misconstrued on the same model. The life that began in a cave ended on the cross, and there was the final conflict between power and love, the idols and the true God, false religion and true religion.[32]

---

[31]Dawe, *The Form of a Servant,* 13–15.

[32]John Macquarrie, *The Humility of God* (Philadelphia: The Westminster Press, 1978) 34.

While this is an image that liberates and fulfills our deepest longings for love and compassion, it is one that we continually resist, both in our lives and in our theologies. We still want God to be a potentate, even a magician. Yet, as Karl Rahner asserts, "[t] he primary phenomenon given by faith is precisely the self-emptying of God. . ."[33] Philosopher Alfred North Whitehead observed that when Christianity came into the Western world its image of God began to be modeled on Caesar rather than on the humble shepherd of Nazareth.[34] The God that Friedrich Nietzsche found so offensive was a moralistic dictator who is primarily interested in moderating human behavior and expropriating our own power. Sigmund Freud thought, quite correctly, that the image of God conveyed by Western theism and religious education is overlaid with Oedipal overtones. Like the superego, this deity issues consolation only at the price of an accusatory coerciveness and restrictiveness. The kenotic God of revelation, on the other hand, unfortunately remains hidden both to believers and unbelievers.

Much contemporary theology has been attempting to undo the assimilation of the idea of God into that of a controlling and dictatorial power. But the work is far from complete. Macquarrie observes:

> The God of Jesus Christ, like Yahweh before him, has been turned back again and again into a God of war or the God of the nation or the patron of a culture. The tendency to idolatry is apparently as strong among Christians as among pagans.[35]

One of the tasks of a theology of revelation today is to restate the meaning of reality, the meaning of mystery, cosmos, history, and selfhood, in the light of faith in the God who renounces despotism and participates as a servant in the lives of those who struggle and suffer.

[33]Karl Rahner, *Foundations of Christian Faith,* trans. by William V. Dych (New York: Crossroad, 1978) 222.

[34]Alfred North Whitehead, *Process and Reality,* Corrected Edition, edited by David Ray Griffin and Donald W. Sherburne (New York: the Free Press, 1978) 342.

[35]Macquarrie, 34.

2

Revelation Theology

Rather than moving directly into the task of developing a contemporary theology of revelation, it may prove helpful to some readers if we pause here and sketch at least a brief outline of the history of Catholic revelation theology. Such background information may help us to appreciate the extent of the struggle the idea of revelation in Catholic theology has undergone in order eventually to be liberated, especially through the work of the Second Vatican Council, from association with theological schemes that tended to narrow its meaning unnecessarily. At the same time such an outline may help to locate more clearly the distinctive character of the present attempt to develop a theology of revelation.

We noted earlier that Catholic theology of revelation has suffered in the past primarily from a "propositional" and correspondingly impersonal tendency. That is to say, it has understood revelation very much as though it were a set of truths and very little as the unfolding of a dialogical relationship between God and the world. Today, on the other hand, most Catholic theologians, along with an increasing number of Protestants, interpret revelation fundamentally as God's personal self-gift to the world. This is a dramatic departure from the dominantly apologetic treatments of our topic since the time of the Reformation.

The new personalist or dialogical emphasis in revelation theology is not incompatible with a propositional understanding, but it goes far beyond it. Gerald O'Collins, who certainly agrees with the new accent, observes that the personalist way of looking at revelation as God's self-disclosure does not exclude the possibility of framing its content simultaneously in the form of statements of truth.

Is there no room left for talk of "revealed truths" and the "content" of revelation? With regard to this question we should recall that the relationship of the revealing God and the believing man is foremost a living experience which shapes man's personal history. But this experienced reality is not so wholly incommunicable that it remains locked up in inarticulate subjectivity. The faith which arises in encounter with the self-revealing God feels the need to formulate true statements of faith both within the community of those who share this experience and also for outsiders.[1]

Still, although traditionally revelation has been understood in a formal sense as God's communication of truths to us, materially and in fact it has never been reducible to the mere transmission of information. In spite of the excesses of the propositional approach at the level of theological articulation, the lived experience of Christians throughout the ages has been one in which revelation, even when it is not called by this name, has been experienced predominantly in a personal, dialogical way. It would be an exaggeration to say that traditional theology has been mistaken in speaking of revelation in propositional terms, for example, during the period in which Scholasticism was virtually equated with Catholic theology. But it has failed, as incidentally all theology has to an extent in every age, by speaking of revelation in a manner that does not adequately thematize what actually goes on in the concrete faith life of Christian believers. The attempt to reduce revelation to propositional statements of truth may serve the cause of apologetics, but it leaves out the main substance or content of revelation as it has in fact been felt and internalized.

Theology has been so preoccupied with what we shall later call "boundary maintenance," the need to guarantee the integrity of revelation in the face of skepticism or alternative religious positions, that it has felt the need to codify its content in the form of credal and dogmatic propositions. This attempt at codification is especially understandable, and certainly forgivable, since the content of revelation needs to be guarded in one way or another. Without conceptually clarified boundaries, any religious tradition risks being dissolved into culture at large and thereby loses its critical edge vis-a-vis the social and political environment. The problem, then, is not with the propositional codification but with the narrow identification of a set of propositions with the sum and substance of revelation. Such an identification is parallel to the fallacy in science of identifying the world of nature with the scientific models that we use to organize our understanding of it. Nature is in fact always much richer and more

---

[1]Gerald O'Collins, *Foundations of Theology* (Chicago: Loyola University Press, 1970) 27.

complex than our imaginative and mathematical models, and we unduly
shrivel our understanding of the cosmos if we equate it in a simple way
with our scientific schemes. Likewise, it is of the very essence of faith that
we acknowledge the transcendence of divine mystery over any of our
propositional and symbolic representations of it. Indeed, not to do so is
idolatrous. And so, if the ultimate content of revelation is the divine mystery of God, then no set of propositional truths can mediate it to us either.
Avery Dulles writes,

> The ineffable experience of the Word holds a certain precedence over
> its doctrinal statement. In the life of the individual believer and in that
> of the whole church, as Blondel observed, "it would be true to say that
> one goes from faith to dogma rather than from dogma to faith."[2]

Few theologians, it turns out, have rigorously equated the marrow of
revelation with any particular set of propositional truths. But especially
under the pressure of apologetical concerns, they have sometimes caused
the theology of revelation to focus so intently on credal formulations that
the life of faith and the intimate relation of God to the world underlying
the statements of dogma have often been virtually ignored. The renewal
of revelation theology, especially since Vatican II, is trying to redress this
imbalance.

We must be careful to avoid caricaturing traditional theology. This is
especially the case with the theology formulated along the lines of Thomas Aquinas' great synthesis. Although Thomistic and later scholastic
philosophies are rightly criticized for their rationalistic excesses, they did
not totally obscure the personal dimension of revelation, but in their own
way kept it alive. Aquinas himself did not lock revelation up in a purely
logical mold, but instead saw it fundamentally as the presence of the Lord
in the heart as well as the mind.[3] As we shall see in Chapter 4, religions
all have an informational component which requires some sort of propositional formulizing, and Christian faith is not exempt from this requirement. But even the most "scholastic" theology of the late Middle Ages
did not entirely reduce revelation to a set of sentences. Hidden beneath
its rigorous preoccupation with dogmatic clarity, there was still the often
inadequately articulated confession of the sense of God's personal presence to the world and to faith. It is this lived faith that revelation theology ideally attempts to clarify.

[2]Avery Dulles, *Revelation and the Quest for Unity* (Washington: Corpus Books,
1968) 59.
[3]*Summa Theologiae* I a. 8, 3; 2, 3, 5, 6.

Revelation Theology Prior to Vatican II

Whenever the main theological concern is one of defending the faith from the threats of outsiders, it is difficult to undertake the work of a truly constructive theology. The latter occurs more readily in circumstances where religious energy can be focused on the development rather than just the protection of doctrine.[4] Before Vatican II, the Church councils and the Roman magisterium spoke of revelation generally in the context of the condemnation of unorthodoxy.[5] At the Council of Trent in the sixteenth century, for example, there was no real theological deepening of the notion of revelation because the main concern was with safeguarding the deposit of faith that the council fathers held to have been passed down in Church tradition under the guidance of the Holy Spirit. And although Vatican I did not explicitly dwell on the topic of revelation, its promulgations on infallibility and faith alluded to the "deposit" that comes to us from the apostles and that needs to be protected by Church authority.[6] Vatican I understood revelation as a fixed body of supernatural truths under the protection of papal authority:

> The Holy Spirit was promised to the successors of St. Peter not that they might make known new doctrine by his revelation, but rather, that with his assistance they might religiously guard and faithfully explain the revelation or deposit of faith that was handed down through the apostles. Indeed, it was this apostolic doctrine that all the Fathers held, and the holy orthodox Doctors reverenced and followed. For they fully realized that this See of St. Peter always remains untainted by any error, according to the divine promise of our Lord and savior made to the prince of his disciples. . . .[7]

The implied view of revelation here is that it is a somewhat manageable body of unchanging truths that can be clearly segregated from the "poison of error." The Council goes on to insist that papal infallibility is itself a "divinely revealed dogma,"[8] thus exposing once again its assumption that revelation comes wrapped in the form of doctrinal propositions.

Perhaps it is unfair of twentieth-century religious thought to be excessively critical of the rather emaciated views of revelation that came to expression at Trent and later at Vatican I and in the many manuals that

---

[4]Sometimes, of course, serious challenges may help to stimulate doctrinal growth rather than retrenchment.

[5]Dulles, *Revelation and the Quest for Unity,* 82.

[6]Gabriel Moran, *Theology of Revelation* (New York: Herder & Herder, 1966) 27.

[7]John Clarkson, S.J., et al., *The Church Teaches* (St. Louis: B. Herder, 1955) 101.

[8]Ibid., 102.

followed. At the same time, however, it is not helpful to imagine that we can find much of a basis for a theology of revelation in these sources. The reason for such a sober conclusion is simply that the apologetic method, almost by definition, leaves too much out. Indeed, while it allegedly defends matters of faith, it typically deals primarily with revelation only from the point of view of what appeals to finite human reason. It rightly allows a place for intelligence and reason within faith, but it simultaneously suppresses much of the very substance of the faith it seeks to defend. Hans Waldenfels observes that in the standard modern manuals of theology, apologetics does not treat the topic of revelation in so far as it is known through faith, but only in so far as it can be grasped in a purely "natural" way.[9] Such a method is bound to abstract considerably from what lies in the depths of faith experience.

While the topic of revelation appears abundantly in apologetic treatises and manuals after Trent, it is impossible to find a fully developed revelation theology in Catholic circles until the present century. A formal theology of revelation does not appear in the Bible, nor in the Church fathers, nor in medieval scholastic theology, either. But this is not surprising since the fact of revelation was so foundational to Christian faith that it did not need to be reflected upon in the deliberate fashion that apologetics requires.[10] We look in vain for treatises *de revelatione* prior to modern times. And even after the Council of Trent in the mid-sixteenth century, the theme of revelation entered into the realm of theological discussion through the doorway of apologetics rather than as a fully developed theological notion. In their opposition to Protestantism, Tridentine and post-Tridentine theologians sought to defend the revelatory role of tradition and the magisterium over against the *sola Scriptura* (Scripture alone) emphasis of Protestant Christianity. In doing so, they and the many manuals that followed understood revelation usually in a starkly minimal sense as the *locutio Dei,* the speech of God. And in order to distinguish the Catholic position from that of the Protestants, they placed enormous weight on tradition and the Church magisterium as vehicles of God's speech. Thus the Bible as God's Word became a subordinate item in Catholic understanding of divine revelation. And in spite of Vatican II's corrections, to this day the Bible is still quite often passed over by many Catholics as they look for the sources of their faith.

In our own century, the famous Dominican theologian Reginald Garrigou-Lagrange, in a massive apologetically oriented two-volume work, *De Revelatione,* gives an elaborate definition of revelation, setting forth its efficient, material, formal, and final causes. According to his defini-

---

[9]Hans Waldenfels, *Offenbarung* (Munich: Max Hueber Verlag, 1968) 27.
[10]See Gabriel Moran, 22–23.

tion, revelation is a supernatural action of God made manifest *"per modum locutionis"* (by way of speech).[11] Such manuals as that of Garrigou-Lagrange typically cite Hebrews 1:1 as a scriptural basis for this understanding: "In many and various ways God *spoke* of old to our fathers by the prophets; but in these last days he *has spoken* to us by a Son. . . ." The notion of God's *locutio* is easily assimilable to that of propositional truth which in turn best suits the interests of apologetics. And it is in this sense that most post-Tridentine Catholic theology prior to Vatican II understood the notion of revelation.

Even though this approach highlighted the "speaking" of God, it was still largely uninformed by, and should not be confused with, the biblical notion of "God's word." And it shows little awareness of the biblical understanding of revelation as history, revelation as event, revelation as dialogical encounter, or revelation as personal relationship. The apologetic preoccupation was with preserving the "truth" of revelation, so much so that the biblical vision of revelation as the generous self-disclosure of God's vision for creation and history was virtually forgotten. What is more, the central biblical experience of God's revelation in the mode of *promise* was almost completely ignored.[12] Even now most Catholic theologies of revelation generally fail to accentuate sufficiently the *promissory* character of the biblical interpretation of God's self-disclosure. In contrast to this puzzling oversight, we shall attempt in the following pages to give the notion of revelation as promise the prominence it deserves.

Protestant and Catholic tracts on revelation began to appear more abundantly in the nineteenth and early twentieth centuries. They were still often written in an apologetic spirit, but by this time the enemy was not so much alternative Christian movements or heresies. Instead, Protestants and Catholics both had to defend the plausibility of *any* revelation whatsoever against the challenges of rationalism and scientific agnosticism. To an extent this apologetic tone still persists in many theologies of revelation, and even in this book we cannot ignore those questions raised by the critical spirit of academic modernity. Chief among these is the question whether revelation itself can be said to be a coherent notion in a scientific age.

When the apologetic emphasis is dominant, however, it becomes difficult to develop a very substantive theology of revelation. If the chief concern is that of defending the facticity of revelation (usually too narrowly defined), then the content and significance of revelation remain unexplored.[13] Accordingly, much that passes as revelation theology prior to

[11]Reginald Garrigou-Lagrange, O.P., *De Revelatione* (Rome: F. Ferrari, 1945) 136.
[12]We are speaking here of the formal theology of revelation and not of the concrete life of faith in which, at least to some degree, the theme of promise remained alive, though not always in the biblical sense.
[13]Moran, 25.

Vatican II has failed to lead us very far into the depth and riches that the notion implies. For this reason, we shall devote most of this work to a setting forth of the nature of revelation, and reserve for our final chapter a brief inquiry into its possible consistency with reason. Such an approach is reflective of the pattern of many recent theological discussions of revelation. We shall not begin with a simple definition of the term "revelation" as the traditional treatises such as that of Garrigou-Lagrange have, defining it as the *locutio Dei*. Instead, we shall spend the largest part of our efforts groping toward a provisional understanding of the notion. Only after reaching at least a fragmentary grasp—"definition" would be too strong a term—of the nature of revelation would it be opportune to inquire into its critical plausibility.

Vatican II and Beyond

The Second Vatican Council's document on revelation, promulgated November 18, 1965, is entitled *Dei Verbum,* the "Word of God." Perhaps nothing signals more directly the new ecumenical and biblical tone of the council's understanding of revelation. Contemporary theologians, attuned as they now are to the renewal of biblical theology, may find the constitution on revelation quite unremarkable. But when we situate it in the context of previous magisterial statements, it takes on the appearance of a dramatic breakthrough in Catholic teaching. It is helpful to know that this document emerged only after a difficult struggle with those at the council who were simply intent upon restating the ideas of Trent and Vatican I. The first draft of the document was honed in a rigorously unbiblical and unecumenical way. Thanks to the intervention of Pope John XXIII and other bishops, the first draft was rejected. The final, approved text, like many other council documents, gives evidence of the modern Catholic Church's intention to keep the lines of communication open to the world, of its willingness to learn from the experience of non-Catholic churches and theologians, and of a refreshing openness to the results of modern theology and biblical scholarship. It is the spirit of this liberating openness that encourages those of us who are theologians to keep probing ever deeper for the meaning of revelation in terms of our own circumstances almost thirty years later.

By accentuating the theme of God's Word, the final text, known as *Dei Verbum,* clearly signals Catholic theology's exposure to Protestant views of revelation in which the theme of God's Word, rather than Church magisterium and tradition, is given primacy. No longer present is the old temptation to separate tradition or ecclesiastical magisterium from Scripture as autonomous sources of revelation. Instead, the document states that

there exists a close connection and communication between sacred tradition and sacred Scripture. For both of them, flowing from the same
divine wellspring, in a certain way merge into a unity and tend towards
the same end.[14]

In this way, the council avoids any narrow biblicism that would tend
to derive all important truths for our lives from the pages of Scripture
alone. It fortunately declares that the Word of God is not limited to the
letter of Scripture: "It is not from sacred Scripture alone that the Church
draws her certainty about everything which has been revealed."[15] At the
same time it emphasizes that the teaching office of the Church "is not
above the word of God, but serves it."[16] Moreover, the council endorses
the methods of modern biblical scholarship which reject literalist and
fundamentalist readings of Scripture. It shows an awareness of the need
to "search out the intention of the sacred writers" by way of form criticism. It acknowledges our need to become aware of the historical context
and different genres of the various books of the Bible. While still conced-
ing points to Trent, Vatican I, and the apologetic orientation of previous
Church documents, *Dei Verbum* overall is an inspiration to those who
are concerned with developing and interpreting anew the notion of revelation. Although many of its articles are now commonplace in modern
theology, the fact that it sanctions new methods and emphases gives one
confidence that the Church's teachers, including its theologians, are commissioned to search for an ever-deeper appreciation of the meaning of
revelation.

In addition to the theme of God's Word, the council also reflects the
Catholic Church's embrace of twentieth-century theology of history in
which God's Word is seen as inseparable from events and deeds. By way
of revelation, *Dei Verbum* states,

The invisible God out of the abundance of his love speaks to men as
friends and lives among them, so that he may invite and take them into
fellowship with himself. This plan of revelation is realized by deeds and
words having an inner unity: the deeds wrought by God in the history
of salvation manifest and confirm the teaching and realities signified by
the words, while the words proclaim the deeds and clarify the mystery
contained in them.[17]

[14]*Dei Verbum,* article 9.
[15]Ibid.
[16]Ibid., article 10.
[17]Ibid., article 2.

Thus revelation is no longer understood here simply as the communication of knowledge, but as a process, involving events as well as words, by which humans are invited into an ever-deeper relationship with God.[18]

Most significantly also, *Dei Verbum*—without developing the point in detail—clearly understands revelation as the disclosure of God's own selfhood: "Placuit Deo in sua bonitate et sapientia *seipsum revelare*. . . ." ("In his goodness and wisdom God chose to *reveal himself*. . . .").[19] Latourelle comments:

> In saying that the object of revelation is God himself, the text thus personalizes revelation: before making known something, that is his plan for salvation, God reveals someone, himself.[20]

The document on revelation goes on to say that the fullness of God's self-revelation becomes manifest in Christ.[21] It is this personalizing of revelation that we wish to highlight. The notion that revelation is God's *self-revelation* has turned out to be one of the most important developments in all of modern theology. Greatly due to the influence of theologian Karl Rahner, Catholic theology of revelation has now shifted dramatically away from the propositional, impersonal, and apologetic features it carried in the past. In doing so, it has merged in substance with much non-Catholic theology of revelation as well.

The Present State of Revelation Theology

Although Vatican II's document on revelation has de-emphasized the propositional approach to revelation theology, much work remains to be done in the area of bringing to clarity the unique content and meaning of biblical revelation. This is now a broadly shared ecumenical enterprise. Increasingly since Vatican II, Catholic and non-Catholic theologians have read and appropriated each others' work in this area. The present book will itself reflect how Catholic theology of revelation can now be animated just as much by the reading of Protestant sources as of Catholic ones. Because of the Second Vatican Council's endorsement of a biblical approach to revelation, with special emphasis on the "Word of God," Catholic theology has been implicitly commissioned to mine the resources of modern Protestant theology of revelation which traditionally has been much more explicitly concerned with the theme of God's word.

[18]Dulles, *Revelation and the Quest for Unity,* 86.
[19]*Dei Verbum,* article 2. Emphasis added.
[20]Rene Latourelle, S.J., *Theology of Revelation* (Cork: Mercier Press Ltd., 1968) 458.
[21]Ibid.

The emphasis that both Protestant and Catholic theology must now develop more forcefully (and Vatican II already took implicit steps in this direction) is that God's revelatory word comes in the form of promise. No contemporary theologian has brought out this dimension of revelation more emphatically than Jürgen Moltmann, a Protestant. And it is especially in relation to his own bold endeavors that a contemporary, ecumenically viable theology of revelation may be constructed.

Another area of revelation theology needing considerable development today is that of how to interpret the Christocentric character of *Dei Verbum*. The council's constitution on revelation implies that the fullness of the divine self-disclosure occurs only in Christ: "The deepest truth about God and the salvation of man shines out for our sake in Christ, who is both the mediator and the fullness of all revelation (*mediator simul et plenitudo totius revelationis*)."[22] How literally does this powerful and sweeping claim, supported by several important texts in the New Testament and by centuries of Christian tradition, need to be taken? This question arises for Christian theology today primarily because of our growing awareness of the revelatory claims of other religious traditions. In our conversations with representatives of these alternative visions of reality, what does it mean to say that Christ is the *plenitudo totius revelationis* (the *fullness* of *all* revelation)?

The issue of how to interpret the alleged finality of Christian revelation is receiving considerable attention in theology today, and in Chapter 4 we shall look into it somewhat more closely. It goes without saying that any efforts we might make with respect to this difficult and controversial matter can only be tentative, not to say clumsy. But it does not seem wise, nor for that matter in keeping with the spirit of tolerance and inclusiveness that we associate with Christian faith, simply to ignore it. The question of the meaning of the traditional teaching about the centrality, finality, and unsurpassability of Christ in revelation needs to be raised and discussed over and over. *Dei Verbum* is not as sensitive to this question as we might have hoped, although in comparison with previous magisterial statements both its tone and content are significant departures from the apologetically bound past. The decree on revelation, as well as other products of the Second Vatican Council, make initial gestures toward acknowledging the situation of religious pluralism, but we need now to go much further.

Finally, the present condition of revelation theology is one in which the kenotic aspects of God's self-revelation are thankfully being accentuated more forcefully than ever before. *Dei Verbum* implies that God's self-revelation is indeed a self-emptying, but it does not make this point very

---

[22]Ibid.

explicit, nor does it develop it. In the present work, therefore, without in any way claiming adequacy for our treatment, we shall bring to the front the theme of God's self-emptying as central to the theology of revelation. When taken together with the biblical motif of promise, the notion of a divine kenosis may provide for our own situation today a solid and compelling foundation for a fresh theology of revelation.

PART TWO

3

Mystery

The idea of revelation in Christian theology is usually associated with a "word" uttered by God. In the Gospel of John, this word, or the *logos,* is said to be fully manifest in Christ, the Word made flesh. So rich is the biblical notion of God's word that we have to seek a variety of terms to capture its meaning for today. No single expression is adequate, but Gabriel Fackre convincingly argues that we might grasp some of its meaning if we translate it as "vision." Revelation, then, is the setting forth of God's vision for the world. God the Father is the Envisager, God the Son is the Vision itself, and God the Spirit is the Power of the vision to transform the world.[1] In Jesus, the vision of God becomes incarnate in our world and history, and in our obedience to and conformity with Jesus' Lordship and the power of his Spirit, we cooperate in keeping the vision alive in our midst.

However, if we follow the biblical traditions closely, "revelation" has primarily auditory overtones. It comes to expression essentially in language. This means, though, that there can be no revelatory "word" without a background of silence out of which it is spoken. The revelation of the word of God would make no sense apart from an ineffable dimension of reality which in revelation becomes articulate. Such a dimension is sometimes called the spiritual, the sacred or the supernatural. It is also known as the realm of *mystery.*

The term "mystery" is not without difficulties. To the modern mind, mystery often implies little more than the unexplored and not-yet-

---

[1]Gabriel Fackre, *The Christian Story* (Grand Rapids: Eerdmans, 1978) 198.

understood aspects of our physical universe. It designates only a range of unanswered questions that science will eventually solve. As human knowledge advances, it seems, the realm of mystery, at least as it is often understood, will gradually shrink and eventually disappear from view altogether. But if revelation is a meaningful possibility, then mystery would have to be something more. In all its silence and fullness it would have to be immune to any process of erosion. And if we are to render the idea of revelation theologically intelligible today, we need first to show that, prior to hearing the word of revelation, we already have some pre-revelational relationship to the silent plenitude of mystery from which any possible disclosure of religious meaning could come to us in the first place.

In former ages, the presence of a dimension of mystery could be taken for granted. It was felt quite palpably as the environing context of the world's reality, and so auditions and visions from that realm were not altogether unexpected events. Indeed, mystery was so much a part of life's presuppositions that there was no need to make revelation the explicit notion it has become today. The disclosure of mystery was so recurrent that it would have been quite superfluous to construct a distinct theology of revelation. As an explicit concern of systematic theology, revelation is a modern development, roughly coinciding with the emergence of post-Enlightenment skepticism. Today, we focus on revelation partly because its very possibility has come under question. And this is in great measure because the reality of an encompassing and incomprehensible mystery, which would be the only "whence" of revelation, is no longer an obvious aspect of everyone's experience.

Therefore, the first step in a theology of revelation has to be what Karl Rahner has called "mystagogy," understanding by this term a "pedagogy" into mystery. We must first determine whether and where a hidden mystery *already* impinges somehow upon our lives, apart from any explicit sense of a special historical revelation. Without the impression that our lives are shrouded in mystery, any notion of revelation will inevitably fall flat. It will have no disclosive intensity unless it comes to us out of the intuited depths of a fundamentally silent but nonetheless real domain of mystery that already bears some relationship to us. Revelation cannot really mean for us an "unveiling," or an "unconcealment" of anything unless we *already* have at least some vague intuition of or access to the unspeakable mystery that it unfolds. As we shall see later, it is too much to expect that the biblical word of revelation will itself bring this sense of mystery along with it, as though we were encountering it there for the first time. Revelation can clarify mystery and tell us what it is really like. It can help us to name the mystery, but it need not be burdened with the task of introducing us to mystery. For we are by our very nature already open to mystery. It is a fundamental structure of our being to be open not only to the world, but also to transcendent mystery, even apart from the experience of any special revelatory vision or word.[2]

The constant presence of this mystery to the world and to human existence is equivalent to what the Christian theological tradition has variously called original, universal, natural or general revelation, which it distinguishes from the special or decisive revelation given in Christ. In Romans 1:19, Paul uses the verb *phaneróō* (to show or manifest) when he says of humans in general, "what can be known about God is plain to them, because God has shown it to them." And he uses the same verb in Rom 3:21 in speaking of the special revelation that comes to expression in Christ: "But now the righteousness of God has been manifested apart from the law . . . through faith in Jesus Christ for all who believe." The New Testament clearly endorses the notion of a universal revelation.[3] In the Prologue to the Gospel of John, for example, the Word is said to be the "true light that enlightens every man" (John 1:9). And in the Acts of the Apostles, Paul is pictured as saying to the Athenians: "What therefore you worship as unknown, this I proclaim to you" (Acts 17:23).[4] In our human awareness of the mystery that enshrouds our existence, there is already a manifestation of God's being that we may appropriately call by the name "revelation."

But, as we have already noted, the sense of mystery often seems to be absent today. Consequently, we must begin our reflections on revelation with an inquiry as to whether and where mystery might already impinge upon our lives.[5] For many people, such mystagogy is unnecessary. They already sense the reality of the sacred; they accept consciously their openness to a dimension of infinite depth, and so the possibility of an explicit revelatory clarification of this mystery seems quite congruent with their experience. For others, however, mystery is not a very meaningful concept. If it signifies anything at all, it is perhaps simply the scientifically unknown world. Mystery, today, often means nothing more than a set

---

[2]See Wolfhart Pannenberg, *What Is Man,* trans. by Duane A. Priebe (Philadelphia: Fortress Press, 1970) 1-13.

[3]Schubert Ogden, *On Theology* (San Francisco: Harper & Row, 1986) 26-27.

[4]Ibid.

[5]Of course, the process of historical, biblical revelation has already in some way shaped the cultural context in which the task of mystagogy is undertaken. There is no purely pre-religious sense of mystery, since in very many ways the biblical revelation, as well as those of other religious traditions, has shaped the sensibilities of all of us. But to many of our contemporaries the intuition of mystery has grown dull. And the apparent circularity of which mystagogy partakes does not exonerate us from the task of elucidating where mystery touches our lives, so that we might appreciate in a fresh way how revelation enters the picture.

of problems that will eventually be solved by science. For example, physicist Heinz Pagels in a recent book on the origins of the universe writes:

> People once worshipped the sun, awed by its power and beauty. Now that astrophysicists understand the physics of the sun and the stars and the source of their power, they are no longer the mysteries they once were. In our culture we no longer worship the sun and see it as a divine presence as our ancestors did. But many people still involve their deepest feelings with the universe as a whole and regard its origin as mysterious. The size, splendor and glory of the universe still provoke the sense of transcendent eternal being.[6]

This popular scientific author goes on to say that physicists will eventually understand the basic laws of the universe, and then, "the existence of the universe will hold no more mystery for those who choose to understand it than the existence of the sun." And then he concludes: "[A]s knowledge of our universe matures, that ancient awestruck feeling of wonder at its size and duration seems inappropriate, a sensibility left over from an earlier age."[7]

Observe that Pagels is using the term "mystery" as the equivalent of "problem to be solved," or "present gap in our knowledge." Accordingly, mystery is a region of the unknown that will shrink away as our knowledge progresses. The term "mystery" is nothing more than a name for our temporary ignorance. And since any religious revelation apparently presupposes a mysterious domain of the unknown, there is little wonder that so many scientific thinkers have serious difficulties with religion in general and especially with the idea of a special religious revelation. The goal of science seems to some of them, at least, to be that of eventually eliminating any mysterious region out of which revelation might occur.

However, to religious experience and theology, the term "mystery" designates much more than a blank space in our knowledge eventually to be filled in by science. It is not just a void begging to be bridged by our intellectual achievements. Such lacunae in our present knowledge should be called *problems,* not mysteries. A problem can ultimately be solved and gotten out of the way through the application of human ingenuity.[8] It falls under our cognitional control and can be disposed of by our intellectual or technological efforts. Mystery, on the other hand, is not open to any kind of "solution." Instead of vanishing as we grow wiser, it actually appears to loom larger and deeper. The realm of mys-

[6]Heinz Pagels, *Perfect Symmetry* (New York: Bantam Books, 1986) 367.

[7]Ibid., xiv.

[8]On the distinction between problem and mystery see especially Gabriel Marcel, *Being and Having* (Westminster: Dacre Press, 1949) 117.

tery keeps on expanding before us as we solve our particular problems. It resembles a horizon that recedes into the distance as we advance. Unlike problems, it has no clear boundaries. While problems can eventually be removed, the encompassing domain of mystery remains a constantly receding frontier the deeper we advance into it.

Albert Einstein is often cited as the exemplar of those scientists for whom mystery means much more than just a set of solvable problems. Though he could not embrace the notion of religious revelation, he still perceived a dimension of mystery so enduring that the advance of science could never eliminate it:

> The most beautiful experience we can have is of the mysterious. . . . Whoever does not know it and can no longer wonder, no longer marvel, is as good as dead, and his eyes are dimmed. . . . It is this knowledge and this emotion that constitute true religiosity . . ."[9]

Einstein saw mystery as real, not just a cover-up for our scientific ignorance. In his view, the sense of mystery will intensify as scientific knowledge advances, for the greatest mystery is that the universe is even intelligible at all. There is little hope for our grasping the possibility of any sort of revelation if we have not, at least minimally, become comfortable in the manner of Einstein with the impression that the universe is shrouded in mystery.

Limit-Experience

An awareness of mystery can make its way into the consciousness of all of us, even though we may not call it by that name. The sense of mystery comes home to us most explicitly in "limit-experiences" and "limit-questioning."[10] Limit-experiences are those happenings in our lives that shock us into a recognition that our ordinary existence is encompassed by a previously unacknowledged realm of the unknown. Often they coincide with moments of tragedy or perplexity, but they may also pop up at times of joy and ecstasy and even during the most ordinary of moments.

In his autobiography *My Confession*, Leo Tolstoy provides a vivid illustration of how mystery-opening questions may interrupt the routine of one's life. At a time when he was already a famous novelist and had achieved great wealth and fame, he found himself drawn irresistibly toward the unsolvable questions: What is the purpose of life? Why go on

---

[9]Albert Einstein, *Ideas and Opinions* (New York: Bonanza Books, 1954) 11.

[10]Tracy, *Blessed Rage for Order,* 91–118; Stephen Toulmin, *An Examination of the Place of Reason in Ethics* (Cambridge: Cambridge University Press, 1970) 202–21.

living? What value lies in continuing one's work? Is life perhaps a stupid cheat? These questions expressed his perplexity about the suffocating nature of an all-too-familiar world. One response to them is a despair that insists on the finality of the ordinary and gives into cynicism. But another is to see such provocations as tortuous openings to the utterly extraordinary and surprising, that is, to mystery.

The presence of limits is felt whenever we find ourselves restlessly asking the big questions to which religions have always been the primary mode of response: What is the meaning of my life? Why am I here? Who am I? What is my destiny? These questions disclose our native openness to mystery even in the midst of the everyday. Functional or pragmatic questions consume the larger portion of our lives, but occasionally things happen that break up the routine and allow us to see our world in a new light. Sometimes these are moments of "earthquake," such as an experience of personal failure or the death of a loved one. Occurring at the edge or "limits" of normal life, they thrust us toward a fearsome but also vaguely promising dimension of reality. They may initially bring a sense of anxiety, but along with it a surprising anticipation of new life. We may even experience a vague longing for such limit-experiences precisely because we have a premonition that they will expose us to new and enriching depths of the unknown.

In the midst of these limit-experiences we are faced with a decision whether to trust in mystery or perhaps give into a despair that binds us even more tightly to the familiar. Limit-experiences bring home to us the boundaries of the ordinary and make us more receptive to the possible presence of another dimension beyond the everyday. But they can also be the occasion for a retreat from the promise of the unknown. They may provoke us to step back into the banal security of the already-mastered world. At any rate, during such moments we seem to brush up explicitly against mystery, even if we then take flight from it.

Our awareness of ordinariness and triviality or tedium can arise only because some part of us has already somehow gone beyond the limits of the everyday world and dipped deeper into mystery. As Hegel, among other philosophers, has put it, to know a limit as a limit is already to be beyond that limit. To recognize and feel confined by the pedestrian quality of our lives is already a hint of our being open to the wider world of a threateningly refreshing mystery. Knowledge of the chains that bind us is the first step in an awareness of our fundamental freedom. A conscious and grateful openness to the mysterious regions beyond our imprisonment may, broadly speaking, be called "religion." The cultivation of a religious attitude, we shall see, is indispensable to the full reception of revelation. Religion is the grateful awareness of and response to a mystery that exposes the limits of the mundane.

A religious detection of the extraordinary can arise out of situations of shipwreck and also at moments of dissatisfaction such as Tolstoy experienced. But we must hasten to add that a sense of mystery can also arise in a very imposing way during moments of deep joy. Ecstatic experiences may actually introduce us to mystery much more emphatically than moments of shipwreck. In a special way, the feeling of being deeply loved by another person can endear one to mystery, as can the experience of great beauty. On such occasions we may intuit a depth of reality that no amount of scientific expertise can adequately probe. The world then appears largely unconquerable by our finite human mental and technological powers. Though such a discovery is intolerable and frustrating to our will to control, genuine religion rejoices in our coming upon a continually surprising region of the unconquerable. Such discovery means that the world is infinitely open-ended, and that the human spirit need never fear the suffocation that would result from a conviction that mystery can eventually be blotted out by our rational expertise or technological prowess.

Limit-Questions

Mystery also shows up at certain points even in our rational, academic, and professional involvement in such disciplines as science and ethics. It becomes most prominent in what Stephen Toulmin calls the "limit-questions" that arise in connection with such disciplines as science and ethics. While we are actively engaged in science or any other intellectual or practical pursuit, we are not usually focally attending to mystery. But an awareness of the dimension of mystery may emerge when we begin to ask *why* we are involved in such pursuits at all.

Usually in our intellectual endeavors, we are not explicitly aware of mystery. For example, in the day-to-day work of scientific investigation, a scientist is preoccupied with questions for which a definite resolution is anticipated. The researcher anticipates that scientific problems will someday be solved and eliminated, and that new problems will take their place. The ongoing search for a unified field theory, a room-temperature superconductivity, or a cure for AIDS, requires no special attention to mystery. In fact, such focal attention might even prove to be a distraction if it were unremitting. But at least occasionally the scientist will likely step outside of the problem-solving mode. She might find herself suddenly asking: why am I involved with science at all? Why have I chosen it as my career? What does my work have to do with the rest of life? What is the meaning of my work? Why do I experience the drive to ask questions and to seek answers? Does the universe ultimately make sense, or is science just a game that leads nowhere? Is it really worthwhile spending my days in pursuit of the truth?

These are examples of what Toulmin and his theological admirers are today calling limit-questions.[11] They are a different kind of question from those that occur *within* science. They do not fall inside, but rather only *at the limits* of scientific investigation. Thus they do not lend themselves to a solution like that of scientific problems. In fact, the deeper one goes with such questions, the more interminable they seem. Such questions indicate how our minds as well as our lives are open to mystery. According to theologians David Tracy and Schubert Ogden, these are the questions to which religion seems to be the most appropriate response.[12] In other words, it is at the point of limit-questioning that mystery begins to appear in relation to our intellectual and academic disciplines. So if any revelatory disclosure of this mystery is a possibility, it would not produce a content that can be placed in the same category as the truths we arrive at through science. Revelation would be a response to the limit-questions that arise at the edge of science. It is not a set of propositions that could compete with or come into conflict with scientific ones. Seen in this light, therefore, there can be no genuine contradiction between science and revelation.

Limit-questions also arise at the boundary of ethical inquiry. Ethics, the discipline that attempts to give answers to our moral problems, can, like science, be carried out without any specific reference to mystery. In fact, today a great deal of ethics is being done in our universities by scholars who apparently have no taste for any kind of religion. Ethicians are similar to scientists, at least in the sense that they too are engaged in a kind of problem-solving activity. They dispute among themselves about whether this or that public policy is the violation of the value of justice, or whether a certain action is the breaking of a contract, or whether a certain decision constitutes infidelity to a promise. They ponder such issues as whether abortion, capital punishment, and war are wrong or right, or in what circumstances a patient may be allowed to die: All of this ethical deliberation can take place with or without a sense of mystery, and with no appeal to religion or revelation.

Once again, however, the ethical problem-solving process, like that of science, eventually comes up against limits that open out into what we are calling mystery. It is difficult to ignore indefinitely such questions as the following ones: Why should we bother about ethics at all? Why be responsible? Why should we adhere to any contracts and promises whatsoever? Why should we be concerned about human life or human rights?

---

[11]Toulmin, 202–21.

[12]Tracy, *Blessed Rage for Order,* 94–109; Schubert Ogden, *The Reality of God and Other Essays* (New York: Harper & Row, 1977) 31.

In short, why pursue the good? Why practice justice? Here the ethician is no longer asking questions that the discipline of ethics, strictly speaking, can itself adequately address. Rather, these are limit-questions. And if we pursue them seriously instead of suppressing them, as we are often prone to do, they may lead us to a sense that both our problems and their solutions are themselves enshrouded in mystery.

If there is any religious or revelatory response forthcoming from the realm of mystery opened up to us by these limit-questions, it would not be an ethical sort of answer. If there is a revelation of mystery it could not give us absolutely clear solutions to specific ethical, political and social problems, any more than we can expect it to solve scientific problems. To do so would amount to a trivializing of the mystery. It is inappropriate for us to expect religion and revelation to compete with ethics, any more than we expect them to compete with science. To look for specific biblical texts as the definitive resolution of questions about war, sexuality, personal rights, public policy, etc., and to present these as revealed truths, is highly questionable. In the final analysis the use of religious sources in this way amounts to a serious repression of mystery and a trivializing of revelation. Instead, we would look to revelation to address our limit-questions, in this case to shed some light on why we should be ethical at all, why we should be responsible, why we should keep our promises to one another.

One way of beginning to understand the idea of revelation, then, is to see it as a response not to our problems but to our limit-questions. It is a crippling reduction of revelation to place its content side by side with the propositions arrived at by way of problem-solving disciplines such as science and ethics. Revelation, we shall see, is the symbol-laden unfolding of the encompassing presence of mystery rather than a magical response to specific sets of problems. Like religion as such, it is more interested in grounding our trust in life than it is with resolving our scientific or ethical dilemmas. Though revelation requires that we take an ethical stance, especially, in the Christian context, that of doing justice, it is not reducible to ethics. And although it gives us a vision that encourages us to seek further intelligibility, it does not fit neatly into the various disciplines of intellectual or scientific inquiry. Its relation to our intellectual pursuits is that of supporting those foundational assumptions that give us a reason for doing science and getting involved in ethics in the first place. To do science we must first *believe* that truth is worth seeking, and to do ethics we must already *assume* that the good life is worth living. Revelation, seen in these terms, is the gift of a vision of, and a word about, mystery that gives us an ultimate reason to seek truth and to live the good life. But it is not just a list of propositional truths or ethical requirements.[13]

[13]See below, Chapter 10, for further development of this point in the context of the encounter of revelation theology with modern skepticism.

To summarize, it is especially at the limits of our experience and problem-oriented questioning that we consciously come up against the truly incomprehensible and uncontrollable mystery to which our lives are inherently open. At these limits, we begin to ask questions that seem unsolvable and irremovable. Our asking limit-questions occurs at all only because mystery has already grasped hold of our consciousness. In a universal or original sense mystery is already revealed to us through these limits. When we reach these limits, however, we often retreat to the safety of mere problems. Or we try to transform mystery into a set of solvable quandaries. We anxiously renounce the inexhaustible depth that becomes evident through our limit-questions. But it is possible that such questions occur to us at all only because we are already somehow situated beyond the merely problematic and because, in the core of our being, we are already abiding within a wider field of self-revealing mystery.

This mystery is present to our lives, but often without being explicitly known as such. We must try therefore to make it more explicit. One way of doing so is to reflect on what Paul Tillich calls the dimension of "depth" that underlies all of our experience of reality.[14] In our relationship to others, to our own selves, to nature, and to society we have all received the impression that there is always something more beneath the surface, no matter how deep we go. In every area of experience we can hardly avoid the sense that we could dig deeper and, after we have done so, deeper still. It is difficult to deny the truism held by both religions and the sciences that things are not what they seem to be.[15] Concealed beneath all appearances, and normally not the object of our focal awareness, there is an inexhaustible dimension of depth. Evidence that we have already experienced this depth lies in the fact that we can now look back and observe how superficial were our former impressions of things, of others, and of ourselves. If we had had no experience of going deeper we would not be able now to recognize the shallow as shallow, the superficial as superficial, or appearances as distinct from reality.

Take, for example, our experience of other people. We may think we know them and understand them, but then they will do something or say something that surprises or disappoints us. We then have to dig deeper into their personalities if we are to continue our relationship with them. And when we have penetrated beneath the surface of their being, we discover that we have still not yet fully plumbed their depth. The deeper our knowledge of the other becomes, the more clearly we realize that we will never fully understand that person. This happens because the other per-

---

[14]For a fuller discussion of Tillich's form of mystagogy see my book, *What Is God?* (New York: Paulist Press, 1986) 11–24.

[15]Huston Smith, *Forgotten Truth* (New York: Harper Colophon Books, 1977) 98–100.

son is grounded in a dimension of depth, enfolded in an unspeakable and silent mystery.

We experience something similar in our efforts to understand our own selves. We may think we know who we are, but as we continue our life journeys we discover aspects of our personalities that we never knew about before. The deeper we travel on the road toward self-understanding the more we realize there is no end in sight. We seem to be borne up by an inexhaustible depth that renders us more and more mysterious even to ourselves. And in our relationship to nature and society we also experience how the appearances they present to us also conceal an infinite depth. The deeper science goes in its understanding of the cosmos, the more it seems to open up wider fields to be explored. And the more we look beneath the surface of our social and historical existence the more we encounter the inexhaustible dimension of depth.[16]

This commonplace experience of depth is not distinct from the experience of mystery. And, as in the case of mystery, once we become conscious of the depth that yawns inexhaustibly beneath our lives we may begin to inquire about what this depth is really like at heart. What is the true character of this misty but ever-present horizon that continues to deepen as we plunge more fully into it? Is this depth simply a bottomless abyss, or does it have a ground to it? Is it an indifferent void, a hostile impasse, or a caring presence? We suspect, with Paul Tillich and many other theologians, that we need a very specific way to encounter the "universal" revelation of the depth or mystery of reality. We look, in other words, for a special or decisive revelation through which we may experience concretely the essential character of this omnipresent dimension of depth.[17]

---

[16]Paul Tillich, *The Shaking of the Foundations* (New York: Charles Scribner's Sons, 1948) 57. The above reflections on depth are suggested by Tillich's important sermon on "The Depth of Existence," 52–63.

[17]Schubert Ogden rightly stresses that there is no "more" in special than in universal revelation. And the New Testament itself does not require that we look at special revelation as a supernatural addition to make up for the inadequacy of natural revelation. Rather, it is sufficient to say that special revelation *makes explicit* the fullness of God's love which is always already poured out into the world. "Although such [explicit] revelation cannot be necessary to the *constitution* of human existence, it can very well be necessary to the *objectification* of existence, in the sense of its full and adequate understanding at the level of explicit thought and speech." *On Theology*, 41. And: "*what* Christian revelation reveals to us is nothing new, since such truths as it makes explicit must already be known to us implicitly in every moment of our existence. But *that* this revelation occurs does reveal something new to us in that, as itself an event, it is the occurrence in our history of the transcendent event of God's love," 43.

Even if we are brought to the point of agreeing that there is indeed a dimension of reality to which the term "mystery" is applicable, we still wonder what this mystery is really like. For it seems to be ambiguous. It is both threatening and promising, and we sometimes wonder whether we can entrust ourselves to it. Perhaps instead we should try to avoid it. It is not surprising that much of our life is indeed an anxious flight from mystery. In the light of this ambiguity of mystery, the quest for special revelation becomes most relevant. The quest for this revelation is at root an inquiry about what mystery is really like. It is not inaccurate to say, at least from the point of view of Christian theology, that the search for such a revelation is the major driving force in the history of religion. And what differentiates one religion from another is the specific set of symbols or myths by which each answers the question about the essential character of the mystery that encompasses us all: "At the base of every religion, as its origin and principle," Schubert Ogden writes, "is some particular occasion of insight, or reflective grasp through concept and symbol, of the mystery manifested in original revelation."[18] To Christian faith, revelation in the special sense of the term occurs decisively in Jesus who is called the Christ.

Nevertheless, the idea of a special revelation can probably have meaning for us only if we have already experienced an orientation to mystery. The experience of a decisive unveiling of a divine vision or the utterance of God's word presupposes on our part at least a dim sense of an expansive realm of the unseen and the unspoken as its hidden source. We have noted, though, that today the reality of such a domain has come under question. Hence, a theology of revelation must begin with at least some effort to awaken us to mystery. A foundational aspect of all theology today is mystagogy.

The term "revelation," as mentioned earlier, comes from the Latin *revelare,* "to remove a veil." Most religions, at least since roughly the middle of the first millennium B.C., have maintained that a veil of illusion or of mere "appearances" normally obscures from us what is ultimately deep, important, or real. And these same religions offer various ways by which our ignorance, alienation, or lack of enlightenment can be overcome. In this sense, all the great religions are concerned at least implicitly with special revelation. And so, in our use of the term "revelation" in this book, we shall be referring primarily to special revelation, and only by implication to original or universal revelation. Special revelation, understood as the symbolic disclosure of what lies in the depths of mystery, is an essential aspect of all religion.

---

[18]Ibid., 40.

Mystery, Religion, and Revelation

The period of history ranging roughly from the eighth to the second century B.C. gave rise to the Hindu *Upanishads* and to Buddhism in India, to the religions of Lao-Tzu and Confucius in China, to the eschatological ideas of Zoroaster in Persia, to the classical biblical prophets in Israel and Judah, and to the philosophy of Socrates, Plato, and Aristotle in the Greek world. This period has been aptly called the axial age by philosopher Karl Jaspers.[19] By the term "axial" Jaspers intends to designate a major transitional period in human history and in our species' understanding of reality. It is a pivotal period because during it there occurred parallel religious revolutions almost simultaneously at different places on our planet. Generally speaking, these independent spiritual developments intensified the sense of the ultimate unity and transcendence of a divine mystery. Or as is especially the case with Buddhism, they gave rise to an unprecedented longing for a state of enlightenment beyond the suffering and unsatisfactoriness of temporal experience. In a broad sense, at least, the major religions and philosophies anticipated special revelatory experiences or moments of enlightenment that would transform human existence and bestow on it a final meaning.

Even before the axial period, archaic or primal religions already had an at least embryonic sense of a sacral dimension that could interrupt life and bestow on it a wider significance than that given in ordinary existence. The religion of early humans focused on the maintenance of stable tribal existence in the face of nature's wild elements and the hostility of other peoples. The purpose of religion was to an extent, though certainly not exclusively, that of world-maintenance. The axial religions, on the other hand, initiated a more explicit longing for a perfect reality *beyond* the immediate world of social and natural existence. Religion became less concerned with maintaining the world than with restlessly transcending it on the way to something infinitely better.[20]

Still, even in pre-axial religion there are the beginnings of a more explicit and adventurous openness to the novelty of mystery. For example, the main religious figure of the pre-axial period, the shaman, characteristically breaks through to a strange but salvific world beyond the ordinary. By way of trances and frenzied actions, the shaman, who functions as a scout of the "other world," discloses or reveals an other-than-ordinary dimension of reality to the members of a tribe. Shamanic mediators of

[19]Karl Jaspers, *The Origin and Goal of History* (New Haven: Yale University Press, 1953).

[20]John Hick, *An Interpretation of Religion* (New Haven: Yale University Press, 1989) 22–29.

a sacred realm abound in early religion. And we fail to appreciate the notion of revelation as it comes down to us in later religious traditions, including the Christian religion, if we forget its primal connections to the visionaries of pre-literate societies. In its earliest forms, even in the Bible, revelation takes place in the ecstatic experience of exceptional personalities who open up an extraordinary realm of mystery beyond the everyday modes of awareness.

However, revelation is present in preliterate religion in an even more fundamental sense than just ecstatic eruptions. In primal religion, revelation has a fundamentally sacramental character. Early religious inklings of "another dimension" were felt especially in those aspects of nature considered important for human subsistence and survival. The aboriginal forms of religious experience may have occurred in the Paleolithic Age going back at least 35,000 years and even beyond. During this hunting-and-gathering period, religious experience was probably tied up closely with the hunt. Because they were indispensable to human survival, animals were endowed with special, perhaps sacral, characteristics. During the Old Stone Age it is quite likely that totemism arose. In totemism, a particular animal or (less often) some other natural phenomenon or artifact is given a special role as the ancestral being around which the social unit's life is structured. Participating in the life of this totem is a way of communing with the sacred. And the totem becomes a symbolic medium through which mystery is disclosed, though perhaps not in the sense of the radical otherness that we discern in the axial and post-axial religious traditions.

Moving closer to modern times, religion undergoes the dramatic transformations we have associated with the axial age. As it does so, the sense of an all-encompassing realm of mystery becomes more prominent in the religious ideas of influential religious visionaries and seers. Ordinary experience of mundane reality becomes more sharply distinguished from and relativized by the awareness of a realm of perfection or of supreme bliss far surpassing anything given in our everyday lives.

For example, the Hindu *Upanishads* which emerged during the axial age inform us that we are normally tied up in a world of *maya* (which means "veil" or illusion). And Vedantic Hinduism seeks to open us up to the fact that we are really at one with *Brahman,* or ultimate reality. The attainment of *moksha,* or ultimate liberation and fulfillment, occurs when our ignorance (*avidya*) is removed and we realize that we are already in union with God. Such a "revelation," which may take place through meditation or other forms of yoga and devotion, shows us retrospectively that we have lived most of our lives in ignorance of ourselves and of the true nature of reality. In the history of religions, revelation often means the removal of a veil of ignorance.

Revelation in the wider context of religion also typically implies some sort of enlightenment or illumination. This, as we have noted, is the primary metaphor by which Augustine understood Christian revelation. But in Hinduism also, the experience of *moksha* entails an experience of unprecedented clarity about things. And in Buddhism, the illuminating moment of enlightenment may be understood as a kind of revelatory experience even though there is no self-revealing God. For Zen Buddhism, the experience of *satori* may not mean the breaking in of new truths from some realm beyond, but it does imply seeing things with a clarity that was previously absent. Even in the case of the Hebrew prophets, the experience of God is an eye-opening one. They are aware of the discontinuity between our perception of the world as we ordinarily experience it through our blindness to injustice, and the world as we may come to see it through the eyes of Yahweh, the God of justice and compassion. Revelation universally implies a clarification of vision. And although biblical revelation is not reducible to enlightenment or the removal of ignorance and unclarity, since this would amount to what is called gnosticism, it nevertheless shares with the wider religious world the sense that we all stand in need of enlightenment. The Christian Church Fathers were especially inclined to understand revelation in this sense.

Mystery and the Humility of God

A theology of revelation must attempt to give an interpretation of the basic data of our experience, including the mysterious. We have an insatiable longing to make sense of the enigmatic features of our personal existence, of history, of the cosmos, and of reality as a whole. We naturally look for some revelatory image that will illuminate reality and make it intelligible. The quest for revelation is inseparable from our perennial human longing for some scheme that will allow things to fit together coherently. Even Albert Camus insisted that it would be dishonest of us to deny that a longing for clarity and lucidity about the nature of reality is an essential part of our existence.[21]

At the same time, however, both Camus, who was an atheist, and the great religious teachers have warned us not to be too hasty in piecing the puzzle of reality together. We run the risk of diminishing the mystery of reality and of ourselves if we plunge precipitously into shallow certitudes. The unraveling we sense at the edges of human existence and of the world must not be prematurely knotted by our own restrictive meanings. If there

[21]Albert Camus, *The Myth of Sisyphus and Other Essays* (New York: Vintage Books, 1955) 20.

is a revelatory key to reality, we must allow it to unfold at its own pace. And at the same time we must be open to surprise at the shape it eventually takes.

In its focus on Jesus Christ as the revelation of God, Christianity claims that the ultimate mystery of reality becomes incarnate in the life of a particular human being at a particular time in the history of the world. In Christianity, a major feature of the sacred is its paradoxical identification with the mundane. The infinite mystery takes on the definiteness of finitude as its mode of actual existence. The eternal identifies with the temporal and perishable. God, in other words, appears to Christian faith as a self-emptying mystery. The mystery becomes definite by limiting itself. In the Christian story, the inexhaustible depth of reality surfaces as a person like us—Jesus of Nazareth—who suffers crucifixion and death.

Interpreting this picture is the main task of revelation theology. In pondering it, we are led to an unprecedented understanding of mystery. The mystery of the world's infinite open-endedness initially strikes us as so frustrating that we try to transform it into an extended set of problems that we can control. But in the light of Christian revelation we are led to believe that the boundless, and perhaps initially terrifying abyss of mystery is in fact the consequence of an infinite God's own humble and loving self-withdrawal. In order to give the world and ourselves the open "space" in which to unfold our existence, the ground of our being absents itself, leaving behind, so to speak, a seeming void or abyss. By concealing its infinity within the limits of particularity, the absolute God graciously opens up for us an unlimited dimension of depth in which to live and move and have our being. The outcome of an infinite self-emptying, then, is an emptiness that seems infinite. This emptiness initially strikes us as a *mysterium tremendum,* that is, an awe-inspiring and even terrifying abyss. So we either shrink back from it in anxiety that we will be lost if we plunge into it, or else we try to domesticate it by reducing it to the merely problematic. In either case we fail to apprehend the absolute lovingness that lies concealed within the infinite void. A Christian theology of revelation instructs us that what might otherwise strike us as the occasion for despair is really the consequence of a boundless love.

That the abyss of mystery can be an occasion for despair is easily illustrated by modern atheism from Friedrich Nietzsche to Jean-Paul Sartre. The most serious forms of atheism interpret the boundlessness and seeming emptiness of mystery as an invitation to nihilism. There is surely an "abysmal" aspect to reality, and nihilistic philosophy and art are intelligible as an articulation of this terrifying face of mystery. But revelation, with its image of the suffering God, allows us to interpret the void not as absurd, but as the consequence of God's self-giving, self-limiting love.

However, the sources of Christian thought, especially the Old Testament, require also that we understand revelation as the disclosure of God's power. Indeed, in a manner of speaking, God's power is the central content of revelation. The one who delivered Israel with a mighty hand and an outstretched arm is the same power that delivered Jesus from death and established him as Lord. The psalmists and prophets constantly implore Yahweh to make manifest the divine power in the face of the attacks of enemies. In light of this dominant theme of God's power in the Scriptures and theology, the specter of God presented in the crucified man, Jesus—so utterly self-limiting—seems contradictory. The image of divine vulnerability and suffering that we encounter in the New Testament and in less dominant strands of theological tradition goes against what we expect God and power to be like. It seems to feed our agnostic suspicions that there is nobody in charge of the world and its destiny. God is supposed to be almighty, all-powerful, that is, capable of doing whatever "he" wills. That God freely suffers self-limitation in order to be one with us and our world is an idea that Christian theology has itself only reluctantly acknowledged. And it has done so only after making very careful qualifications. Its Trinitarian theology confesses the "communication of idioms," according to which the features and actions associated with one person of the Trinity are attributable to the others also. Accordingly, the sufferings of the Word made flesh cannot be viewed as though they occur outside of God's life. But long ago the Church also rejected patripassionism, the view that the suffering of the Son can be attributed to the Father also. And in many other ways the theological tradition has kept its distance from the idea of a kenotic God, even though to an increasing number of theologians today it has always been essential to Christian revelation.

How can we make sense of this apparent contradiction? Perhaps behind its reluctance to speak of a suffering God, there lies a legitimate concern that if suffering and death are ascribed too literally to the Godhead, the very foundations will be taken out from beneath our world. Moreover, we might wonder whence would come the capacity to deliver us and the world from evil, to bring the divine promise to fulfillment, if the person of God is itself so beset by defenselessness. Dietrich Bonhoeffer's famous remark, "only a weak God can help," sounds too extreme to many. And Jürgen Moltmann's recent revival of the theme of the crucified God, has been criticized as misleading even by such progressive Catholic theologians as Karl Rahner and Edward Schillebeeckx.[22]

[22]And yet Hans Urs von Balthasar, who in many respects appears more cautious in his theology than either Rahner or Schillebeeckx, has endorsed, through his reflections on Trinitarian theology, the notion of a suffering and dying God much more strongly than most other Catholic theologians: "the death, and the dying away into silence, of the Logos so become the centre of what he has to say of himself that we have to understand precisely his non-speaking as his final revelation, his utmost word:

On the other hand, the enormity of suffering by creatures on this earth, and perhaps especially the human suffering of the present century, makes it difficult for us to return to any concept of divine omnipotence in which God stands silently and apathetically beyond the world's evolutionary and historical struggles, able but unwilling to intervene. Such an idea seems theologically and spiritually bankrupt nowadays, even if at one time it was credible. On the other hand, the image of a self-limiting God who joins in utter solidarity with the suffering, the sinful, and the dying is more significant than ever today.

The earliest Christian sources already display an awareness that the philosophers and the wise of "this present age" will not easily entertain the paradox that power is made perfect in weakness. The identity of power with vulnerability is a great stumbling block to our ordinary sense of what is rational. But the revelatory image of a self-emptying absolute may just be the revelatory scandal which, if accepted in faith, can make all else intelligible. Even though the image of God's humility is paradoxical to human reason, we may be enabled by it to make much more sense of our world than we could without it.[23] The kenotic image of God provides a surer access to mystery than the more dominant idea of a coercive and domineering divine power. And, as we shall see later, our being grasped by the image of the self-limiting God promotes a heuristics (an impulse toward further discovery) that allows us to bring into our picture of the world, society, and ourselves elements that are usually excluded as unintelligible. In other words, the revelatory image of a self-limiting, self-giving, self-emptying God fosters a continually widening coherence in our understanding of reality and mystery. It evokes a distinct form of enlightenment that lets us see the possibility of redemption in the world and in history, and it provides an empowerment for a human praxis that helps to bring this redemption to pass.

and this because in the humility of his obedient self-lowering to the death of the Cross he is identical with the exalted Lord." *Mysterium Paschale*, 79.

[23]Perhaps the best approach to the problems we have raised is that of John MacQuarrie. He proposes a "dialectical theism," according to which we would avoid the conclusion that any statement about God can be understood as the whole truth. Dialectical thinking requires that whenever we make a statement about God, such as "God is all-powerful," we also allow that in some sense that God is weak and powerless. Such dialectical thinking pushes us toward some "higher" resolution, even if we never quite arrive there. *In Search of Deity: An Essay in Dialectical Theism* (New York: Crossroad, 1985).

4

Religion and Revelation

The conviction that mystery is revealed to us is not unique to Christianity and biblical religion. Religion in its entirety can be viewed generously as the disclosure of a transcendent mystery. In our own cultural context we call this mystery by the name "God." But peoples of other times and places have also experienced the breaking of mystery into their lives, and they have related to it, talked about it, and worshipped it through many different verbal and iconic designations. We cannot appreciate the Christian understanding of revelation unless we keep this wider religious world before us. A Christian understanding of revelation will become distinctive to us only if we view it in the context of other kinds of religious awareness.

Searching for distinctiveness, however, need not imply looking for ways in which Christian revelation might be better than others. Any singularity we may find in Christianity does not necessarily imply "superiority" to other faiths. Such a comparison would be pointless and arrogant. There is, of course, a considerable body of Christian opinion that still insists on a comparative devaluation of other religions. But we are now beyond the time in our global religious evolution when we need constantly to be so exclusivistic. This is not to say that all religions are the same, or that they can be reduced to some common essence. Such a simplifying perspective would enormously diminish the rich diversity of religious paths that history has bequeathed to us. Religions are not the sort of realities that can easily be comparatively graded. Perhaps aspects of them, such as their ethical implications, may be compared, but as total approaches to mystery, to human existence, and to the world, it makes little sense to say that one is clearly better than another. None of us occupies a neutrally objective perch, above or outside of all traditions, from which we could ever securely make such an assessment.

Fortunately, there is now developing, here and there, a new spirit of mutual openness and respect among influential religious thinkers representing the various faiths. For Catholic theology, the ecumenical movement and the Second Vatican Council have signaled the end of the old "apologetic" approach to revelation.[1] In the past, a defensive style of theology, remnants of which still unfortunately live on, sought to preserve an often rather narrowly conceived Christian notion of revelation from attack by alternative positions, whether religious or secular. As a result of the self-enclosure of this kind of theology, its treatment of revelation could not receive much nourishment from other traditions. Such isolationism is no longer acceptable in Christian theology.

Still it may be useful at this point for us to speculate on why religions are so vigilant in defense of what they perceive to be revealed truth. Such an examination may go some way toward helping us understand why the idea of revelation has been set apart by theology for special treatment in the first place. Why do Christians and members of other faiths stand guard so securely over their respective deposits of faith?[2] The following explanation of religion's preoccupation with apologetics is offered by British theologian John Bowker. It is certainly not intended as an adequate account, but it does offer a rather novel perspective, and it is one that we shall draw on at other points in the present book.[3]

Whatever else they may be (and they are other things besides), Bowker claims that religions are, at the very least, systems for processing information. They are living structures with boundaries built up over the course of sometimes many centuries for the purpose of encoding, storing, retrieving, and transmitting to the next generation a very important kind of information. This information is usually connected explicitly with some notion of revelation. It is a very special kind of information. It may be non-verbal as well as verbal, but it is not trivial. It has to do with salvation, liberation, and fulfillment, the goals that have traditionally mattered most to the majority of the earth's human inhabitants. Religion responds to the deepest and most urgent of all human concerns. It answers questions about the final meaning of life, and in doing so it shapes the identity of individuals. It responds in a decisive way to the need to be loved or forgiven and to the longing to discover the purpose of the universe.

---

[1] See the Council's document on revelation, *Dei Verbum.*

[2] The Greek word for bishop, *episcopos,* literally means "overseer."

[3] John Bowker, *Is Anybody Out There?* (Westminster, Md.: Christian Classics, Inc., 1988) 9–18; 112–43.

Religions are so important because they provide information about how to negotiate the most intransigent roadblocks we encounter in life. Whereas other techniques, like those of science and engineering, can remove more mundane obstacles, religions attend to the most irremovable limits on life: fate, guilt, meaninglessness, and death. Since religions deal with such important matters, the information they convey to their followers is the most valued of all. And so it needs to be carefully protected, more than any other kind of information. It is no wonder then that religions are so defensive—and for that reason also at times so dangerous.[4]

Information, Bowker says, does not just float about aimlessly in the universe. It has to be ordered and processed if it is to carry any meaning.[5] But for this purpose it requires a system, an organized channel through which content can flow and be reliably passed on to receivers. Any information system must be allowed to sustain a definite identity throughout the passage of time. It requires some degree of stability. And for that very reason it has to have clear *boundaries* consisting of sets of constraints. Without such limits the channeling system would collapse, and any revelatory information would dissolve into the noise of indefiniteness. A cell without a membrane would be too shapeless to carry the information essential for life. A computer without the constraints of its circuitry or a specific program could not organize and process information. The informational component in a cell, organism, or computer has to be constrained if it is to be informative. Clear boundaries must be imposed upon a system in order to allow for the processing and transmitting of information. And since religions are information systems (or, perhaps more accurately, complexes of informational sub-systems), they are not exempt from the need for definite constraints to protect the information they seek to transmit.[6]

The term "constraint" often has a negative ring because it seems to imply oppressive limitation. But modern information science insists that constraints are a positive and necessary feature of any information system. Without our adhering to the constraints of grammar, for example, we could not communicate information in speaking or writing. Our verbalizing would be unstructured and unintelligible. Religious systems are no exception to the informational need for limits. Were it not for their doctrinal constraints they would have no distinct identities. To be something definite, and not just a vague spewing forth of data, an information system requires clear borders. In the case of religions, doctrinal, ritualistic, and scriptural limits are necessary to protect the information

[4]Ibid., 15–18.
[5]Ibid., 114ff.
[6]Ibid.

about ultimate questions that they each consider important enough to pass on to the next generation of believers.

Especially in the early phases of a sect or religion's existence, a period of relatively narrow and restrictive self-definition seems necessary. A religion needs to get its sense of revealed truth under some control lest it fade off into indefiniteness. But even in later phases, the boundaries need to be maintained in the face of various threats to a tradition's identity. For that reason, religions will often tend to be conservative and apologetic. After all, they are absolutely convinced that they have information worth preserving. Not that they are totally immune to change. For they are each the product of a winnowing process which sometimes only over the course of many generations establishes clearly the constraints within which they assume distinctive shapes. Witness, for example, the tortuous history that culminated in the Nicene Creed or in the formulations of the Council of Chalcedon. But once doctrinal essentials are established, religious communities will not casually erase or redraw the revered boundaries that protect and channel the information they hold to be indispensable for ultimate fulfillment. So whenever a religion's boundaries are being attacked, either by insiders or outsiders, they must apparently be fortified.

This tendency to exclusivity has been present throughout the history of religion. It is apparently the role of bishops, popes, imams, gurus, and other officials to monitor the flow of information in a religious system by carefully patrolling its borders.[7] It is the function of codified doctrines and authoritative teachings to determine who is in and who is outside the system. Offensive to particular individuals and to outsiders as they may sometimes be, some sort of boundaries seem to be essential, informationally speaking. They are needed in order to keep the religious system from melting into a shapelessness that would prevent the ordering and transmitting of any information at all. A religion without boundaries simply could not function as a vehicle for passing on the revealed information.[8]

The problem, however, is that some religions draw their boundaries more sharply than others. And some subsystems within a tradition are stricter about doctrinal constraints than other subsystems. This is clearly the case with various factions of Islam. Or, to give a more familiar example, within Christianity Roman Catholicism is generally more concerned about boundaries than is Anglicanism.[9] At times a religion's or a denomination's borders can become unnecessarily hardened. And when this oc-

---

[7]Ibid., 14.

[8]And yet, we shall observe later how Christian revelation also has within it an impulse to transcend all boundaries in the interest of the inclusiveness manifested in the life and teachings of Jesus. See below, Chapters 6 and 9.

[9]Bowker, 129.

curs, religion can become exclusivist and self-protective to the point of being a menace to others.

The point here, though, is not to dwell on the negative implications of religions' concern for constraints. Rather we may be content for the moment simply to acknowledge that some kind of boundary maintenance is essential in order to protect the saving or revealed information that religions value so highly. Even in the most liberal forms of Christianity, traditional religious teachings, sacraments, and Scriptures exercise some sort of constraint on what people teach their children about the meaning of life, death, and reality as a whole. Religions can never be completely a case of "anything goes." They require "membranes" with at least some degree of thickness. Otherwise they spill over into such vagueness that they lose their identity altogether.[10]

Thus, information theory helps us understand the apologetic tone of so much religion and theology. It allows us to see why the concern for a specially revealed deposit of truth can be so important in the shaping and maintaining of a religion's identity. And it also suggests why religions often claim that their respective revelations are superior to those of others. Such a claim can be a very effective means of boundary maintenance.

However, we may now take a step beyond Bowker's illuminating use of the new information-systems model. For information theory also instructs us that religions, like other systems, cannot sustain any vital flow of information if they remain absolutely conservative and defensive. Information theory also requires that there be an element of *unpredictability* in any truly informative message. In order to be informative, a system has to avoid not only the chaos or "noise" of indefiniteness, which boundary maintenance is designed to assure, but also the monotony of excessive redundancy. Of course, some redundancy, that is, a tendency to repetitiveness, is a requirement for the flow of information in any system. For it is in such redundancy that informational constraints and boundaries are embedded. For example, the constant and repetitive adherence to the rules of grammar is essential for linguistic communication. But if the redundancy is excessive it will drown out the unpredictability and novelty that the passing on of information also needs.

This holds true for the obvious reason that if information were totally predictable it could not really be informative. If a system were simply an "order" without any openness to novelty, it would be frozen into a single identity and would therefore be incapable of anything other than self-duplication. It would be incapable of mediating any genuine revelation. Its absolute rigidity would inhibit the entrance of novel, surprising content. The same material would be repeated over and over, impeding the

[10]Bowker, 124–32.

flow of real information to present recipients. If I already know the content of the message coming across a telegraph wire, I can hardly call it informative or revelatory when it finally arrives. Absolute predictability inhibits the flow of information since everything is already fixed irreversibly in a stationary pattern. Only an entropic disassembly of the elements involved in information can allow for a reassembling into truly novel and informative patterns. A leaning toward disorder is necessary if information is to have the surprising character it requires in order to be information. As a system processes information it needs randomizing moments or trends in order for wider and more intensely informative patterns to emerge.

Thus any kind of information, revelatory or otherwise, has to walk the razor's edge between noise and redundancy, between chaos and monotony, between unintelligibility and repetition. Without a certain amount of redundancy, information would have no intelligible shape. But without a system's capacity for moments of deconstruction, no meaningful or relevant information could be inscribed in it. A periodic veering toward the state of "noise" loosens up a system to receive new life and information. Without such a capacity for randomization, a code would be too "stiff" to carry a message. If religions are information systems, then their revelations must also be in some way continuously open to novelty, precisely in order to sustain their informational character.

The extant religious traditions all began when the boundaries and constraints of their historical predecessors had become too restrictive to mediate the saving information required to interpret new historical circumstances. Buddhism, for example, originated when the Buddha perceived Hindu religious practice to be too confining to bring the fulfillment and release from suffering for which living beings longed. Islam began when Muhammad became sensitive to the dehumanizing implications of the idolatry of popular religious practice. And Christianity started in the fresh experience of the compassion of God by Jesus of Nazareth. Gautama, Muhammad, and Jesus all transgressed the boundaries and constraints that had shaped and channeled the flow of religious information in their respective cultures. It is clear then that religion and revelation are more than the passing on of a fixed tradition. The beginnings of influential religious movements are usually tied up with acts of rebellion and revolution. However, adventurous religious movements at some point typically abandon the innovative openness of their originating moments. They circle the wagons not only to contain their well-winnowed traditions, but also in order to seal themselves off from novelty. Too much novelty would lead to chaos, but without some opening toward surprise a religious system eventually stifles the traditional information it seeks to transmit.

Christian Attitudes Toward the Religions

As we move forward in our inquiry into the nature and plausibility of revelation, it will be helpful to keep before us the rules by which all systems process information. The transmission of ideas associated with revelation will be especially bounded by protective constraints. But a religion's understandable concern with clear borders may at times restrict the very novelty that originally made the ideas seem to be specially revealed.[11] Even though emphasis on doctrinal constraints is an inevitable phase in the formation of a tradition, there comes a time in its unfolding when a purely defensive posture leads to stagnation arising from under-nourishment. At such times a relaxation of the apologetic approach and a new openness to the foreignness of alternative ways of looking at mystery become essential simply for the sake of the vitality and survival of the tradition's revelatory capacity.

We are now living at such an exciting time for religions. World history is bringing the various traditions together into such mutual proximity that they can no longer ignore one another. Simply thickening their protective membranes and emphasizing doctrinal constraints, or the normative superiority of one deposit of faith over the others, now leads only to an obstruction of informational flow. In the final analysis, sheer defensiveness becomes an impediment to the communication of revelation.[12]

Although there is still considerable resistance on the part of many devout Christian believers to the new openness now being extended toward other religions, there is also a great deal of enthusiasm about it on the part of many others. Religion on our planet is now embarking upon a new and adventurous stage in its history. To an unprecedented extent, members of the various faiths are today in conversation, seeking to learn

[11]In order then for revelation to remain truly alive it must always be a source of new surprises for each generation of believers. We shall see later that our conceiving revelation in the form of "promise" allows for just this novelty, whereas a purely antiquarian retrieval of a "deposit of faith" from the past is by itself inadequate as a way of understanding the self-disclosure of God.

[12]As we shall see later, the openness of authentic Christian faith to the future, to novelty, and surprise invites it therefore to undergo considerable transformation in its encounter with other traditions. Christianity, following Jesus and Jesus' God, should be expected to be somewhat vulnerable and "defenseless" in any relational encounter with other faiths. If it defends anything vigorously it should be its own defenselessness and inclusiveness. Informationally speaking, this would entail a willingness to allow its boundaries to shift in response to new information in its encounters. In this way it preserves its identity instead of losing it. Like persons, a religion must "die" (abandon any non-relational exclusivism) in order to live.

new things from one another. This occurrence is too threatening for large segments of some traditions and subsystems, and so they have retreated into themselves, building thicker walls against the invasion of alternative points of view. But in other respects, the new inter-religious encounters are already changing the religious landscape of our world in a wholesome way. And they are inviting us to rethink our ideas of revelation in terms of inter-religious conversation.

Today, most Christian theologians have rejected, at least in principle, a purely exclusivist approach which would deny the revelatory value of other religions. Where significant controversy now exists, it involves the so-called "pluralists" on the one hand, and the "inclusivists" on the other. Informationally speaking, the pluralist theological option radically relativizes the importance of distinct religious boundaries, proposing that different religious traditions may all be equally valid ways of experiencing the revelation of an ultimate reality transcending the comprehension of any particular tradition.[13] The inclusivist approach in Christian theology, however, without denying the value of other traditions, is more concerned with boundary maintenance.[14] It is open to dialogue with other traditions and willing to have Christian faith enriched by ecumenical encounter and exposure to the sacred texts of other traditions. But it is not willing to sacrifice this teaching, expressed as early as Acts 4:12: "There is salvation in no one else [except Jesus Christ], for there is no other name under heaven given among men by which we must be saved."[15]

Whether one takes the pluralist or the inclusivist position, it is generally agreed that any Christian theology of revelation that we construct today has to be sensitive to the new consciousness of religious plurality emerging in our time. Previously, it was especially in the theology of revelation (and also Christology) that Christian theologians argued apologetically for the eminence of the Christian religion. They maintained that it has this status by virtue of a privileged access to God given in a special

[13]See the essays in John Hick and Paul Knitter, eds., *The Myth of Christian Uniqueness* (Maryknoll, New York: Orbis Books, 1987).

[14]See, for example, Gavin D'Costa, ed., *Christian Uniqueness Reconsidered* (Maryknoll, New York: Orbis Books, 1990).

[15]We are far from resolving this very important debate. Both the pluralist and the inclusivist positions are making important points. The perspective taken in this book (especially in Chapter 8) is that of an evolutionary cosmology in which the universe itself is the primary revelation of mystery and in which religions and their symbols are seen as expressions of the cosmos (and not just of isolated, cosmically homeless human subjects). Religion is something that the universe does through us in its evolutionary journey into mystery. Contemporary theology, including discussions between pluralists and inclusivists, is still hampered by a pre-evolutionary, acosmic understanding of religion.

revelation withheld at God's discretion from other religions. Much Christian theology still has overtones of this apologetic approach, but it is being challenged by a more ecumenically minded sensitivity to the revelatory possibilities in all the religions.

The traditional language of Christian religion and theology emphasized the centrality and normativeness of Jesus Christ as the decisive and final revelation of God. For centuries, Christians have been taught that the fullness of God's being becomes manifest *only* in Christ. And this teaching seemed to imply that we need not look elsewhere for any further data of revelation, least of all in the other religions. Our theologies of revelation focused almost exclusively on the Christ-event and its biblical environment. The exclusively Christo-centric character of revelation theology made it difficult for us to take seriously the revelatory character of primal religions, of Hinduism, Buddhism, Islam, and other religious ways.

The simple dynamics of human psychology provide some explanation for the tenacity of an exclusivist Christo-centrism. A devotee's concentrated commitment to Christ is not entirely different from one person's loyalty to another in ordinary situations of friendship or romance. Because of the limitations of our existence, it is difficult for us to divide our loves indefinitely. We normally need a central focus of devotion, and in our commitment to one individual we may sometimes devalue or deny the reality of others. In romantic love, sometimes it is as though virtually nobody else exists outside of the beloved. And even though to some degree one may outgrow sheer obsession, the normal predilection for a select person or group will still persist. The awesomeness of the world requires that finite beings "partialize" it in order to relate to it at all. We have to bite it off in little chunks, or else risk madness.[16] We simply do not have the capacity to consume it in all its depth and complexity. It would not be surprising, therefore, if this limitation overlays our grasp of any possible revelation of the mystery that encompasses us.

In the enthusiasm of devotion to Christ, a Christian will often insist that Jesus *alone* is savior and Lord. Such exclusivist language is consonant with the state of being enraptured or in love. Indeed, if it were absent one might even question the intensity of the devotion. When Christians proclaim Jesus Christ as universal savior, is this entirely distinct from the excessiveness of all love-language?

Still, when John's gospel testifies that in the incarnate Word *all* things have their being and when St. Paul extends Christ's lordship to the entire universe, are we not beyond the kind of exuberance that pertains to romantic expression? Is there not something more literally cosmic and metaphysical here? In any case, the universalism accompanying Christo-centric

---

[16]Ernest Becker, *The Denial of Death* (New York: the Free Press, 1973) 244.

exclusivism constitutes a major problem in today's inter-religious encounters. It is also a major issue in the theology of revelation. In what sense can Christians call Jesus Christ the decisive revelation of God, the savior of all humanity, or the Lord of all the universe, without treading on the religious toes of Hindus or Buddhists or others who sense no such universality in Christ?

In all honesty, today Christians have to ask whether their own concepts of salvation are any more universal in intention than those implied, for example, in the Buddhist ideal of the *bodhisattva,* one who is portrayed as having such sentiments as these:

> All creatures are in pain. All suffer from bad and hindering karma. All that mass of pain and evil I take in my own body. Assuredly I must bear the burden of all beings for I have resolved to save them all. I must set them all free, I must save the whole world from the forest of birth, old age, disease, and rebirth. . . . For all beings are caught in the net of craving, encompassed by ignorance, held by the desire for existence; they are doomed to destruction, shut in a cage of pain.
>
> It is better that I alone suffer than that all beings sink to the world of misfortune. There I shall give myself into bondage, to redeem all the world from the forest of purgatory, from rebirth as beasts, from the realm of death. I shall bear all grief and pain in my own body for the good of all things living. I must so bring to fruition the root of goodness that all beings find the utmost joy, unheard of joy, the joy of omniscience.[17]

At the moment when *nirvana* is about to occur, the *bodhisattva* (as portrayed in Mahayana Buddhism) pauses on its threshold, deciding that it is not yet the right time to enter fully into the blissful state of fulfillment. The mass of living beings still remains stuck in the cycle of rebirth and suffering. Other living beings have not yet attained the bliss of *nirvana,* so it would be inappropriate to enter into the rapture of final liberation as long as even one of them remains suffering outside. Thus the *bodhisattva,* filled with almost infinite compassion, renounces salvation until *all* living beings have been liberated. Would it be surprising if a Buddhist tendered the same sort of devotional regard toward the salvific person of the *bodhisattva* that Christians give to Jesus?

Following Chapter 1 of Paul's Epistle to the Romans, Christian theology has traditionally taught that revelation is present in a general sense throughout creation. In some way or other, all things are manifestations of God's glory. More recently, theologians have allowed that other religions, which are also a part of God's universe, have a special role to

---

[17]*Siksasamuccaya,* adapted from William Theodore de Bary, *The Buddhist Tradition* (New York: Vintage Books, 1972) 84–85.

play in manifesting the Creator. The Second Vatican Council explicitly affirmed the revelatory value and significance of the great religious traditions. But following mainstream Christian teaching, it continued to affirm the decisiveness and finality of the revelation given in Christ. It maintained that the prevalence of sin has blinded us to the full glory of God, and it seemed to imply that other religions can give no more than a glimpse of it. Only in Christ has sin been decisively vanquished and the fullness of God's being been made manifest.[18] And this seems to be the consistent teaching of the Christian churches.

Thus, along with the element of universality mentioned above, the doctrine of the unsurpassability of Christ as the final revelation of God has come to be a crucial point of controversy in inter-religious discussion involving Christians and other traditions. But do we not now have to keep in mind, even more than the Second Vatican Council, what a Buddhist or Hindu might think of our theologically exclusivist language? Should we make any theological statements today, even amongst ourselves, that will antecedently rule out the possibility of deeper conversation and eventual agreements with sincere members of other faiths? None of us can yet give definitive answers to these questions, and it may be years and even centuries before theological discussion has moved us close to any kind of resolution. But the question of how to interpret the doctrine of the universality and unsurpassability of Christ in the context of inter-religious dialogue is now with us for good, and the fact that it will not go away means that we may be at least a little closer to an answer than we were before.

A priori, of course, we cannot rule out the possibility that God can make one phase or moment of history more decisively revelatory than others. In fact, to suppose that every period in history or every person is just as transparent to mystery as any other seems quite implausible. In the evolution of an emergent universe, each "higher" development can make its initial appearance only at *one* particular time and place. There is something singular and unique about every new breakthrough in evolution and history. Perhaps the same could be said concerning the revelation of mystery through the religious traditions of humanity. It is not inconceivable that there would be degrees of revelational intensity at various phases in the religious dimension of the cosmic process, especially if there is a discernible axis of "progress."[19] That God's love, manifest in diverse ways

[18]At the Second Vatican Council both *Lumen Gentium* and *Dei Verbum* reaffirmed this traditional conviction.

[19]Whether the evolving universe is a progressive development is highly disputed. Generally speaking, scientific skeptics, like Stephen Jay Gould, repudiate the notion of evolutionary progress. Religious scientists, such as Teilhard de Chardin, however, discern clear lines of progress, at least in terms of the emergence of complexity-

throughout the duration of the universe, might come to a full and unsurpassable self-expression in an individual human being who lived and died in the Middle East almost two thousand years ago does not seem incongruous with what we now understand about the nature of an evolving universe, especially if we regard religion as a phenomenon emergent from the universe rather than just something done on the earth by cosmically homeless human subjects. Nor can we rule out the possibility that one aspect of God's total self-revelation is normative for all the others. Indeed, most Christian teaching in the past seems to have made exactly this claim for the Christ-event.

But in our religious situation today can we continue to maintain such an exclusivist Christo-centrism? Is honest dialogue with other religions possible as long as the cards of conversation are stacked in such a way as to make the dialogue partner's position inferior to ours from the start? Does not "dialogue" then become just another word for a not-so-subtle proselytizing? Do we not implicitly subordinate our conversation partners to ourselves if we insist from the start on the definitiveness and unsurpassable character of Christian revelation? Can Christians plausibly continue to affirm the revelatory supremacy of the Christ-event and at the same time be fully open to other traditions that have their own unique convictions about religious meaning and truth?

Before any of us undertakes to address these questions it may be well to recall two facts about religion that have become more visible in theology and other disciplines especially in the last one hundred years or so. The first of these facts is that religious reference is always *symbolic* rather than direct and literal. The character of mystery is mediated to human beings only by way of concrete aspects of the world. These may be called symbols or "sacraments" of mystery. Objects, persons, events, metaphors, analogies, and stories are the vehicles through which we first encounter the divine. Even "God," Paul Tillich says, is a symbol for God.

The fact that religious expression is symbolic, however, does not mean that it is inferior to direct, non-symbolic language. To say that religious expression is "merely symbolic" implies that non-symbolic reference to mystery is the ideal. But a completely clear or literal representation of ultimate reality would trivialize mystery to the point of idolatry. Accepting the symbolically vague nature of religion is not a surrender to softheadedness, but an implicit affirmation of the transcendence of the mystery that no human expression can capture adequately. Religion, we shall see, requires silent or apophatic moments precisely as protection against our taking symbols too literally. If we think carefully about the symbolic

consciousness. While it is impossible to discuss this controversy here, it is at least worth noting that it is not irrelevant to the question whether one historical revelation may be taken as an advance over others.

nature of religious language, it may lead us to acknowledge its inadequacy. And if we accept its inadequacy, this will leave an opening for us to learn things about mystery from other traditions that our own symbols may not convey.

The second axiom contemporary theology has to accept in our religiously plural context is that religious consciousness, no less than any other aspect of human awareness, is *historically conditioned*. All religious thought, utterance, and practice grow out of particular times and circumstances. They are bound up with specific localities and are subject to the cultural and linguistic constraints that prevail at the time they come to expression. Thus, there is a certain perspectival limitation or *relativity* inherent in all human attempts to affirm the absolute.

Acceptance of this relativity, however, does not mean that theology is forced to accept *relativism,* the view that nothing is absolute. It only means that any religious *representations* of the absolute are themselves relative. That is, they must be interpreted in terms of the cultural and linguistic patterns out of which they originate. If they are taken as completely timeless—in the sense of being immune to the conditional character of historical existence—they then become idols themselves instead of pointers to the mystery that transcends history and culture. To accept the contingent character of our religious language may seem at first to threaten its informational boundaries, and so in reaction we may be tempted to elevate our particular traditions to a status of timelessness that they in fact do not possess. But alternatively we might also take the new awareness of the relativity of our own doctrinal constraints as an opportunity to open ourselves to a wider world of revelation as it is mediated by other similarly conditioned religious traditions.

After all, there is no reason to insist that the Christian religion and its theological language are an exception to the two rules we have just enunciated. In the first place, Christianity, like most religions, is tied up with specific symbols or sacraments. Think, for example, of the wide variety of images and ideas by which the New Testament itself seeks to interpret the life and person of Jesus. The specificity and culturally shaped character of religious symbols is necessary if a saving mystery is to be communicated in a rich way to a particular people at a particular time. And second, even by virtue of its own doctrine of the incarnation, Christian faith accepts its thorough immersion in the particularity of concrete historical circumstances. This means that there is a certain relativity (not relativism) at the very heart of its own understanding of mystery. To confess this relativity is religiously necessary. And at the same time, it is the indispensable condition for honest dialogue with other traditions. There is little hope of our learning, appreciating, and appropriating the content of other religions unless we first accept the relativity, and that entails the revisability, of our own standpoint. If we assume from the start that we cannot learn anything from others because our own position has no room for growth, then entering into dialogue would be dishonest. And as pointed out earlier, it would also unnecessarily contract the informational character of our own faith tradition.

However, to return to the main issue before us, it may seem that we are being disloyal to traditional Christian teaching if we in any way cast doubt on the universal and unsurpassable character of Jesus the Christ as decisively revelatory of God. So in what sense can we continue to proclaim the special authority of Christian revelation while at the same time fully embracing the implications of our two axioms: on the one hand that our religious language, including our Christological categories, is never adequately representative of God, and on the other that it is always conditioned by historical relativity?

A Mystery-Centered Approach

Perhaps the best approach to take in this matter is a "mystery-centered" one. Without reducing all religions to a quest for one common essence—which the pluralist position is often accused of doing—and without making the simplistic claim that all religions are saying or doing "the same thing," it nevertheless seems that in their own widely divergent ways they all seek and express union with something like what we have been calling "mystery." In our dialogue with other traditions, the key to sustaining conversation (rather than cutting it short by claims that others will interpret as arrogant) is to keep before ourselves the possibility that in some way or other all religions may be relative, culturally specific ways of looking toward an ineffable mystery. Intuitions of mystery are universally possible and not confined to specific cultural-linguistic frameworks, simply by virtue of the fact that all people have limit-experiences and occasionally at least ask the limit-questions that transport us beyond the confines of the everyday. Indeed, it is awareness of limits that allows us to share human experiences across widely diverse cultures. Whatever transcends these limits, whether it be an emptiness, an abyss of nothingness, or a plenitude of being, is what we are calling mystery. This dimension of mystery is not a "common essence." However, the experience of limits is universal in human experience, so it seems reasonable to suppose that all religions bear some relationship to this experience.

According to this hypothesis, what is all-important is not our religions themselves, but the mystery of which they speak and to which they point. In the final analysis, what is really "unsurpassable" in *all* religions is the mystery that they mediate, and not the religions or theologies that speak of this mystery. And this is a point upon which, it seems, the greatest voices of all the traditions have already agreed.

Sensitive religious people have always been more oriented toward mystery than toward their own religions. Jesus, for example, clearly pointed his disciples toward an ultimate reality beyond himself and beyond the conventional religious certitudes of his day. And even though the New Testament expresses a Christo-centrism, its focus on Christ is best understood as a sacramental mode of *theo*-centrism. Without its general orientation toward God, Christology, like any kind of religious symbolics, would be idolatrous. It is clear that Jesus himself was God centered. The gospels indicate that like all humans he struggled with the temptation to self-assertion, but that he conquered the urge to make his own personality into a cult object. So if there is something unsurpassable about him for believers, it is ultimately derived from the mystery that he sacramentally mediates. Whenever a religion speaks of the "unsurpassability" of its central revelatory event, personality, or doctrine, religious wisdom exhorts us to acknowledge that only the unfathomable mystery to which these realities point is indeed unsurpassable. Jesus, for example, would never have insisted that his own being is unsurpassable. Rather, he would have given this status only to that ultimate mystery he referred to as "abba."[20] If Jesus' own person is unsurpassable it is so only in the sense that it is for Christians the primary sacrament of the encounter with the infinite God.[21]

But as we have already observed, from the point of view of Christian revelation, the unsurpassability of the divine mystery itself consists in the limitlessness of its self-emptying love. If we keep this kenotic aspect of mystery in mind whenever we use the adjective "unsurpassable," it may be possible to enter into religious dialogue in a spirit of openness and humility rather than with a doctrinaire inflexibility.

Moreover, it is not a requirement of authentic Christian faith to hold that the Christ-event is the only way through which divine mystery is mediated to human consciousness, including that of Christians themselves. Although there has been much controversy and even bitter dispute on this issue, Christian doctrine has never insisted that our sense of mystery is bound exclusively to the Christ. Mystery becomes transparent to people through the mediation of numerous aspects of nature, society, and human experience. It would be contrary to the spirit of Jesus' own faith, life, and teachings to tie our sense of the divine to the relativity of a single sacramental matrix, even if it is Jesus himself. The Christ-event can still

---

[20]See Leonard Swidler, "Jesus' Unsurpassable Uniqueness," *Horizons* XVI (Spring, 1989) 116–20.

[21]Edward Schillebeeckx, O.P. *Christ the Sacrament of the Encounter with God* (New York: Sheed and Ward, 1963) 7–45.

legitimately be taken as sacramentally normative for Christians without entailing a symbolic exclusiveness.

Today, in fact, the idea of revelation must be unfolded with an eye toward rendering intelligible the very fact of the plurality of religions themselves. In the past, apologetic presentations of revelation theology sought to suppress the significance of any religion but Christianity itself. It was almost as though the large majority of human beings have lived in total darkness, unillumined by the light of Christ. Now, however, we may acknowledge with more sincerity than before that the light that illuminates us in Christ also shines through other faith traditions in other ways.[22] Not to acknowledge this possibility is itself a kind of idolatry that obscures, as does all idolatry, the self-revelation of mystery. Idolatry is the elevation of a particular and relative approach to mystery to the status of sole and exclusive representation of it. Such idolatry can be as much a part of exclusivist Christianity as of any other efforts to tie the mystery of God down to the particularity of a single culture and time in history. On the other hand, by viewing the plurality of faiths from the point of view of our central revelatory image, that of God's self-emptying love, we may effectively confront the temptation to idolatry. Indeed, in the light of this image, we would be surprised if there were not a rich variety of revelatory religious paths. This point will be developed below.

The Four Ways of Religion

In Christianity, Jesus the Christ is the primary symbol or sacrament of our encounter with God. The distinctiveness of Christianity from other traditions lies especially in its choice of this particular "sacrament" as central. Most of the differences among the religions have to do with their understandably one-sided attachment to the particular sacramental images, events, experiences, or persons that they choose as representative of mystery.

But there is more to any religion than just the sacramental constituent. Religion of course always requires at least some symbols. But in addition to being sacramental, it is also mystical, silent, and active. Only a cursory look at the story of religion is needed to see that there is more than one way of orienting ourselves religiously toward mystery. And this diversity must influence our ideas of revelation as well.

We may present the four main "ways" of religion in the form of a simple typology suggested by a comparative study of distinct emphases found respectively in four different kinds of religion: early (or "primal") religion, Hinduism, Buddhism, and the prophetic religions (Judaism, Chris-

[22]See *Lumen Gentium,* Chapter II, #16.

tianity, and Islam).[23] The sacrificial practices of preliterate peoples suggest one way, the *sacramental*. The Hindu *Upanishads'* quest for union with the "One" implies another, namely, the *mystical*. The Buddha's renunciation of selfish craving together with his silence about theological issues offers yet another, what we shall call the *apophatic* (or silent). And finally, the intense social concern of the prophets provides yet another way, the *active*. If religion in general means an adventure toward mystery, it is now clear that there is more than one way of moving toward this goal.

More specifically: 1. Primal religion takes a predominantly sacramental or symbolic approach to mystery. It senses mystery only in relation to concrete objects, persons, and events. 2. Hinduism, especially *Vedanta*, exemplifies what we shall call the mystical tendency present in all religion. Mysticism, as we are using the term here, perceives more explicitly than sacramentalism the presence of an ultimate unity of mystery *beyond* finite realities and seeks to enter into this unity immediately and intensely, at times with little apparent need for sacramental mediation. 3. Buddhism, with its "way of renunciation," is characteristically silent (scholars would say "apophatic" or "hesychast") with respect to the nature of mystery. The "way of silence," which is likewise an ingredient, at least to some degree, in all religion, is so alert to the inadequacy of any sacramental images of mystery that it sometimes puts them completely aside, intending thereby a radical purification of religious consciousness. 4. Finally, Judaism, Christianity, and Islam (to oversimplify for the moment) may be taken as exemplars of the active side of religion. For them, the approach to sacred mystery is inseparable from a transformative *praxis* in the world of political, social, and economic existence.

Sacramentalism, mysticism, silence, and action are the four main religious "ways" of entry into mystery. To some degree they are each present in all the religions, but often with differing emphases. The history of religion teaches us that religion will preserve its integrity only if it keeps all of these four ways in mutual tension and relationship. Each of the four ways must be critically connected with the other three, or else it runs the risk of losing its religious character altogether (if by "religion" we mean a receptivity to the reality of sacred mystery). As we construct a Christian theology of revelation in the context of our growing awareness of the plurality of religious revelations, it will be helpful to keep this picture of the fourfold complexion of religion before us. It will enable us to see better the connections Christianity has with other religious traditions, and it will also assist us in clarifying the diverse ways in which mystery reveals itself in Christian faith.

[23]An expanded version of this typology is given in my book *What Is Religion?* (New York: Paulist Press, 1990).

Corresponding to each of our four religious components there is a representative sociological role or institution. Sacramental religion generates the office of *shaman* or *priest* as the representative of a divine order. The mystical way produces the type known as the *contemplative*. Our third religious type, represented especially by Buddhism, is based on the ideal of detachment, renunciation, and silence. These ideals are associated especially with the *ascetic,* one who renounces any clinging to the things of the world (traditionally represented in the institution of monasticism). And finally, prophetic religion inspires a fourth religious type, the *activist,* whose life is dedicated to the transformation of the world and society into a more just context for human life.

The activist, of course, may also be a priest, contemplative, and ascetic, all at the same time. But often the activist lives in tension with the other three types. The activist may criticize the priest, contemplative, or ascetic for not caring enough about the process of political and economic renewal of the social world. And the priest or mystic may question whether activists, preoccupied as they are primarily with the secular realm, are sufficiently oriented toward sacred mystery. But the activists, such as the biblical prophets, claim that the life of social concern is thoroughly religious, and they make "doing justice" the very heart of any authentic religious relation to the sacred mystery of God.

Each of our four ways also has its corresponding manner of interpreting the world of "secular" reality. Sacramental religion's attitude toward the world may be characterized as one of *enjoyment.* It rejoices gratefully in the goods of creation and interprets their giftlike character as a hint or revelation of the ultimate beneficence of God. Mystical religion exemplifies the religious *relativizing* of the world. It senses the ultimacy and unity of mystery more dramatically than sacramentalism, and it seeks to move more decisively beyond particular things, thus relativizing them in the light of the transcendent. Apophatic or silent religion, exemplified by the Buddhist renunciation of clinging, and also by the hesychast strains of other religious traditions, is significant for its patient *letting be* of the world. And activist religion seeks to change or *transform* the world. Strains of all four attitudes are found in any of the major religious traditions, though they are present with distinct emphases.

Finally, each of our four types is subject to its own peculiar *temptation.* As mentioned earlier, the four ways need to communicate with each other in order for religion to be healthy. If any one of them loses contact with the others, it degenerates into a caricature that eventually divests it of its revelatory character, of its transparency to mystery. For example, if sacramentalism is uninformed by the mystical tendency to relativize the things of the world, or by the apophatic suspicion of symbols, or by the activist need to change the social world, it will inevitably degenerate into idolatry and empty ritualism. When this occurs, it forfeits its mediating or revelatory character. If mysticism loses touch with sacramental symbols, with apophatic patience, and with the needs of the social world, it becomes a form of religious escapism. If the ascetical way of silence is not carefully qualified by at least some degree of sacramentalism, by the mystical sense of transcendence, and the activist concern for the world, it tends toward nihilism, the view that all things are empty of value. And finally, if religious activism breaks its ties with sacramental, mystical, and silent religion, it becomes indistinguishable from secular humanism, such as Marxism for example. These four temptations of religion, all of which in the extreme would frustrate any revelation of mystery, can be thwarted only if each religious way allows itself to be nourished by the other three.

Awareness of all four ways of religion and of their respective temptations allows us to approach the subject of revelation in such a way that in inter-religious dialogue, areas of religious agreement may show up more obviously than when we look only at the obvious sacramental differences. Of all four, it is in the sacramental arena that differences stand out most sharply. It is especially here that disputes and controversies arise. Different cultures will choose correspondingly different media by which to focus their sense of mystery. For example, in Christianity the primary sacrament is Jesus as the Christ, whereas Hindu *bhakti* might choose *Krishna* or *Kali* or numerous other deities. (It is likewise in the sacramental dimension that conflicts arise concerning the gender of God.)

It is extremely difficult, and probably impossible, for all peoples on earth to reach agreement all at once on the appropriateness, decisiveness, or normativeness of a specific *sacramental* mediation of mystery. However, this impasse need not prevent us from acknowledging the convergence among religions regarding the other three aspects of religion. The sacramental is only one of four essential religious ingredients. Some religious agreement may occur in reference to the mystical, apophatic, and active modes even where it is lacking in the sacramental.

For example, there has already been some convergence among representatives of the various traditions regarding the *mystical* dimension of religion. Likewise, we may look for more and more agreement on at least some of the *active* components of religious life. Regardless of a faith's sacramental peculiarities it is still possible to recognize some overlapping with other traditions on the question of what needs to be done in our world today. Buddhist monks, for example, are now engaging in protests against social injustice. And a convergence on the issue of planetary environmental ethics is very promising for the future.

Most important, however, is the possibility of inter-religious agreement flowing out of a common sharing of the religious way of silence. Here, more than anywhere else in religion, there can be virtual unanimity. The theme of the "ineffability" of mystery is taught to one degree or another by all the religious traditions.[24] To the extent that they are at all open to mystery they unanimously agree that no set of sacramental expressions can ever adequately communicate the content of religious experience. They are sensitive to the inadequacy of any images of, or language about, ultimate reality, and so they all make room for silence as an authentic religious corrective. Thus the occasional *avoidance* of images and symbols is a distinct and venerable religious "way" of opening ourselves to mystery. Authentic religion requires that at least at times we cease our habitual verbalizing and imagining what mystery is like, and silently allow it to be itself, purified of our always inadequate symbolic representations. The way of silence becomes the opening to an ever deeper sense of mystery. Thus it is an indispensable disposition for opening our lives to the revelation of God.

The fact that sacramental religion employs a multitude of symbols, rather than just one, already implies a wholesome conviction that no single concrete object, personality, or event can all by itself correspond completely to the unknown and unnameable mystery. And a sure sign of the informational openness of a religion is its willingness to experiment with a wide variety of metaphors. But the most obvious way in which religions acknowledge the reality of divine mystery is by their assuming the posture of pure silence. Like sacramentalism, mysticism, and action, silence is an essential condition for the reception of revelation.

In Buddhism, the emphasis on silence leads to a distinct world religion. Gautama, the Buddha, considered theological discourse to be utterly inappropriate. Talk about God or nirvana gets in the way of the process of bringing actual people salvation from suffering here and now. Other religious traditions share at least some of the Buddhist reserve about religious talk. There is an apophatic strain in Hinduism, Taoism, Judaism, Christianity, and Islam. And it is in their meeting on the plain of stillness that these very diverse traditions manifest their deepest sharing of mystery. In that sense their common reversion to silence renders sacramental differences somewhat less significant than they might otherwise appear to be.

Religious Pluralism and the Humility of God

In terms of a Christian theology of revelation, however, the sacramental normativeness of Christ is still the main issue. So we repeat now the question asked earlier: How can we enter seriously into inter-religious dis-

[24]See my book *What Is Religion?*, 113–27 for examples.

cussions while clinging to the doctrine of his uniquely normative and universal significance?

We cannot respond to this question without recalling, as we shall do in each of the following chapters, what we take to be the startling imagery presented by the Christian understanding of the revelation of mystery. Earlier we noted that the central content given in the Christian understanding of this mystery is summed up in the theme of the humility and self-abandonment of God. When ultimate power conceals itself in apparent powerlessness and when mystery "loses" itself in the particulars of history or in the uniqueness of a particular personality, there is already a ratification of the symbolic and the relative as the media of revelation. The fact that we have to resort to symbolic language and commit ourselves to a relative perspective in our thinking about God is not a defect for which we need to apologize. Rather, it is a direct implication (and imitation) of the humility of God. It follows from God's own eternal decision to forsake any domicile located exclusively outside of our time and space. The concrete sacramentality and historical relativity in our speaking of God is, therefore, not a problem to be solved in spite of our Christo-centrism. It is a direct expression and consequence thereof.

The image of God's self-humbling generosity is also the key to the plurality of religions. Given the extravagance of God as manifested in the evolving universe at large, it would indeed be surprising if there were not also a splendid variety in the religious unfolding of the cosmos as well. Nothing would be more out of character with mystery, with nature and its evolution, or with history and selfhood, than a drab homogeneity in any phase of cosmic emergence. And religions, we have to remember, are part of this cosmic emergence. In God's letting-be of the world by humble self-limitation, there is established the probability that there will be a plurality of (relative) paths toward the one Absolute. Each one of these paths is unique, and it would be unfruitful to measure them as though only one of them is in full possession of the truth and is thereby clearly superior to the others.

However, acknowledging plurality does not require that we suppress the Christian intuition of something unique, decisive, and unsurpassable in the Christ of faith. Yet this unsurpassability needs to be understood in such a way as to avoid the connotation of a superiority that negates the revelatory value and validity of other religious traditions. If there is anything decisive for faith in Christian revelation, it is the unsurpassably self-sacrificing character of the God who becomes manifest in Christ. The crucified Christ is the sacrament of a God who renounces omnipotence in order to "let us be."[25] This Christian image of God's humility and "let-

---

[25] This "letting be" does not mean that we ourselves become totally free of limits. In the first place, no being could be actual without being determinate, and that means

ting be" can also be our guide when we encounter other religions. We too can adopt an attitude of letting them be. Indeed this is the model for all human conversation. Adopting a tolerant and humble approach in inter-religious conversation is our own way of sacramentally representing the God revealed in Christ. Faith in revelation is at heart a commitment to imitating the self-absenting God who lets the world be, in order that it may flourish in rich and luxuriant spontaneity and variety. That the world of religion also manifests this florescent diversity should not surprise us. Instead, it can be another of the many reasons we have for rejoicing in the extravagance of the mystery revealed in biblical religion as the one who makes and keeps promises.

limited. There is, of course, the possibility that in our hubris we will demonically go beyond our proper limits in the wake of God's loving self-renunciation. But God's own self-sacrifice is itself the criterion of human existence as well, and in our imitation of God's own self-emptying, we would discover our own proper limits. See Geddes MacGregor, *He Who Lets Us Be* (New York: Seabury, 1975).

5

Promise

In the previous two chapters we sketched the broad religious and symbolic context out of which the notion of revelation may be understood. We noted that without our having an antecedent sense of the silent and mysterious depths of reality, the idea of revelation has little meaning. An awakening to mystery, then, is the first step in a theological appreciation of revelation. Religions in general are ways of bringing mystery to awareness. They generally appreciate the necessity of mystagogy as the condition for opening up our consciousness to the possibility of revelation. Through their sacramental representations of the sacred, in their mystical longing for transcendent unity, in their experience of the demand to act justly and lovingly in the world, and in their assuming the apophatic posture of pure silence, religions place us before the possible unfolding of a holy mystery.

Because of their diverse sacramental features, religions differ considerably from one another in the ways by which they formulate for their followers the fundamental character of this mystery. Although they generally agree that mystery is in some sense gracious, salvific, and fulfilling, there are endless variations in their imaginative envisagements of the nature of ultimate reality. It is not our task here to summarize these differences. We must leave that enormous undertaking to the historians of religion. Instead, we shall focus here only on the manner in which biblical religion, and particularly Christianity, unfolds its own unique experience of the dimension of depth to which the many religions witness in their widely dissimilar ways.

Mystery as Promise

All religions have some vision of "salvation," fulfillment, or liberation. Because of the universal experience of suffering, people have naturally sought a definitive solution to sorrow and evil. They have looked toward some final state of deliverance. And religions have attracted so many followers because they provide ultimate ways toward release from suffering, death, and other limits. But they do not all propose the same route to redemption. The religions descended from Abraham, for example, have a unique appreciation of mystery and a distinctive understanding of the salvation that coincides with it. They experience mystery especially in terms of "future," and they understand deliverance or salvation as an experience whose definitive occurrence resides not in the past or present, but only in the future.[1]

This vision of the ultimate futurity of reality sets biblical religion apart from the other traditions. Primal religion was chained to the cycle of seasons. Its sacramental relation to animals, fertility, and earth gave it a cyclical character based on the repetition of natural occurrences. It was not yet aware of the radical openness of reality to the future. It remained bound to the soil, the sun, the moon, the forests, rivers, and seasons. This sacramental attachment to nature still lives on as an important layer within many religions. And it would be a considerable impoverishment of religions if they ever forgot their origins among the ancient hunters and gatherers of the Stone Age and the more recent planters and harvesters of the agricultural period originating about ten thousand years ago. The sacramental life of religious people to this day carries with it metaphors (such as the dying and rising of a god) that owe their original meaning to the religious imaginations of our forbears of the early agricultural period.[2] Although biblical religion overlays the natural world with historic meaning, it nevertheless does not completely abandon the natural-sacramental mode of religion. This is a point worth holding on to as we search for a response in the religions to our global environmental crisis.

All of the axial religions, in fact, maintained some connection to nature's rhythms and cycles. But they also nurtured a new restlessness that loosened them from early religion's immediate connection to nature. The

---

[1]See Jürgen Moltmann, *The Experiment Hope,* edited and translated by M. Douglas Meeks (Philadelphia: Fortress Press, 1975). Much of the interpretation of mystery given in this chapter follows ideas of Moltmann. However, the writings of Ernst Bloch, Teilhard de Chardin, Wolfhart Pannenberg, Karl Rahner, and their many followers have also influenced the ideas presented here.

[2]It is possible that the metaphor of "resurrection," for example, was originally nurtured by the experience, going back to the neolithic period, of planting in the ground seeds which "die" and then "rise" to new life.

Vedantic quest for the One, the Platonic postulation of an ideal world of being beyond the becoming of the sensible world, and the Buddhist renunciation of the religious clinging to concrete worldly objects—these and other developments in the first millennium B.C. augured a new and more disturbing understanding of mystery while showing the provisional and imperfect character of the world of ordinary human existence. Simultaneously they relativized the sacramental orientation of early religion by warning of the narrowing effects of idolatrous attachments.

The religion of Israel developed a unique version of the axial disengagement from purely nature-oriented religion. Filled with an unprecedented hope for a *future* fulfillment within the context of history, it no longer thought of the cycles of nature as the primary sphere in which fulfillment is to be found. As noted above, it did not entirely abandon nature. It is impossible to do so. But it began to think of mystery more in terms of a vision for *history* than in terms of the sacral dimension behind natural phenomena. And it learned to think of God as one who continually holds out a fresh promise for the future, as one who calls us to hope in a vision yet to be fulfilled.

Hans Küng summarizes the temporal and futurist slant that biblical religion gives to the axial intuition of a transcendent mystery:

> Transcendence . . . is conceived no longer as in ancient physics and metaphysics, primarily spatially: God *over* or *outside* the world. Nor is it to be understood on the other hand as idealistically or existentially interiorized: God simply in us. No, in the light of the biblical message transcendence must be understood primarily in a temporal sense: God before us. . . . God is not to be understood simply as the timeless eternal behind the homogeneous flow of coming to be and perishing, of past, present and future, as he is known particularly from Greek philosophy; but it is precisely as the eternal that he is the future reality, the coming reality, the one who creates hope, as he can be known from the promises of the future of Israel and of Jesus himself: "thy kingdom come."[3]

This religious attitude of looking toward the future for deliverance is known as *eschatology*. Thus Judaism and Christianity may be called eschatological religions. The term "eschatological," derived from the Greek

[3]Hans Küng, *Eternal Life,* trans. by Edward Quinn (Garden City, New York: Doubleday & Co., 1984) 213-14. Küng acknowledges the debt that Christian theology owes to the Marxist philosopher Ernst Bloch and to Bloch's main Christian theological follower, Jürgen Moltmann, for retrieving this futurist aspect of the biblical understanding of God. For centuries it had been lost beneath the metaphysical categories Christianity inherited from Greek philosophy.

noun *eschaton,* literally means "final" or "last." In Christian theology, the term "eschatology" formerly meant a study of the "last things," i.e. death and life beyond death. But in its broader and more biblical meaning, it designates the hopeful looking forward to a future salvation.[4] The notion of revelation, we shall be emphasizing, needs now to be grasped again in its profoundly eschatological nature.[5]

Eschatological thinking appeals to believers partly because it provides a response to the perennial problem of suffering. The solution to suffering in eschatological religion begins with a *hope* that the God who comes to us from the realm of the future will bring the end of frustration. By hoping for a future deliverance, biblical eschatology renders present misery only temporary, and even though distress may still remain, the prospect of an eventual solution at least makes pain more bearable. Without such hope, suffering is intolerable.

In the face of suffering, eschatological religion conjures up a rich array of images pointing to future salvation. It speaks of *shalom,* of the "day of the Lord," of the coming of the Son of Man, of the "reign of God." But perhaps its fundamental contribution to the history of religion is its idea of a personal, caring God who makes promises and intends to deliver people from their suffering. It is in the realm of the future that this God's reality most fully resides. The esoteric Marxist philosopher Ernst Bloch observes that the God of promissory religion "has the future as the mode of his being."[6] This God is the source of endless surprise, holding out the vision of a realm of fulfillment and joy far surpassing all present anticipations. The image of a promising God who meets us out of the mysterious future subverts the archaic religious instinct to seek fulfillment in nature or in the present moment alone, or in an escape from history into timelessness. The promising mystery holds out a new vision of creation's possibilities and thereby sabotages our instincts for securing our existence only in the predictability of natural recurrences.

The invasion of promise into human consciousness has proven to be quite disturbing, as the biblical texts testify. Promise is troubling because it demands of us a willingness to let go of the present and to forsake our tendency to define reality only on the basis of what has already happened in the past. Its God is one who makes all things new (Rev 21:5): "For behold I create new heavens and a new earth. . . ." (Isa 65:17).

What is meant by promise? Jürgen Moltmann, who—perhaps more thoroughly than any other contemporary theologian—has retrieved the

---

[4]For a summary of recent theological interpretations of eschatology, see Zachary Hayes, *Visions of a Future* (Wilmington: Michael Glazier, Inc., 1989).

[5]Moltmann, *Theology of Hope,* 37–94.

[6]Quoted in Moltmann, *The Experiment Hope,* 48.

biblical theme of promise and hope as central to the Christian vision of revelation, answers as follows:

> A promise is a pledge that proclaims a reality which is not yet at hand. A promise pledges a new future, and in the promise this new future is already *word-present*. If a divine promise is involved, it means that this future does not result from those possibilities which are already present, but that it originates from God's creative possibilities. God's promise always points to a new creation as the word for divine "creation" in the Old Testament, *barah*, indicates. . . . The *word* of the promise itself already creates something new.[7]

In the Bible, God's transcendence is located not so much "up above" as up ahead, in the realm of the future. Moltmann seeks to recapture the biblical notion of the future as the realm of divine transcendence. But he emphasizes that the future can be conceived of as the primary abode of God only if we allow that it contains possibilities and surprises that we are incapable of calculating on the basis of present experience.[8] The future is God's, and God's future is not a simple unfolding of potentiality latent in our present or past. Rather, in its transcendence it comes to us in a way that we cannot predict or control. It cannot be completely planned. And genuine hope, the fundamental consequence of biblical faith, possesses an openness to this future and a willingness to undergo the transformation that it requires as we go to meet it.

By offering a new future, the biblical word urges us to move actively toward the realization of the promise it announces. The revelatory word of promise not only announces, it also transforms. Opening ourselves to the novelty of God's future requires an active struggle with those inclinations in us that seek security in a settled past or an untroubled present. So we often resist the futurity of being. But in so doing we obscure the goal of our deepest and most intimate yearnings. In disclosing undreamed-of possibilities for us, revelation seeks to expose the very core of human longing as well. This process can be quite uncomfortable even while it is very promising. The mysterious depth of God's future may first present itself to us as an abyss to be avoided rather than as a ground of consolation. The future appears to us a *mysterium tremendum*.

For this reason, contrary to what many critics of religion have claimed, accepting the promise held out by eschatological faith is by no means an easy or childish escape from the difficulties of human existence. The uncertainty of a future that appears only in the form of promise rather than

[7]Ibid., 49.

[8]Jürgen Moltmann, *Zukunft der Schöpfung* (Munich: Chr. Kaiser Verlag, 1977) 21-22.

as an instantaneously complete manifestation of the sacred is terrifying. Accepting the unpredictability of the future is too much for us at times, and so we seek refuge in the more certain and predictable realm of nature or in our past achievements. Trusting in an uncertain future is much more challenging than is a religiosity based on the securing of ourselves to present certitudes. Eschatological religion does not appeal to the human instinct for safety as much as to our passion for adventure. Much that goes by the name "religion" is little more than a sanction of the status quo or a flight from the messiness of historical existence. Our religiosity easily reverts to an idolatrous sacramentalism or an aversion to temporality and history. But eschatological faith is intolerant of such escapism.

Abraham

We gather from the Bible that the promissory vision of existence originated in the dreams of a semi-nomadic people in pre-axial Mesopotamia. Among the natives of the Fertile Crescent during the second millennium B.C., perhaps there was a "wandering Aramean" known as Abram.[9] Like all semi-nomads, he was required by seasonal changes to shift his herds and family constantly in search of new resources. Such a restive life allowed no final settling down into one fixed place. Thus the nomadic existence nourished a spirit of anticipation. Fresh possibility loomed constantly on the horizon. In such disquiet there may have occurred the first hints of the futurity of mystery that would culminate in a new and distinct religious tradition.[10] The biblical understanding of God would eventually blossom from this ancient intuition of reality's promise.

According to the Bible, Abram used to travel the caravan routes linking Ur, Haran, Damascus, Shechem, Hebron, and Egypt. At a certain point in his wanderings, he experienced a summons from God to leave his ancestral home and go forth to a new life of unknown promise. In some of the most memorable words of the biblical tradition, God is said to have called Abram:

> 'Go from your country and your kindred and your father's house to the land that I will show you. And I will make of you a great nation, and

[9]We are not concerned here with questions of the historical facticity of the ancestor narratives in the Bible. Rather, we are concerned only with the way in which such accounts express the promissory faith of Israel.

[10]Even when Israel finally abandoned the nomadic life of her ancestors, the wandering spirit remained at the heart of its God-consciousness, and this served to make Israel's religious experience unique among the nations. See Moltmann, *Theology of Hope,* 79.

> I will bless you, and make your name great, so that you will be a bless-
> ing. I will bless those who bless you, and him who curses you I will curse;
> and by you the families of the earth shall bless themselves.' (Gen 12:1-3)

It is impossible to determine the exact circumstances surrounding this
calling. The biblical narratives about the ancestors are colored over with
religious and political ideals of later periods of Israel's history and hopes.
It is conceivable that there was an historical Abram who experienced mystery in the mode of a future promise. In any case, the picture presented
in Genesis portrays him as one who felt God's future beckoning him toward the uncertainty of a whole new way of existing. Perhaps he felt a
deep uneasiness about abandoning himself to its promise. But he is pictured as surrendering himself to God's promises in an attitude of trust
that has remained the norm of authentic piety to this day in the Jewish,
Christian, and Islamic traditions, all of which claim him as their father.

As the book of Genesis tells it, God periodically renewed the promise
to Abram: "To your descendants I will give this land." (12:7) "All the
land which you see I will give to you and to your descendants forever"
(13:15). "Look toward heaven, and number the stars, if you are able to
number them. So shall your descendants be" (15:5). "Behold my covenant is with you, and you shall be the father of a multitude of nations"
(17:4). And in Abram's old age, God bestowed on him a new name:

> 'No longer shall your name be Abram, but your name shall be Abra-
> ham; for I have made you the father of a multitude of nations. I will
> make you exceedingly fruitful; and I will make nations of you, and kings
> shall come forth from you. And I will establish my covenant between
> me and you and your descendants after you throughout their genera-
> tions for an everlasting covenant, to be God to you and to your descen-
> dants after you. And I will give to you, and to your descendants after
> you, the land of your sojournings, all the land of Canaan, for an ever-
> lasting possession; and I will be their God' (17:5-8).

As we have already noted, the biblical stories about Abraham express
the sentiments of later stages in the history of Israel. So it is hard to sift
out the events as they actually happened or to distinguish them from later
interpretations. But, for our purposes, such otherwise significant scholarly effort is not necessary. It is sufficient to emphasize the distinct mode
of the appearance of mystery as it is portrayed in these passages. What
stands out is that revelation comes in the mode of a promise of *future*
fulfillment to which we can relate only by adopting the posture of hope.
Promise is the *form* of revelation, and hope is the indispensable attitude
for the *reception* of revelation. Revelation is not, biblically speaking at
least, a vertical interruption from above. It is not a passing of informa-

tion from "up there" to "down here." Nor is it a mystical rapture with the One such as we find, for example, in Vedantic Hinduism. Neither is it Buddhism's sudden entrance into *nirvana*. Revelation is not the present uncovering of the nature of ultimate reality, as much traditional theology would have it. The fullness of the future cannot be exhaustively disclosed in any particular present moment within history. For that reason, it is difficult for theology to maintain that revelation has yet been completed. Thus revelation may best be understood as the disclosure of God's vision of the future in the form of a promise. And in any present moment, we attune ourselves to this revelation only if, like Abraham, we let go of the present and renew our hope in the promise of an open, uncertain, but fulfilling future.

Characteristics of Promise and Hope

The main features of the divine promise are its *gratuity, extravagance,* and *surprise.* These three persistent elements of revelation are already present in the story of Abraham, and they recur in numerous other biblical narratives. Revelation's gratuity—its undeserved nature—is manifested, for example, in Abraham's doing absolutely nothing to earn the promise bestowed on him and his posterity. The promise always arrives in a most unexpected way, often when conditions seem to be impossible and incapable of redemption. "Grace" is the name that Christian theology has given to this freely bestowed promise of fulfillment. The gracious character of the promise implies that we ourselves are not in a position to wrest any revelation from the heart of mystery. We can make no claim upon it, even by the most virtuous of our actions. We may open ourselves to it in hope, but we cannot exact it. It comes as a gift.

Second, revelation is extravagant. There is no apparent limit to the abundance promised to those who trust in God's promise. Abraham's posterity will be numberless. The land his posterity will inhabit will be bounteous to the point of overflowing. Throughout the Bible, God's revelation is constantly portrayed in images of excess. This immoderate nature of revelation is a quality that our parsimonious human habits of religiosity find quite disturbing at times. Usually our expectations of how any conceivable revelation might confront us are framed in terms entirely too narrow to contain its superabundance. But it always spills over the upper limits of our apparatus for receiving it. And so we typically filter it out and shrink it down to our own size rather than embrace it in its fullness.

In the third place, and precisely because of its gratuity and extravagance, the revelatory promise catches us by surprise. It goes beyond our wildest expectations and imaginings. None of our present anticipations of the mystery of the future can adequately forecast the actual shape it will take as it comes into conformity with God's vision for the world.[11] The consistent biblical teaching, which becomes most explicit in the apocalyptic literature, is that the future is ultimately God's future. Biblical religion, therefore, requires that we always keep ourselves open to the possibility that this future will surprise us. The indispensable condition for the reception of revelation is an openness to the possibility of being surprised.[12]

The appropriate response to the free, extravagant, and surprising promise of God is hope. Hope is a radical, unquestioning openness to the breaking in of God's future. It is not the same as mere wishing, or naive optimism, although hoping does not necessarily exclude wishing and optimism either. But wishing without hoping can, as Freud shows, easily become nothing more than illusory projection. And wishing may be little more than the fantasizing of a future whose shape is determined exclusively by what *I* (first person singular) would like *now* (present tense).[13] Such an attitude, insofar as it is devoid of hope, closes one off from any possibility of being surprised by the actual arrival of a truly transcendent future. Though we cannot and perhaps should not even try to purify our hope of all elements of wishing,[14] we may still distinguish it from less expansive modes of desire. Hoping is understood here as openness to the radically new. It is a willingness not necessarily to renounce but at least to relativize the optimism of wishing, which is usually oriented entirely from the point of view of our present situation and needs. Instead, hope transforms our natural human desiring into an openness to that which present awareness may not even begin to envisage as possible.

Hope is a posture that embodies all four of the religious ways discussed in the previous chapter. First, it generates a highly sacramental aspect in its rich images of the future. For it is through our images of hope that God's future first comes to birth in our world. Human imagination is the vehicle of divine revelation.[15] Such an observation might seem at first to arouse an enormous number of epistemological difficulties. For if revela-

---

[11]For this reason, the theology of Karl Barth, with its emphasis on the otherness of God's word, is a healthy corrective to the straitjacketing effect of many of our hermeneutical efforts.

[12]This is a point that has been made more consistently in the works of Andrew Greeley than in the writings of most theologians.

[13]H. A. Williams, *True Resurrection* (New York: Harper Colophon Books, 1972) 178-79.

[14]See William Lynch, *Images of Hope* (Notre Dame: University of Notre Dame Press, 1974.

[15]Ray Hart, *Unfinished Man and the Imagination* (New York: Herder & Herder, 1968) 180-266.

tion is so closely tied to our faculty of imagining, how do we know that
it is true to reality? How can we tell when our images of the future arise
out of hoping rather than solely out of wishing? How do we know when
imagination is exclusively projective and when it has elements of radical
openness to a transcending future?

It would seem that our longing for the future is genuine hope rather
than mere wishing, only if, along with its images of the future, it also
includes mystical, apophatic, and active elements that keep these images
from being frozen into absolutes. As we argued in the preceding chapter, religion is most wholesome when it balances its four elements—
sacramentalism, mysticism, silence and action. The same criterion of
authentic religion—namely, that of keeping the four aspects in dynamic
tension—can be used to distinguish hope from unrealistic fantasy.

Hope, as we have just noted, has a sacramental character in that it is
always embodied in images of the future. Without a lively imagination
there can really be no hope. Hope cannot take root in our lives without
very concrete imaginative representations of the future. For example, as
we shall observe, Israel's hope in God's promise takes on the vivid shape
of a search for a secure homeland. But hope's openness to the futurity
of mystery is ensured especially by its including also a mystical willingness to transcend endlessly the particularity of sacramental images. Moreover, its realism is grounded in an apophatic patience and capacity to wait
in silence, as well as in its embodiment in concrete action, or in what contemporary theology calls *praxis*. It is by maintaining a healthy tension
among these four aspects that hope avoids escapism and opens itself to
the revelation of God's promise.

Let us look a bit more closely at the mystical, apophatic, and praxis-
oriented aspects of hope. Hope manifests its mystical side in its longing
for ultimate *union* with the future and therefore deliverance from the relativity of the present. Prophetic religions have often been sharply contrasted
with Asian religions because the former seem to be less interested in mystical union than the latter. Such a comparison, however, is difficult to
sustain. For in hope's reaching out to the future, it is also seeking intimate union with sacred mystery, which in the prophetic context happens
to have the shape of "future." The fact that mystery bears the character
of futurity, however, does not make prophetic religions less mystical than
any others, if by mysticism we mean a longing for and experience of union
with ultimate reality. There is even a sense in which the person who hopes
seeks thereby to lose or abandon herself to God, taking on the attitude
of complete surrender that is typical of mystical experience everywhere.
In that sense at least, the desire for union with God is no less passionately
mystical in biblically based religions than it is in the Asian traditions. The
difference is that hope does not insist upon a full epiphany of God, nor

does it pretend that in any historical moment we can ever achieve complete and total enjoyment of God.

Hope also gives evidence of an apophatic or renunciatory aspect in its willingness to let go of the present and in its patient *waiting* for the genuine arrival of God's future. This willingness to wait is clear evidence of a mature hope's openness to the graciousness, extravagance, and unexpectedness of revelation. Hoping, we have noted, is not an easy attitude to assume. It may indeed be quite painful.[16] The first implication of hope, after all, is that the present must be abandoned. Hope carries its own kind of asceticism.[17] It requires that we cease our clinging to the way things are. Genuine hope, moreover, is faithful to the apophatic requirement of authentic religion in its willingness to forsake obsession with any single sacramental image or vision of the future. As it allows the mysterious future to enter into the present, it abandons any exclusivist fixation on previously consoling images and begins to experiment with new ones. It seeks to transcend utopian visions of the future that had been built up out of our previous wishings. It lets go of the present in order to receive the open, surprising, and inexhaustible reality of the future. In its exposure to surprise, genuine hope yields to the future in a way that allows the latter to retain its "otherness" and ineffability. It does not try to coerce, but expresses its willingness to let go of comforting and optimistic imaginings spun too abundantly out of our own narrowness of perspective. It does not seek to force mystery to take on the shape of our desires. For that reason, it is entirely appropriate for us to speak of an apophatic dimension of hope. No less than Buddhism, a religion of hope must be ready to renounce those cravings that tie us down to the present. Its adoption of the "way of silence" guarantees the realism of hope over against the short-sightedness of mere optimism.

Finally, hope contains an active aspect in its refusal to wait in sheer passivity. Hope realizes that the arrival of the future requires our energetic involvement in its coming. The vision unfolded in biblical revelation can become incarnate in our world only as we cooperate actively with

[16]As Moltmann indicates, the Greeks even saw hope as an evil to be avoided, because it is an attitude that time and again leads to disappointment. According to the myth of Prometheus, hope is the last and greatest of the evils that escape from Pandora's box: "In addition to all other evils, man acquired yet another: hope. It deceives him with illusions and thus intensifies all his sufferings. If we were able to be free of hope, then we would be able to come to terms with all forms of our suffering. We would no longer experience our suffering as pain. We would then have no more fear; without fear and without hope we would be invulnerable like the Stoics. Hope is a fraud. Only if one sees through this deception is he or she at peace. Give up hope, then you are happy!" *The Experiment Hope,* 16.

[17]Williams, 178–79.

the power behind that vision. For this reason, Christian teaching rightly rejects a quietism that leaves our human activity and creativity out of God's revelatory vision. Of course, it spurns any "works-righteousness," according to which our own actions are made the sole criterion of salvation. But it also finds unacceptable the notion of a faith that fails to challenge us to a praxis corresponding to God's plan for the world and its future. Concretely, this implies that we incarnate our hope, for example, in action for justice on behalf of the poor and abandoned.

In summary, then, if we follow the Bible, hope in God's promise is the core of authentic religion. The story of Abraham's fidelity to the promise is the model of fidelity to God. Stories of such unflagging loyalty are necessary to fuel our own faith in revelation's promise. For Buddhists, the story of Gautama is the central model for their own persistence on the path toward enlightenment and final freedom from suffering. When Buddhists hear about Gautama, with all his struggles and temptations, they are encouraged to sustain their own life quests, keeping in view the fact that Gautama eventually reached his true destiny. All religions contain narratives of such courage, and it is in these heroic accounts that the character of a religion is most vividly represented. For Jews and Christians, as well as Muslims, it is Abraham's enduring faith in God's promise that constitutes our shared model of faith and hope.

We notice that Abraham had many apparently solid reasons to abandon his pursuit of the promise. His own wife's infertility hardly augured well for one who was promised descendants that would outnumber the stars in the sky. He was commanded, by the same God who had given him the promise of enormous progeny, to sacrifice his own son Isaac. Yet Abraham continued to trust, and his perseverance remains the standard of religious fidelity in the prophetic faiths.

Judaism

Revelation, as we observed above, takes the shape of very concrete images of God's vision for the world's future. In order to have any content, it requires a symbolic or sacramental component. In Hebraic religion, the ideal of a *land* in which to dwell at peace is the great sacrament of hope. Through it, the mystery of the future enters concretely into the religious consciousness of the people. To this day, much Jewish faith requires a specific homeland as the indispensable sacrament of its encounter with the mystery known as God. Its need for sacraments of promise explains the symbolic power of the land of Israel or the city of Jerusalem as an emblem of hope. Without such visible and tangible monuments to the future, existence as a people would become inconceivable to many Jews.

The importance of a homeland for this people cannot be appreciated aside from the deep religious need for sacramental representations of a future in which to hope. Hope must be embodied in concrete realities if it is to arouse all levels of our longing.

The story of the Jewish quest for the "land" is well known. Most of what Christians have traditionally called the Old Testament centers around the quest for a Promised Land, the successful occupation of this land, the struggle to hold onto it, the anguish at losing it, and the prospects of reclaiming it. Often, Christians and other religious people have difficulty understanding the seeming obsession with geography and locality in Jewish religion. Many religions have so spiritualized the object of their aspiration (as have even some later developments in Judaism itself) that the Jewish concern for a rather small Middle Eastern territory, today the state of Israel, seems utterly secularistic (as indeed it often is). However, we have suggested that there is a need for at least some sacramental representation of mystery in all religion. Though it is not without its own temptations, some degree of sacramentalism is indispensable to the very integrity of religion. Without a sacramental component, religion—or religious hope—can easily take flight from our earthiness and from the reality of bodily existence. It will then be transformed into the style of religious escapism known as "gnosticism." Gnosticism itself, however, merely translates the desire for some special place in history or among the nations to a longing for an elite spiritual status in the eyes of God. The sad consequence of gnosticism is that its etherealized piety and its demand for esoteric knowledge make it largely irrelevant to human history. Without some bonding to the earth and to the political and economic realities of our existence, hope turns into reverie or romantic utopianism. And from such unrealistic aspirations, the road to cynicism and despair turns out to be very short. The great lesson Christians can learn from Judaism is the importance of some visible, bodily representation of a future in which to hope.

Let us recall briefly the main episodes in the story of the Jewish quest for the land. The ancestors of Judaism lived a servile existence in Egypt without a home to call their own and without a clear national identity. Then Moses rose up in their midst, initiated a revolt against the pharaoh's regime, and crossed over the "Sea of Reeds" in a liberative event known as the Exodus. He led his band of followers into the wilderness where they wandered for a period. All the while, the dream of a new land sustained them. Eventually, as the story goes, they arrived in Canaan where they merged with the inhabitants and gradually became the biblical people of Judah and Israel. Moses himself never reached the Promised Land, but his liberating efforts, his hope for the future, and his fidelity to the "promise" have made him the central ancestral figure in Judaism.

Judaism traces its existence as a distinct nation or people to such dreamers of the future as Abraham and Moses. And with them, it still continually looks toward the future. Along with Christianity, it anticipates the breaking in of a free, extravagant, and surprising future. The primary historical basis for its hope in the future lies in the deliverance from Egypt as recounted in the biblical Book of Exodus. The narratives comprising this book seem highly exaggerated when we view them simply in terms of scientifically historical standards. In fact, there may have been only a relatively small band of people who followed Moses out of Egypt, whereas the Book of Exodus speaks of thousands. But we would be missing the point of Exodus if we concentrated only on the question of whether it actually happened that way. For its purpose is to arouse trust in the future, and it looks back to the past liberation of the Hebrew people and to their settlement in a new land as the sacramental and narrative basis for our hoping here and now in the mystery of a future that is still dawning.

Having fled from slavery and the threat of losing their identity as a distinct people, Moses and his followers gave thanks to Yahweh, the deity to whom they attributed their new freedom and their creation as a people with a new future. The Exodus, we should note, occurred long before what we have called the axial age. During the thirteenth century B.C., the religious consciousness of the Hebrew people had not yet fully developed the axial yearning for a transcendent Oneness with its intolerance of a multiplicity of gods and goddesses. Yahweh, therefore, was not originally the one-and-only transcendent being that he was later to become. Initially, he may only have been Moses' tribal or family deity, but as Israel's religion developed during the following centuries, the name of Yahweh took on a more comprehensive and eventually monotheistic character. Finally, during the axial period, Yahweh began to be seen not only as the great promiser, liberator, and mighty warrior who had fashioned a distinct people, but also as the creator, savior, and ruler of the entire world. Judging by the writings of Second Isaiah, strict monotheism, which is intolerant of trust in a plurality of deities, arrived decisively somewhere around the sixth century B.C.

According to Exodus, after the deliverance from Egypt, Moses and his followers continued their relationship with the God of freedom and hope. At Mount Sinai, Yahweh forged a "covenant" with his elected people. Once again, the theme of the land was central. Yahweh graciously promised the Hebrews their own home and high status among the nations if they on their part would but put their trust in him and in the future fulfillment of his promises. They would have to show their loyalty by turning away from idols, from gods that would only enslave them once again. They must place their trust in Yahweh, the liberator and promise-keeper, alone. The Ten Commandments and the Law in its entirety make explicit what it means to live freely and trustingly as a community of hope. The imperative to turn away from idols is in fact an invitation to freedom. Any obsessive clinging, including any exclusivist possessiveness toward the land itself as though it were a right and not a gift, leads away from the free life and back to slavery.

During the wilderness journey, the Hebrews are said to have "murmured" in defiance of the divine promise given through Moses. Unwilling to adopt the patience and waiting that always accompany authentic hope, they fell back into idolatry, forsaking the dream of freedom. Meanwhile Moses struggled valiantly to sustain their hope in the promise. But, in a way characteristic of all humans, the people yearned for security in the present and the past. They expressed their distaste for freedom and the uncertain future by a longing to return to Egypt. It would be better to be slaves again than to wander in the wilderness devoid of safety. In slavery there is at least a kind of security, while the call to freedom and the unknown future is full of risk. The Bible credits Moses and his faithful followers, however, with not allowing their vision of future deliverance to die. And it is in great measure to their steadfastness that the Jewish and the Christian faiths owe their vision of the unconquerable power of hope in God's future.

The struggle against despair remains a constant one in all religion and in human life as such. In Israel, it is especially the prophets who take up the cause of Moses and Abraham and insist that God's people not give into the temptation to hopelessness. It is especially on the prophets that there falls the obligation of keeping the promise pure and alive in the people's religious life. There is a natural tendency for a nation living close to the land and making its living from the earth to consort with the gods of nature and fertility. From the perspective of our awareness of the history of religion, such devotion seems quite understandable and forgivable. But to the prophets of Israel it was an abomination because it signaled an abandonment of the revelatory promise given earlier to Abraham and Moses. In sum, it was a forsaking of the liberating mystery that had disclosed itself as a personal God of promise. Returning to nature symbolized a despair about history and its possibilities for fulfilling the deepest longings of creation and of human existence.

In fact, the fulfillment of history's promise always seems too far off, whereas the gods of nature offer immediate satisfaction. It is very tempting to lose ourselves in the natural and to anesthetize any deeper longing we may have for a wider vision. But the prophets, speaking authoritatively on behalf of the God of Abraham and Moses, challenged the people to trust in the promise unconditionally. They protested any flirtation with the gods and goddesses of nature. They even objected to the establishment of a monarchy that would tempt people to settle for the superficial sacramentalism according to which divine mystery is represented only in the image of monarchical political power. If Yahweh is King, it is not in the same sense as the typical despots who have so little concern for justice.

It is in their demand for justice that the prophets stand out most sharply. In the eighth century B.C., a young dresser of sycamores named Amos from the southern kingdom of Judah experienced a calling to journey to the northern kingdom of Israel in order to protest the social injustice, especially the widening gap between the rich and the poor, that had become prevalent there. He thought of himself only as a humble farmer and did not identify himself with the professional prophets of the day. But he was consumed by a passion for righteousness, and he spoke out on behalf of the God of justice. He observed that the Israelites "trample the head of the poor into the dust of the earth, and turn aside the way of the afflicted" (Amos 2:7). He attacked them for their presumption that being chosen by God from among the nations is a guarantee of salvation rather than a call to responsibility. Israel had failed to abide by the conditions of the Sinai covenant, and now the promised "Day of Yahweh" would spell doom rather than joy.

The prophetic message is that God is faithful to his promise but that the promise is not to be taken lightly. It requires that people adopt the same concern for the needy as Yahweh had done in electing Abraham and in rescuing his people from Egypt. But Israel and Judah had failed to follow the demands of the election and covenant, and had thoughtlessly turned back onto themselves. The land had become an idol rather than a sacrament of the future. The praxis required by authentic hope had been ignored. The neglect of justice had led to an obscuring of the religious heritage of hope. Revelation, at least in the biblical sense, can be experienced only if justice prevails. Where justice does not yet reign, the appropriate sense of God is also absent.

In the prophetic outcries of Amos, Hosea, Micah, Isaiah, Jeremiah and Ezekiel we see yet another instance of axial religion's critique of a piety based only on sacramentalism. About the same time that the *Upanishads* were expressing an uneasiness with Vedic ritualism, Amos and Micah were excoriating the superficial sacrifices of the Israelites. While the Buddha was reforming religion in India, even to the point of abandoning the ancient Hindu rites altogether, the prophets of Judah and Israel were impeaching the superficial piety of their own culture. They rejected any sacramental religious solace that was not accompanied by positive social, political, and economic implications. A more thunderous indictment of ineffective religiosity is hard to find than the one preserved in the book of Amos. Here God reproaches Israel:

> 'I hate, I despise your feasts, and I take no delight in your solemn assemblies. Even though you offer me your burnt offerings and cereal

offerings, I will not accept them, and the peace offerings of your fatted beasts I will not look upon. Take away from me the noise of your songs; to the melody of your harps I will not listen. But let justice roll down like waters, and righteousness like an ever-flowing stream' (Amos 5:21-24).

Like the Buddha, the prophets insisted that religion cannot be separated from compassion for those in need. Sacramental, mystical, and silent religion must also have implications for life in this world. Trust in the promise requires an attitude of inclusiveness that embraces all and excludes none.

The Vision

The biblical idea of revelation as God's promise has both auditory and visual overtones. Usually we think of revelation as a disclosure of God occurring through the mediation of the spoken word. The prophets, for example, called upon their listeners to hear the "word of the Lord." In the Bible, the *dabhar* or the *logos* of God appears to be the primary medium of divine revelation. But revelation may also be understood as the unfolding of a *vision*. The latter notion has not been as prominent in the theology of revelation as has the former, but it is no less biblical. The prophets leave us with vivid pictures of God's plan for the future. They require that we use our own imaginations to portray, however inadequately, the freedom, extravagance, and surprisingness of God's eternal vision for the world and humanity. The concept of God's vision for history, and for the entire cosmos, is indispensable for a genuinely biblical understanding of revelation.[18]

Although "vision" does not capture everything implied in "word," it allows us to focus on the pictorial features implied in the revelatory promise. It enables us to assimilate revelation to the notions of dreaming and imagining without which we can have no vivid sense of what is promised to us. In dreaming and imagining we form pictures of the future. The eschatological age, according to the prophet Joel, will feature those who dream dreams and see visions. Since the future has not yet fully arrived, it can come into our lives now only on the wings of dreams and imaginings. Biblical religion, unlike our naive "realism," actually encourages us to dream about the future. And although we must be critical of our

[18]As noted earlier, this idea is worked out most explicitly in Gabriel Fackre's *The Christian Story.*

dreams, since they may easily become unrealistic, the reception of revelation requires on our part an actively visionary way of thinking.[19]

Once again, though, we must ask ourselves how we know when our visions are simply projections of childish wishing, rather than images more truly revelatory of mystery. We shall address this question at greater length in Chapter 11, for around this issue the question of the plausibility of revelation revolves. But even here, we may invoke the simple criterion implied in the teachings of the prophets themselves: we can trust our visions if they are all-inclusive ones, open to the assimilation of ever new, surprising, and alien elements. In other words, the authenticity of our visions is a function of their heuristic breadth.[20] Earlier we spoke of mystery in terms of depth. Here, the notion of vision invites us to think of mystery also in terms of breadth. Accordingly, the "truthfulness" of a vision resides in its capacity to spread out and integrate coherently into itself elements of experience that would otherwise remain unnoticed and unintelligible.

Most of the time our visions of and plans for the future tend to leave something out. And this is why, in retrospect, they seem so naive. They are misguided because they have failed to consider items that in a wider perspective turn out to be indispensable for genuine wholeness. For example, when we close our eyes to elements of society such as the homeless, the unemployed, the mentally ill, and others who do not seem to fit into our idealization of social order, or if we forget the sufferings of past generations, we end up with sketches that are inadequate to God's own vision of the future. Much evil, including the slaughter of millions of innocent people, has been wrought, especially in the present century, by "visionaries" who were not expansive enough in their dreams of social order to include those too weak, poor, or ideologically unsuitable to fit into the plans of the powerful for the future.

In order to avoid such narrowness and naiveté, the biblical prophets, unlike their obsequious establishment rivals, did not turn toward the future with rosy-eyed optimism. Their hopes were tempered by a sober realism about the current state of affairs. They took note of present injustice, particularly the exclusion of the poor, and proclaimed the inadequacy of any vision of the future that failed to include the suffering and the marginalized victims of society. The prophets called for a continual widening

---

[19]On the importance of day-dreaming as our access to the dawning of future possibilities, see Ernst Bloch, *The Principle of Hope*, Vol. I, trans. Neville Plaice, Stephen Plaice, and Paul Knight (Oxford: Basil Blackwell, 1986).

[20]As we indicated several times earlier, authentic religion must have an apophatic dimension. It is in its move toward silence that it acquires a breadth that is lacking in sacramentalism as such.

of what it means to be a community of hope, and they did so by refusing to allow any forgetting of the poor and outcasts. Social planning that excludes certain groups for the sake of efficiency and homogeneity is in the long run completely unrealistic. The prophets forbade such narrowing of social ideals. They refused to let the children of Abraham forget the dark side of history, the sufferings of the past, or the poverty of their own origins. To them, the vision of future *shalom* had to be all-inclusive.[21]

Although the prophets were speaking primarily of social and economic inclusiveness, we are called upon by revelation to extend their criterion of inclusiveness to other arenas (such as race and gender, for example) today. If a vision is to be realistic it must be open to an ongoing expansion that continually takes more and more data into account and fits these data together in increasingly more meaningful ways. In our own day this means that a vision of the future cannot ignore what the sciences tell us about reality. And now, more than ever, it must be attentive to what other religions are saying. Without losing its distinctive boundaries (which are essential for the passing on of information) a "truthful" revelatory vision must nevertheless be continually open to new data. Of course, none of us can ever hold the breadth of reality within the narrowness of our own awareness. But at least we may be open to the possibility of a wider vision, one far surpassing our own. And we may even speak of an ultimate vision, one in which there are no limits whatsoever on inclusiveness.

Such a limitless breadth of vision is sacramentalized in the biblical image of *shalom*. Authentic faith is the search for an ever-widening vision of peace.[22] It is the quest for a perfection too grand to be contained in any present moment, a vision that only the uncertain future is adequate to hold. Faith's vision, because of its infinite scope, cannot be squeezed into the narrowness of the "now." It can be approached only through the mediation of an imagination suffused with a hope held in common with others.[23] Revelation, therefore, is the disclosure not only of the depth but also the breadth of mystery. Such breadth would be intimated only by the vision of a future in which *all* can hope. Such a vision would thereby provide a meaning not only for our own lives but for all of history and even of the universe as a whole. The function of revelation is to set forth such a vision.

---

[21] It is especially in the company of the prophets that we shall locate the revelatory role of Jesus. See below, Chapter 6.

[22] This is a major theme in Alfred North Whitehead's understanding of religion. See *Science and the Modern World*, (New York: The Free Press, 1967) 191–92.

[23] See Teilhard de Chardin, *The Future of Man* (New York: Harper Colophon Books, 1969) 75.

The Image of God's Humility

God, as Karl Rahner puts it, may be understood as our "absolute future."[24] But the absoluteness of the future hides itself, and it is sacramentally approachable by us only in the concrete particularity of our present experience with its always limited images of the future. But whereas psychology might suggest that these images are our own creations, faith allows us to see in them an incarnation and revelation of God, our absolute future. The infinite mystery of the future, notwithstanding its ultimate hiddenness, condescends to dwell within the restrictive arena of our present human imaginings. It does so by limiting itself and taking on, after a fashion, the shape of our own hopes in order eventually to lead us further into the depth and breadth of God's own vision for the world.

The theme of the "land" in Judaism is one such sacramental incarnation of God's future in the religious life of a particular people. To our overly spiritualized religious sensibilities, a geographically limited locality might seem to be a too secular and even materialistic way of symbolizing that which is promised to us. And yet the restrictedness of such symbols is quite consistent with our central image of the humility of God. The biblical understanding of revelation is thoroughly incarnational, and not just in the New Testament. The sons and daughters of Israel also believe that the eternal mystery of the world does not keep itself separate from the temporality of our particular world. It grasps hold of us and elicits the response of hope only by embodying itself in something so concrete as a homeland in which to hope. It is through our relationship to such mundane longings that we begin to construct our visions of the future. To separate hope from the bodily, social, and geographical realities in which we abide will lead us away from and not toward the God of promise.

In order for revelation to be a meaningful notion to us, we must experience the promise of the future in the particularities of our own lives and our own times. The promise of God, if it is still to be effective, must enter into the warp and woof of our existence here and now. Otherwise, it is nothing more than an abstraction. Perhaps it even needs to come alive in a new way every day of our lives. This means that we will not experience revelation simply by reading the Bible or attending a religious service. Although these are indispensable, the concrete situation of our encounter with the futurity of mystery is our everyday life with others in the world of today. If the idea of revelation is as intimately tied up with the theme of promise as we have argued in this chapter, then any appreciation we might have of it has to begin with an honest reflection on what *our own hopes* are.

[24]Karl Rahner, *Theological Investigations,* Vol. VI, trans. Karl H. and Boniface Kruger (Baltimore: Helicon, 1969) 59–68.

The Bible and the tradition of the Church cannot all by themselves tell us what we can hope for. We read and remember the stories of God's promises in the Bible. Yet we do so not in order to go back in time and repristinate a lost culture, but to look forward *with* the stories of God's past promises in order to hear them again challenging us in our own language and in terms of our own needs and aspirations. Revelation is not fundamentally a codified set of beliefs written down in Scripture or doctrinal formulations. We can happily move beyond such an idolatrous notion of revelation today. Since it comes to us from an inexhaustible future, revelation is potentially as fresh every day of our own lives as it was to Abraham, Moses, the prophets, and Jesus. But only by acknowledging our own hopes can we begin to allow it to enter into our present.

Our sense of revelation, therefore, must begin with a scrutiny of what we long for in the hidden depths of our own being. In our encounter with revelation, we must be open to having these longings transformed from private wishing into communal hoping. But the beginning of an understanding of revelation requires an admission that we have concrete and often mundane wishes, beneath which there may already lie the seeds of a hope that will become increasingly more receptive to God's vision.

In Abraham's and Israel's experience, the mystery of God's promise is felt palpably through the image of a new land, through anticipation of a multitude of progeny, through the hope of a long and blessed life for the people, through a vision of *shalom*. Accordingly, God is understood as the one who makes and keeps the promises we live by. Although our earthy sacramentalism can easily be vitiated by our inclination to idolatry, this is not a valid reason for completely mystifying religion. The value of sacramental images of hope is that they keep our religious life firmly planted on the terrestrial ground from which we have ourselves sprung. And at the same time, they remind us of the humility of the mystery that condescends to meet us in the concreteness of our ordinary human hopes and desires. When Christian faith discerns the limitless *logos* (or vision) as becoming "flesh," this linking of the divine to the corporeal is not entirely unprepared for in the sacramentalism of Israel and even of the world's other sacramental religions.

We can now begin to see how our twin themes of revelation as promise on the one hand and the image of God's self-emptying on the other converge. The revelatory image of a self-emptying God explains not only the fact of reality's mysterious openness, as we noted at the end of Chapter 3, but also why mystery presents itself to us in the mode of a promising future. The futurity of mystery is grounded in the humble self-absenting of God. The gift of a future to hope in is a consequence of God's self-concealment in such mundane realities as the land or an infant, a humble shepherd, a crucified man, a community of the oppressed. For our sake and for the world's future, God renounces any impulse to make the divine mystery a totally present, completely available reality. Such a presence would overwhelm the world and paralyze any possibility of its further becoming. It would inhibit the self-creation and self-transcendence essential to ourselves and an evolving universe. The self-effacement of a God who withdraws into the future, and who meets us in the humble guise of sacraments of promise, allows our world to exist as relatively autonomous and self-coherent. At the same time, this faithful and humble God of promise continually offers the possibility of redemption and new creation, for the world often fails to choose the appropriate paths toward its true destiny. At each point along the journey of its movement toward the future, the world meets the responsive grace, extravagance, and surprisingness of an always new and unexpected future. Revelation means the arrival of this future in our midst in the form of promise. The biblical understanding of revelation as promise invites us to understand this future as "God."[25]

[25]In this sense, Moltmann is correct in saying that the content of the promise and its author are one and the same. *The Experiment Hope,* 50.

6

Jesus and the Vision

The sense of mystery and its promise would remain too vague without concrete sacramental mediation. Though it is a necessary corrective to ensure the breadth of our hope, an exclusively apophatic religion or theology would fail to connect us to our future. Promise requires images that can arouse our hope in very specific ways corresponding to diverse times and circumstances.

It is true, of course, that Islam, Judaism, and Buddhism, as well as some significant strains of Hinduism and Christianity, have all expressed suspicion about the excesses of images and sacramentalism. The apophatic strand present in all of these religions justifiably cautions us that our clinging to particular symbols can at times be an obstacle to deeper encounter with sacred mystery. The *via negativa,* the way of silence, is intended to repair such narrowness. Silence opens us to the radical otherness of mystery. There is a place in all religions for the dialectical negation or subduing of words and images. Revelation involves much more than just a sacramental or verbal manifestation of mystery. It also requires, as a necessary condition of its reception, moments of silence, renunciation, and waiting. Silence prevents our anticipations of revelation from being dominated by our own predictions and keeps open to us the surprising aspects of mystery's promise.

Nevertheless, people are first brought to an explicit sense of sacred mystery through sacraments or symbols. And even when their religion assumes mystical, apophatic, and active aspects it still has to remain connected to a sacramental base.[1] The distinct shape that mystery takes in Israel's experience, we have seen, is that of a promise sacramentally mediated through images of *shalom,* that is, through vivid pictures of peace, righteousness, and abundance on the land. That is why the holy city of Jerusalem and the land of Israel have remained to this day powerful and palpable symbols of the presence of God's promise. Without such concrete imagery, hope might remain too vague, devoid of context and content.

In Christianity, the sacramental form in which mystery and promise are embodied is preeminently the compassionate person of Jesus of Nazareth.[2] "He is the image of the invisible God, the first-born of all creation. . . ." (Col 1:15). "In him all the fulness of God was pleased to dwell. . . ." (Col 1:19). "He reflects the glory of God and bears the very stamp of his nature. . . ." (Heb 1:3). "He who has seen me has seen the Father. . . ." (John 14:9). Thus the New Testament expresses the early Christian conviction that the person of Jesus symbolically reveals to us the reality of God. Jesus is the "human face of God."[3] In the faith of the early Christian community, as Rudolf Bultmann notes, the "proclaimer became the proclaimed."[4] The one who announced the breaking in of the Good News of God's reign turns out to be, in his very own person, the incarnation of God's promise. The New Testament speaks of revelation as the making known of a *mysterion* (Rom 16:25; Eph 3:3-4; 6:19; Col 1:27; 2:2; Mark 4:11). For Christian faith, this "mystery," hidden in God from all eternity, becomes most fully manifested in Jesus.[5]

To Christian faith, Jesus himself is the primary sacrament of our encounter with the divine mystery of promise. To the Church, Jesus is the "Christ," the Word of God, God's self-revelation. But what is the nature of revelation when viewed in terms of Jesus' own personal experience? How did he apprehend the revelation of God? Difficult as it is to give confident answers to such questions as these, we must ask them here

[1] See above, Chapter 3.

[2] See Monika Hellwig, *Jesus, the Compassion of God* (Wilmington: Michael Glazier, Inc., 1973) 121-23.

[3] John A. T. Robinson., *The Human Face of God* (Philadelphia: Westminster Press, 1973).

[4] Rudolf Bultmann, *Theology of the New Testament,* trans. Kendrick Grobel (New York: Charles Scribner's Sons, 1951) 33.

[5] With Moltmann, however, we must emphasize that Jesus himself still has a future. So we do not need to interpret Jesus' coming in history as though there is nothing left for us to hope for. If we see him as the fulfillment of the quest for revelation, it is not in a static sense, but as the one in whom we now orient ourselves toward the future.

nonetheless. For it would seem that revelation has its proper origin in Jesus' own consciousness of the arrival of God's future.[6] Revelation, in the Christian sense at least, is born in the crucible of the Jewish mind, soul, and imagination of the man Jesus of Nazareth with his unique vision of the "reign of God."

Where did his powerful vision of this reign (or "kingdom") of God come from, and what does it reveal to us today? In asking such questions, we are of course also taking up once again the perennial theological quest for who Jesus really was and what possible meaning he might have for our lives. That is to say, we are entering into the area of Christology.[7] A Christian theology of revelation depends in a special way on the insights of this branch of theology. If it has not yet become evident to the reader, we must here emphasize that a theology of revelation embraces every other realm of the theological enterprise. It includes within itself contributions of all the other fields of theological inquiry. It is closely related to soteriology and pneumatology as well as Christology. And by identifying revelation with promise, we have already seen that it embraces eschatology as well. In the following chapter, moreover, we will observe that cosmic creation also may be interpreted as revelation. Its breadth, therefore, makes it logically misleading for us to list revelation simply as one theological category alongside others. It is a broad concept that includes, in some sense at least, the other divisions of theology as well.

But this comprehensiveness raises the question whether we can legitimately distinguish revelation theology from theology as such. Why have a *distinct* theology of revelation? Is not all Christian theology revelation theology? Why set revelation apart for special treatment? After all, during most of the Christian centuries, revelation received very little if any formal attention. It did not become a clearly distinct theme in theology until modern times. Apparently for the larger portion of its history, Christianity has been able to get along quite well without an explicitly formulated theology of revelation. So why do we need one now?

Not all theologians are of the opinion that we do. Some of them are reluctant today to speak of revelation because it seems to be too apolo-

---

[6]The location of revelation centrally in the consciousness of Christ has been most explicitly highlighted by Gabriel Moran, *Theology of Revelation* (New York: Herder and Herder, 1966).

[7]Recent Christian theology has increasingly placed Christology first in the order of theological disciplines, insinuating that we can have no more than a vague knowledge of God prior to an encounter with the man Jesus. The approach taken in this book, however, emphasizes the theological priority of a disclosure of mystery as the whence of revelation, prior to doing Christology. It seems that Christology is overburdened when it is forced to do all the work of mystagogy.

getic and particularist, especially in light of the plural nature of our religious situation. Others avoid the notion because it appears to exaggerate what faith can now perceive only dimly. They would prefer to use the notion of revelation only with reference to what we will experience eschatologically.[8] So far, they insist, nothing has been disclosed with sufficient clarity to qualify as revelation. Everything is still too cloudy and ambiguous. We must await the end of history in order truly to experience revelation.[9] Until then it would be more modest and unassuming if we did not use the term at all. Others are embarrassed by the idea of revelation because it conjures up obsolete and scientifically unacceptable images of a supernatural world that comes down to us from another realm and arbitrarily interrupts the closed continuum of natural and secular reality. And still others find it problematic because their experience indicates no domain of mystery or sacred hiddenness from which any "unconcealment" or "unveiling" could possibly occur. Obviously, skeptical thinkers have serious reservations about the idea of revelation. But not even all Christian theologians are convinced that a special theology of revelation is helpful.

Still, while remaining sensitive to these objections to the concept of revelation, we must insist on its enduring appropriateness. Christian theology needs to have a special treatise on revelation if for no other reason than to emphasize the indispensable biblical doctrine of the prevenience of God's promissory vision for our lives and the world.[10] The awareness that God's promise exceeds or outdistances anything we could ourselves construct is the very foundation of faith. There may be no better term than "revelation" to accentuate faith's conviction that we ourselves are not the authors of the promise we live by. Were we to abandon the notion, as some have urged us to do, we would once again have to wonder whether there are any real reasons for our hope. Could the content of Christian faith then be construed as anything more than our own creation? For if revelation were taken to be no more than our psychic or social projections, our beliefs would surely lose their hold on us. If our images of God and the divine promises were seriously taken to be nothing more than

[8]This is the position, for example, of F. Gerald Downing, *Has Christianity a Revelation?* (London: SCM Press, 1964) 239-90.

[9]Wolfhart Pannenberg is open to the notion of revelation provided that we understand it in the present as "indirect" revelation that awaits the full disclosure of God at the end of history. See the collection of essays *Revelation as History,* edited by Wolfhart Pannenberg, Rolf Rendtorff, Trutz Rendtorff, & Ulrich Wilkens, trans. David Granskou (New York: Macmillan, 1968).

[10]This is the main theme of Ronald Thiemann's controversial but helpful book, *Revelation and Theology* (Notre Dame: University of Notre Dame Press, 1985).

religious or theological constructions,[11] they would forfeit their "other-ness" and along with it their capacity to criticize and transform our situation. If we viewed our religious symbols as *nothing but* our own imaginative inventions, we would be forced to wonder whether we could really be challenged by them or whether we could take them at all seriously. A set of ideas or images that we suspected to be no more than an emanation of our own imaginative powers could hardly summon us to new life or to genuine hope, no matter how charming they may be. The idea of revelation points to the graciousness, extravagance, and surprisingness of a future that always lies somehow beyond our calculation and control, and that breaks into our midst with a form and content that has not been anticipated in its every aspect. It carries with it the implication that this future is always a judgment on the paltriness of our own aspirations. And so, by virtue of its having this character of prevenience, it is an indispensable notion for any theology that takes seriously the biblical theme of promise.

At the same time, however, we may be permitted to entertain reservations about some interpretations of revelation, such as that of Karl Barth and his followers, which make revelation so absolutely interruptive and "different" that it casts all of our natural aspirations in a suspicious light. Barth thinks of God's word as so completely "other" than what we naturally long for, that when revelation bursts forth in Christ, it crushes all our former (perverse) longings and replaces them with new ones that were in no sense there before. Such a radical reading of revelation may at first sight seem to be quite appropriate in the face of our human frailty. The sinful distortions of our lives and consciousness twist and divert our longings and aspirations in such an idolatrous way that we are forced at times to distrust them completely. For that reason, the critiques of culture by Barth and other representatives of neo-orthodoxy should not be erroneously mistaken for fundamentalist retrenchment. Their call to attend to the element of judgment and new creation accompanying God's word is an indispensable ingredient in any authentic theology of revelation.[12]

However, the neo-orthodox demand that we repudiate our natural hopes and imaginings is, in the final analysis, excessive. At heart it is an insult to the creativity of God and to the natural visionary capacity that sustains human existence. Official Christian teaching has consistently emphasized that creation is good and that this goodness exists as a permanent stratum of our own human existence as well, even in a sinful world. The propensity to dream, wish, and hope is an essential part of our creatureli-

[11]As they are taken to be, it seems, by theologian Gordon Kaufmann, *An Essay on Theological Method* (Missoula: Scholars Press, 1975).

[12]See Karl Barth, *The Epistle to the Romans* (London: Oxford University Press, 1972).

ness. To pull up by the roots and cast away as worthless our inborn visionary habits would be an act of violence toward the created order. If revelation brings something new and unanticipated, it must still somehow connect with the structure of our present expectations as well as with those of all the past generations of human searching. Otherwise, it would amount to a complete annihilation of our created being and consciousness. It would throw all previous history into utter futility. If revelation were to come to us without already having at least some resonance with the natural core of our longings it would hardly be the Good News we take it to be. What James Carpenter states about the neo-orthodox attribution of *absolute* novelty to Christ applies to the whole of revelation:

> To posit the "absolutely new" in Christ . . . is to take him out of the
> context of life, to see him as having no part in human emergence, a non-
> participant in the created processes of existence. It is to divorce him from
> prior history and to separate him from all those in other religions who
> have had a little something to say about hope.[13]

Nevertheless, after voicing this reservation, it still seems correct to maintain that revelation does bring something new and unanticipated.[14] Its promise awakens in us longings that, though they may already have been somehow present, were inactive or needed to be clarified, focused and purified. Revelation is a "disclosure" event in which we are confronted with a picture of reality which faith makes out to be the good news we have *always* been longing for but which we could never have conjured up all by ourselves out of our own ambiguous lives.[15] It is an essential theological notion because it expresses our sense that the imagery of faith places what we may hope for in a continually new light. It has the power to make sense of things in ways that would be historically impossible without its intervening images of our future. The theme of revelation brings out how faith can help us see things in an ever wider and deeper perspective. It is this illuminative aspect of faith that a theology of revelation seeks to make explicit. It is faith's discernment of a new *vision* of reality

[13]James A Carpenter, *Nature and Grace* (New York: Crossroad, 1988) 92.

[14]This does not contradict Schubert Ogden's interpretation, endorsed above in Chapter 3, according to which special revelation is not something "more" than or in addition to what is called original revelation. The two are ontologically inseparable. Special revelation, however, has the character of novelty in that it is encountered in our finite, culturally relative historical and categorical existence. The mystery of God's love and promise is always, ontologically speaking, fully present to the world, but in terms of our historical existence, it takes on the character of surprise and unpredictability.

[15]The argument of this book is that it is especially the image of God as self-emptying love that confronts us in this interruptive, yet deeply longed for, manner.

that encourages us to think of revelation as a distinct theological theme, though certainly not unrelated to the other branches of theology.

What native Americans, such as the Sioux Indians, refer to as a "vision quest" is to some degree representative of the longings of our common humanity. Built into us there is a profound appetite for "vision." We long to see things more and more clearly, truthfully, and meaningfully. "Vision" means the imaginative representation of meaning, truth, and, above all, beauty. Beauty, in turn, refers to a "harmony of contrasts." Our natural quest for a continually wider beauty is a most important aspect of our vision quest. We have a natural instinct for adventurously widening our horizons, expanding our picture of reality's beauty, and for continually heightening our vista's contrast and harmony. We are born with creative imaginations that seek to bring increasingly more nuanced harmony into the sweep of our awareness by way of a continually broader variety of symbols, images, and metaphors.

This visionary capacity is given with our existence and cannot be eradicated without great stress to our constitution. Satisfaction of our longing for "vision" is essential to human vitality. But at the same time, experience instructs us that we have strong inclinations to acquiesce in unnecessarily narrow and mediocre images of the future. As Whitehead says, we tend to substitute a sketch for the whole picture.[16] Our desire for order and harmony can smother our need for breadth of contrast and novelty. This is the same tendency that leads sacramental religion toward idolatry. We often try to exclude the contrast that makes for wider vision,[17] and so we remain content with excessive rigidity, settling for a harmony without contrast, order without nuance, and unity without complexity. It is in opposition to this complacency that Jesus introduced his disturbing vision of the kingdom of God. His religious faith and awareness are marked especially by an intense longing to expand our purview of human life and of reality as a whole. This concern for breadth of vision appeared especially in his words and parables about the dynamic "reign of God."

Just how disturbing, but also promising, his vision of the reign of God was can be brought out in a fresh way if we interpret it in terms of the four interrelated modalities required by any integral religious vision. In order to be receptive to the revelation of mystery, religious faith must have sacramental, mystical, silent, and active ingredients. If any of these is exaggerated at the expense of others, or if any one of them recedes too far

[16]Alfred North Whitehead, "Mathematics and the Good," in Paul A. Schillp, ed., *The Philosophy of Alfred North Whitehead* (Evanston and Chicago: Northwestern University Press, 1941) 679.

[17]Today such exclusiveness may take the form of a refusal to encounter the challenging plurality of religions, thus narrowing our understanding of revelation and forfeiting opportunities for a widening of our notion of the mystery of God.

into the background, distortions will appear that either diminish or deny the reality of mystery. The revelation of mystery, we have been emphasizing, requires our careful cultivation of all four ingredients of religion. And when mystery takes the shape of promise, as it does in biblical religion, then hope, the Bible's characteristic response to mystery, must also balance all four ways according to its own logic.

Jesus' repertoire of images of the kingdom, his habit of presenting what we can hope for in the idiom of parables of God's reign, is an exceptional illustration of these four revelatory aspects of religion. We shall focus on the sacramental, mystical, silent, and active aspects of his proclamation of the reign of God. In this way we may be able to link his teachings to the wider world of religious revelation, while at the same time bringing out their freshness and distinctiveness.

Before doing so, however, it may be useful for us briefly to expand on our earlier suggestion that the religious posture of hope in God's promise embodies the four ways of religion, and that the failure to integrate all of them leads to the perversion of hope.[18] In the first place, hope has to come to expression in quite specific and concrete sacramental images in order to connect with present reality and thereby to avoid the docetic and gnostic temptations to escape from the present altogether. But if our fixation on a particular imagery is too exclusivist, then our sense of the future decays into a restrictive obsession with the sheer givenness of things. This narrowness rules out the attainment of wider vision. It turns into an idolatry of the present or past, and it is content to live without the tension and challenge of a new and surprising future. On the other hand, a healthy hope is willing to entertain a wide variety of images of the future. We shall see that this is one of the remarkable features of Jesus' religious imagination. Genuine hope allows our vision to expand to the point of an inclusiveness that takes into account the future of those other than ourselves, indeed of the whole of creation. It avoids fixation on particular symbols that would end up shrinking our sense of the future to a size too small for our deepest aspirations. We may understand the Spirit of Christ as the power that seeks to extend to the ends of creation and its future this all-inclusiveness.

Hope is also mystical. It is mystical in the sense that it seeks union with, and longs to be lost in, the futurity of God. If it blossoms to maturity it surrenders to an "absolute future."[19] But if the mystical component of hope (its experience of union with this absolute future) becomes disengaged from a specific sacramental context, or if it ignores the requirement of present praxis and the necessity of silent, patient waiting for God's

[18]See Chapter 5.

[19]Karl Rahner, *Theological Investigations,* Vol VI, 59–68.

future, it shrivels into sheer reverie. The mystical aspect of hope then turns into a premature flight from the world of the present. It abandons earthy imagery and worldly reality too early, and this forfeiture amounts to a gnostic denigration of creation. Hope withers when it loses its connection to nature, to time and place, and to the need for action here and now. It turns into an escapism that leaves the present and past world out of the picture of promise. We should note that Jesus' imagining of the reign of God remains closely connected to the earth and the mundane. It does not yield to mysticism's characteristic temptation of flight, but remains tied up with the sacramental, silent and transformative ingredients of hope. It seeks the establishment of God's reign *on earth* as well as in heaven. It invites patience as well as action.

Hope also has an apophatic dimension. It entertains a justifiable suspicion that its images of promise are always inadequate. Thus it is at times reduced to silence out of respect for the unpredictability of the shape the future will actually take. Because of our petty pictures of reality's possibilities, it makes us seal our lips in the manner of Job and occasionally quiet our imaginations and thoughts in the fashion of all so-called "negative" theology. It is aware that only God can present to us our true destiny. The apophatic instinct arises out of hope's concern for breadth, for a *wider* beauty and perfection than that encompassed by our current visions of utopia. Genuine hope brings with it an intuition that none of our present imaginings could ever adequately represent the full graciousness, extravagance, and surprisingness of the mysterious future we call God. Therefore, it is willing to undergo an asceticism whereby it renounces fixation on any particular human images of the future and opens itself to God's vision of the world's possibilities. The need for renunciation in the interest of breadth is one of the main features of Jesus' own teaching. He speaks, for example, about the need to subordinate our own desires to God's will, and about the importance of watchfulness in place of calculations: "You know not the day nor the hour."

But there is also a danger hidden in the apophatic side of hope. We may, out of frustration, turn vengefully against *all* images of the perfection we seek. An exaggerated hesychasm may either decay into an absurd silence, or it may experiment with such a wild array of images, discarding one after another, that it leads to despair. Apocalyptic projections manifest the longing for an undreamed of future, but the chaos of apocalyptic imagery sometimes stops just short of confusion. If it were not still tethered to the sacramentality of present experience, and to the mystical and active aspects of hope, it could easily pass over the border to an anarchical hatred of present reality. Such transgressions have occurred more than once in the history of religion and Christianity. Here again it is worth noting that Jesus' preaching, though it shared aspects of apocalyptic expectation, avoided the extreme of world hatred to which this genre is at times disposed.

Finally, genuine hope also requires an element of praxis, a need to be embodied in transformative action in the world. Hope is empty unless it leads to cooperative action that tries to make the vision of God's future more explicit and sacramentally present in our world here and now. The heirs to biblical faith have often overlooked the prophetic call to social justice. Indeed, a case may be made that the major religious failing of Western theism has been its slighting and even repressing the summons to action central to the prophets' teaching. Without the *doing* of justice in the present, it is questionable whether we can experience much of the revelation of God's future. There can be no full verification of revelation apart from the wager of direct involvement in the praxis of the reign of God.

Still, like the other three elements of religion and hope, the way of action is also subject to its own peculiar kind of temptation. In the case of action, a possible failing is impatience. An activism divorced from sacramentalism, mysticism, and silence may attempt to seize the mysterious and incalculable mystery of the future and make it a present possession subject to human control. In doing so, it will inevitably shrink hope down to the level of mere planning. Planning is essential, but it does not exhaust the meaning of hope. For hope also has sacramental, mystical, and silent aspects that open us to the self-disclosure of an unfathomable future. Genuine hope points our social existence toward an ever wider vision. It makes us aware of the narrowness of all our current images of the future. Hope is most authentic when it displays a capacity, when necessary, simply to wait in silent expectation. It is healthiest when it sustains a balance of all four religious ingredients.

Jesus as the Revelation of God's Promise

Jesus' life and his teachings about the reign of God give evidence of this balance. In his person as well as in his vivid images of the kingdom, Jesus sacramentalizes the compassionate God whose promise is coming to fulfillment. In his urgent vision of the unity of humanity with God, presented especially by John, we see the mystical side of his hope. In his continually turning his will, his longings, and his future over to God we observe the apophatic tendency of his hope. And in his connecting the reign of God to our present praxis of justice, thereby subordinating ritual to justice and piety to caring for the poor, he links hope to action. In sum, the life and words of this remarkable man open up the mystery of the future to his followers in such a radical fashion that he functions for them as the very revelation of God.

In the Gospel of Mark, Jesus opens his ministry with these words: "The time is fulfilled, and the kingdom of God is at hand; repent, and believe in the gospel" (1:15). When placed within the context of expectation that runs from Abraham through the prophets, Jesus' announcement that the time is now fulfilled is indeed dramatic. It implies nothing less than that the absolute and unsurpassable future promised by God from the beginning is now entering into our life in a decisive way.[20] What is noteworthy here is how Jesus links his own anticipation of the arrival of God's future to the contemporary standards of expectation that he inherited from his culture. In interpreting God's promise, he does not uproot previous patterns of hope but instead seeks to transform the traditional images of Israel's understanding of its prospects. He came not to destroy but to fulfill.

There is, however, an apparent impatience in Jesus' declaration that the long-awaited kingdom is *now* at hand. We have seen that one of the temptations of all religions is that of a refusal to wait patiently for the fullness of mystery to disclose itself. Such a refusal can lead to a shrinking of the transcendent into the narrowness of our own contemporary designs. Judaism stands forth to this day as a powerful witness to our need to wait in hope until the time is ripe for the messianic age, which to Jewish faith has not yet arrived. During the Jewish Passover meal these words are still uttered: "I shall wait resolutely for the coming of the Messiah. And even though he tarry, yet shall I wait for him." Theologian Paul Tillich emphasizes this point about waiting: "We are stronger when we wait than when we possess."[21] Is it possible then that the eschatological teachings of Jesus violate this imperative to wait? Is there too much impatience in his message? And, moreover, is there perhaps a premature closure of history in Christian faith's identification of Jesus as the conclusive fulfillment of God's ageless promises?[22]

These are difficult questions, and they can only be addressed inadequately here. For Jesus, however, it is clear that the time is *always* ripe for the coming of the kingdom. The kingdom, which stands for the reign of justice and peace, is needed at every moment of history, if for no other reason than that people are suffering. "All life is suffering" is the First Noble Truth of Buddhism. And Jesus shares with the Buddha a compas-

---

[20]See G. R. Beasley-Murray, *Jesus and the Kingdom of God* (Grand Rapids: Eerdman's, 1986) 73.

[21]Paul Tillich, *The Shaking of the Foundations,* 151.

[22]Moltmann says: "The existence of the Jews again and again forces Christians to the knowledge that they are not yet at the goal, that their church is itself not the goal, but that with eschatological provisionality and brotherly openness they remain on the way." *The Experiment Hope,* 66.

sionate desire to cut right to the heart of human suffering and to eliminate it as soon as possible. If this is impatience it is not the sort that
diminishes the divine. Rather, it is an impatience that grows out of profound contemporary compassion for the abandoned, the poor, and the
lost. If anything is clear in the gospels, it is that the pain of others vehe-
mently violates Jesus' sensitivity. And to Christian faith, his deeply human
caring stands sacramentally for the ultimate caringness of God. In its all-
inclusiveness it opens us up to a vision far wider than our own efforts
and plans could allow.

The Buddha's departure from previous religious and theological patterns was the consequence of his profound longing to eliminate suffering
as soon as possible. And in the case of Jesus, we would hardly be stretch-
ing things if we surmised that his own reshaping of religious and eschatological expectation was the result quite simply of his own exceptionally
intense compassion for the needy, the poor, the outcasts, the guilt-ridden,
and the forgotten whom he encountered every day. His longing to remove
their misery compelled him to announce that the God of Moses, who long
ago had heard the Hebrew people's loud outcries and had responded to
them, was now once again near at hand and ready to rescue the people
from their pain. It is Jesus' special discernment of human tribulation that
makes his proclamation seem to be a bit "impatient."

When he stood up to read the Isaiah scroll at the beginning of his ministry (Luke 4:16-21), Jesus announced that the time of liberation for all who
are imprisoned in any way had dawned on "this very day." Christian faith
has deciphered in this man's exceptional outpouring of empathy for the
poor, the captives, the abandoned, and the sick, the consummate entrance
of an ultimate love and mercy into our world. In our experience of Jesus'
compassion, we experience the compassion of God. If there is something
"impatient" about all of this on Jesus' part, it is an impatience born of
compassion and not out of a will to control the mystery of the future.

In fact, the empathy evident in Jesus' life, action, and teaching does,
after all, require at its roots a profound religious patience with respect
to our social, political, and economic schemes. What the gospel, as well
as the teaching of all the prophets, rejects is the kind of impatience we
find in most social planning. Such planning seeks to establish a smooth,
unblemished order as quickly as possible. But almost inevitably when we
begin to implement our envisagements of the ideal social arrangement,
we end up excluding some groups and individuals whose presence in our
system keeps it from running as effortlessly as we would like. The homeless, the insane, the non-conformists, and the economically disadvantaged
tend to mess things up, and so we ignore their presence. In Jesus' vision,
though, no arrangements are ideal or adequate until and unless they have
included all segments of society and have not left any groups or individ-

uals out of the picture. Since such an arrangement has not yet appeared, and since it will never be perfectly approximated on the plane of pure history, Jesus' "impatient" eschatology shows how far the fullness of God's future is yet from complete realization. By his being such a radical departure from our ordinary accommodation to suffering and injustice, Jesus prophetically sets forth our future possibilities. He demonstrates that an impatience born of compassion does not conflict with, but actually supports, the apophatic posture of patience and concern for breadth essential to all authentic religion and hope.

Furthermore, the religious temptation to flee impatiently from history is also offset by the sacramentality of Jesus' teaching, especially in the parables. Jesus typically employs earthy, mundane, and natural images to communicate the intensity of his hope. He discerns a religious depth in such simple realities as the anticipation accompanying the sowing of seed. The promise hidden within the inauspicious origins of a mustard tree gives him an image of the disproportionality between present reality and the full flowering of God's future. But Jesus tempers such sacramentalism, in turn, with an apophatic posture of patience. In the interest of breadth, his vision of the kingdom, as exemplified in his parable of the sower and the seed, demands that our own trust put down its roots deeply into the ground and that we be wary of the shallowness of any too-hasty sprouting. He urges us also to allow the weeds to grow together with the wheat, and to avoid any premature harmony and "purity" at the expense of the nuance and complexity of the full harvest of God's vision. He does not try to separate the just from the unjust, but sees God's goodness and compassion encompassing both.

Finally, his parables are also invitations to action in the present. They announce the breaking in of God's future, and they call us to a *metanoia,* to a transformation of our lives into vehicles of the spirit of inclusiveness that refuses to leave things the way they are. The balance of sacramentality, mystical openness to the future as God's future, silent waiting, and vigorous action ensures the revelatory power and religious integrity of his gospel of hope.

Especially noteworthy in Jesus' life and teaching is the announcement of what we are calling, in the terminology of Whitehead, the "wider vision." It is worth quoting in full here the famous philosopher's enunciation of what he took to be authentic religion:

> Religion is the vision of something which stands beyond, behind, and within, the passing flux of immediate things; something which is real, and yet waiting to be realized; something which is a remote possibility, and yet the greatest of present facts; something that gives meaning to all that passes, and yet eludes apprehension; something whose posses-

sion is the final good, and yet is beyond all reach; something which is the ultimate ideal, and the hopeless quest.[23]

Jesus' personal sense of the present and coming reign of God is an opening to and revelation of this wider vision. He does not seek to uproot our natural instincts and desires but only to direct them toward a wider fulfillment. In his parables of the kingdom, we observe a blending of the most familiar imagery with a summons to an unimaginable breadth of vision and hope. His religion is not one that encourages withdrawal from the world of our senses. Instead, it seeks to extend the sensuality and earthiness of our experience toward a divine mystery that embraces all things. Jesus requires a kind of renunciation, not for its own sake, but only for the purpose of allowing ourselves to be embraced by a wider and eternal panorama. It is not a puritanical, spiritual athleticism that he prescribes, but an asceticism of the future that opens us to the enjoyment of a wider vision. What he asks us to renounce is not our enjoyment of the good things of this world, but our failure both to share this enjoyment with the poor and to imagine and trust in the infinity of goodness and compassion that transcends and grounds the good world.

In order to keep his vision of God's future connected to present reality, Jesus' teachings employ a vivid imagery based on the worldly experience of his day. Although there is considerable controversy among New Testament scholars about the authenticity of many of the sayings and teachings of Jesus himself, there is little doubt about his passion for proclaiming the nearness of the reign of God. The image of a reign or kingdom, we can readily observe, is a very worldly one. The practice of embodying the sense of promise in such secular imagery as a *basileia* is thoroughly Jewish, thoroughly worldly, and at the same time thoroughly religious. Jesus' teachings about the dynamic "rule" of God consistently make reference to present reality. His parables take as their symbolic basis not only natural occurrences but also the social, domestic, political, and economic realities that shaped the lives of his contemporaries. In his sacramentalism of the reign of God, he refers to fathers and sons, to kings and servants, to the use and abuse of money, and to many other purely "secular" realities. "The reign of God is like. . ." is an expression he uses often. And it is remarkable how, in his articulation of what it is "like," he employs the most pedestrian of characters and locates them in the most commonplace of circumstances. This sacramental style is indicative of one who did not despise the earth but who loved it dearly. While he was deeply disturbed about the injustice and poverty that prevailed, he did not seek a future that would have no roots in or consequences for present realities.

---

[23]Whitehead, *Science and the Modern World,* 190-91.

At the same time, however, Jesus' imagining of the kingdom pulls us and our world beyond the mere givenness of the present. It exhibits a deep discontent with the status quo. Jesus' profound mystical and apophatic sense of divine love and the otherness of God's compassionate plan for the world give his teaching a critical dimension that unsettles all who invest too much in the way things are. His intuition of a wider vision continually demands that the present stretch itself to include the unprecedented novelty of God's reign. He is especially sensitive to how the social conditions of his time tended to crush the life and self-esteem out of entire groups of people. This situation, rooted in both the political and religious ideology of his time, was intolerable to him. And so his most powerful teachings were directed at those conditions that bring misery and hopelessness to so many.

The social situation in which Jesus lived was one in which a distinctively Jewish identity had to be constructed in the face of constant pressures to become assimilated into the Roman Empire.[24] In order to resist this pressure, several religious alternatives for affirming one's Jewishness were proposed by such groups as the Essenes, Sadducees, Pharisees, and Zealots. Each of them offered a "way" of solidifying Jewish identity so that it would not be absorbed into the Roman culture. However, in order to follow any of these "ways," specific rules and regulations had to be followed closely. Only in this manner could one prove that he or she fully belonged to a particular religious sect or political faction. At times the requirements for membership in such an affiliation were so exacting that many who were financially poor, or mentally, intellectually, or physically impaired, or who felt morally disqualified, could not participate in any of the dominant religious groupings. Consequently, they were unable to take advantage of the cultural and sub-cultural opportunities for gaining a sense of personal and social significance that were available to the more fortunate "belongers." They inevitably felt left out of any respectable "system," and therefore were especially vulnerable to the feeling of shame. These were the outcasts, the poor, the abandoned, the despised, or the "sinners," those who did not "belong." They were what today's sociological terminology would brand the "marginalized."

It was especially to such people as these that Jesus announced his Good News concerning the reign of God. In addressing his gospel to those who were not only in but also outside the various systems, he indicated that religious boundaries now had to be stretched beyond what was conventional. In fact, there could no longer be any social or religious demarcations at all that would elevate one group to superiority over others. All

---

[24]For the following see Marcus Borg, *Jesus: A New Vision* (San Francisco: Harper & Row, 1987) 79-96.

alike are God's children. Unlike the sectarians who had made membership dependent upon fulfilling religious, ritualistic, political, or economic prerequisites, Jesus' wider vision of the kingdom was expansive enough to include all, even the excommunicated. It was not necessary for those abandoned by society to fulfill any special social or religious conditions in order to belong to the kingdom proclaimed by Jesus. In Luke's gospel Jesus says: "It is your Father's good pleasure to give you the kingdom." (12:32) Here the emphasis is probably on the word "give," indicating the absolute gratuity of God's gift, and that one does not have to earn one's deliverance by fulfilling a list of obligations.

Both in word and action Jesus attempted to convince his disenfranchised listeners of their unconditional worth. "Blessed are you poor," he proclaims in Luke's version of the Beatitudes. And at the beginning of his public ministry he says, "The spirit of the Lord is upon me, because he has anointed me to preach good news to the poor" (Luke 4:18). Jesus understood his public vocation to be that of announcing the limitless breadth of the divine vision. Only as such can we understand his passion for extending the circle of religious and social belonging. Thus his parables teach the all-inclusive nature of the future reign of God that is now dawning.

Moreover, his own life embodies in action what he proclaims in word. He becomes a living parable of inclusiveness and belonging, especially in his table-fellowship with sinners and rejected people. In Jesus' culture, sharing a meal—and especially a banquet—with someone was a highly charged symbol of acceptance of that person. And so when he sat down to eat with tax-collectors, prostitutes, and other non-belongers, and with Pharisees and wealthy too, he clearly signaled God's unconditional acceptance of them all.

The revolutionary implications of this parabolic speech and behavior have yet to be thought out fully, much less applied in real life. Many different images and concepts are required to unfold it. We are merely suggesting here that the Whiteheadian notion of a "wider vision" goes some way toward interpreting the revelatory meaning of Jesus' consciousness and action. Jesus' inclusive images of the kingdom and his mission to seek out those who are lost in order to make them part of the wider picture is, to Christian faith, the vehicle of God's revelation. By making room for the incongruous, the unqualified, and the disparate within the dimensions of a single religious society under God's fatherhood, Jesus' words and actions shatter all conventional views of human reality. His proclamation of the reign of God requires the painful dismantling of all non-inclusive arrangements of social and religious reality. In our own time, there are at least some efforts to include women, ethnic minorities, the homeless, and other previously repressed and excluded minorities as fully belonging to social and religious circles. Jesus' teachings and actions on behalf of the kingdom surely support such endeavors, and we can hardly expect to experience his Spirit today apart from our own involvement in such processes leading toward complete inclusiveness.

But where did this incorporative vision of Jesus come from? Ultimately, we must surmise that it came from his own unique experience of sacred mystery. Just when his sense of an all-inclusive reign of God was solidified we cannot say. Was it when he was still a child? When he was alone in the desert? When he was baptized by John? During his episodes of prayer in lonely places? We simply do not know for sure. What does seem certain, scholars generally agree today, is that the distinctive character of Christian revelation bears a close relationship to Jesus' unique experience of God as "abba" (usually translated as "father" but expressive of the deepest familiarity and trust). The term "abba" was in Jesus' day apparently used as an intimate and familiar address to elders in whose presence one felt completely secure. In Jesus' use of this religiously unusual appellation, he showed that for him the ultimate character of mystery is nothing other than the most intimate and inclusive love. His sense of God as "abba" is the font that nourishes his vision of the kingdom as well as his own inclusive actions. We may infer then that Christian revelation begins to receive its own specific shape in Jesus' consciousness of God as "abba."

The point of Christology, as Schubert Ogden has clarified, is not so much to tell us who Jesus is as it is to tell us who God is.[25] Or to put it in terms of the present book, its point is to clarify for us what the ultimate character of mystery is like. Humanity's religious quest, with its innumerable sacramental representations of incomprehensible mystery, receives a unique answer in Jesus' revelation of God as "abba." And when the New Testament poses the question "who is this man?" or "who do you say the Son of Man is?," the point is not to have us focus on Jesus as much as on the mystery whose character his life and teaching are revealing to us. The point of our dwelling on Jesus as the Christ, then, is to bring us to a clear sense of the meaning of the mystery of God revealed in him. Perhaps nowhere does the character of this promising mystery present itself more graciously, extravagantly, and surprisingly than in Jesus' exhortation to think of God as "abba."

Cross and Resurrection

According to Christian faith, the Jesus who was crucified early in the first century now lives. Indeed, his life—according to Paul and John—is

---

[25]Schubert Ogden, *The Point of Christology* (San Francisco: Harper & Row, 1982) 20–40.

our own life. Jesus' resurrection means that he is still present to us, no less than to his disciples who gathered in Jerusalem and Galilee after his death on the cross. And the life that he has now with us in the Spirit is our access to the ultimate mystery he called "abba." God's promise and the world's own aspiration toward a new vision come together in the Jesus who is now risen from the dead. His resurrection is the promise on which Christian hope is based. But as Carl Braaten says, "The resurrection as an event is not only a basis of hope in the future; it *is* the power of the future becoming present now. . . ." The resurrection ". . . not only points to the future; it *is* the future entering the present."[26] Thus, because it is the definitive (though not conclusive) arrival of the mystery of the future, for Christian faith the resurrection is, in its inseparability from the Cross, the central event of revelation.

The articulation of Christian belief throughout the ages confesses that in Jesus there exists the very reality of a God become human. Ultimately, therefore, the unfolding of Christian faith leads to the unanticipated and indeed scandalous conclusion that, in Jesus, the Godhead took up our own struggles and aspirations, suffered frustration, and experienced all that it means to be a finite human being who suffers and dies. The content of revelation includes at its very core the idea of a self-humbling God who experiences suffering and death in the crucifixion of Jesus.[27] And yet, the other side of this self-gift is resurrection. In the resurrection is prefigured the prospect of a future for the cosmos, for humans, and, we may even say, for God.

Jesus died as a sacrifice to an all-inclusive vision of the world's future. But in spite of this death, the vision still lives on in the Spirit. The cross is followed by resurrection. And the Spirit of God in Christ remains alive in our midst. We can detect the reality of this Spirit most vividly in present social, political, environmental, and religious movements that seek the full inclusion and unity of those beings and persons who have been left out by our restrictive social, political, economic, environmental, and religious practices. We become vehicles of this Spirit and its vision whenever we ourselves live a life of concern for social and religious unity and inclusiveness (and as we shall emphasize later, a concern also for reconciliation with the natural world).

[26]Carl E. Braaten, *Christ and Counter-Christ* (Philadelphia: Fortress Press, 1972) 50, emphasis added.

[27]Dermot Lane remarks: "It is difficult for us today to understand a love that is not capable of some form of empathy, sympathy and suffering. From a purely human point of view, a love that does not suffer is somehow something less than love. It was this kind of love, the love that suffers out of love, that was revealed in the passion and death of Jesus on the cross." *Christ at the Center* (New York, Mahwah: Paulist Press, 1990) 72.

The seeking out, embracing, and including of the lost and forgotten is the main thrust of Jesus' life and teaching. Such a life requires the renunciation of any special or separate status on the part of the includer. As long as the one who initiates the act of inclusion insists on preserving a special status there can really be no inclusion or relationship of empathy after all. We cannot really embrace others as on an equal footing with ourselves unless we forfeit any attempts to define ourselves as more privileged than they. What allowed Jesus to attract to himself so many of those lacking social or religious credentials is his self-effacing desire to exist alongside of them rather than above them. Though he clearly exemplified moral excellence, he never condemned those who lived immorally, but regarded them as partaking of his own sonship with his heavenly Father. The gospels portray him as resisting all temptations to privilege, and this renunciation allowed outcasts to approach him and to belong to his open circle without fear. It was a posture that eventually led him to his death on the cross.

But if Jesus is the sacrament of God's own reality, as Christian faith teaches, we must conclude once again that the essential content of revelation is nothing other than the *kenosis* of God that opens up the future to an all-inclusive vision promised in the resurrection. What finally becomes manifest in Jesus, and especially in his death, is that the promising mystery that embraces our world is, at heart, utterly self-emptying love. Eberhard Jüngel writes that:

> [S]hortly after his death, *Jesus himself was proclaimed as the nearness of God,* and as the Son of God. Faith in God, which Jesus had made possible in a new way, now became valid as faith in Jesus Christ. After his death, Jesus was no longer only the witness to faith in God. Like God himself, he had become the object of faith.

Then Jüngel adds that faith in God did not end with the flight of the disciples after Jesus' death:

> There arose faith in Jesus. And faith's own explanation for this is that God had revealed his glory through the dead Jesus. The nearness of God's rule, that which had determined Jesus' earthly life, that to which he appealed and cried out in his death, showed itself to be immediately present in the death of Jesus. This was the experience of the Easter-faith, and it was this that men had to experience: in death, the Proclaimer and the content of his proclamation *have become identical.* The Proclaimer has now himself become the Proclaimed. Thus faith's own ground and

presupposition for faith in Jesus is God's *identification* with him in his death.[28]

By identifying with the dead Christ, God experiences the negativity, the alienation, the relationlessness of death. But in God's self-emptying identification with a dead man, there is also the unassailable reality of an eternal love that promises victory over death. Death means essentially a state of relationlessness, but the love of God expressed in the unbroken divine relationship to a dead man overcomes the alienation. As Jüngel goes on to say,

> To be for someone means to stand in relationship with him. However, when God's relationship to us remains unbroken even in death, when he identifies himself with the dead Jesus in order to demonstrate his gracious concern for all men through the crucified One, then out of the midst of the relationlessness of death there emerges a *new relationship* between God and man. And we must be careful to note that this new relationship of God to man consists in God himself bearing the relationlessness of death which alienates man from him. It is when relationships are broken, when the relationships between men are ruptured that God takes up man's cause. As pledging himself for man in this way, God *reveals* his very being. By identifying himself with the dead Jesus of Nazareth to the benefit of all men, he reveals himself to finite man as a being of infinite *love*. For it is when everything has become relationless that love alone creates new relationships. When all relationships have been broken, only love can create new ones.[29]

The historical life that Jesus lived was clearly one devoted to the overcoming of relationlessness. The sense of not belonging, of being unaccepted by the social, ethical, and religious requirements of his times led him to identify in a special way with the outcasts in order to give them a new and more secure sense of relationship, and therefore of life. But even while Jesus' chief passion was to restore broken relationships, he himself became increasingly the victim of efforts to break his relationship to the world. And in his own death by crucifixion, Jesus himself died the death of an outcast abandoned even by those who had been closest to him. He experienced the very depths of relationlessness.

Relationship, as we now see more clearly in the emergence of ecological consciousness, is the substance of all being and of life itself. Without relationship among entities—whether at the levels of matter, life, or per-

[28]Eberhard Jüngel, *Death: The Riddle and the Mystery,* trans. by Iain and Ute Nicol (Philadelphia: The Westminster Press, 1974) 107–08.

[29]Ibid., 109–10.

sons (and in Trinitarian terms, of God also)—there is simply no reality. This is why death is so abhorrent. For it means the loss of relationship, the experience of being cut off from life, loved ones, and seemingly of God, too. In the Hebrew Scriptures, death is clearly seen as a state of being estranged from one's people, from participation in the promise, and also from God. God is a God of the living, and the dead no longer appear to have a relationship to the God of life.

Christian faith discerns in Jesus' death, that is, in an event of utterly broken relationship, the revelation of God's eternal love and its power to restore relationship. The resurrection then is grounded in the love of God entering into and appropriating relationlessness so as to overcome it. Revelation is the disclosure of the self-humbling of God and with it the promise of ultimate reconciliation and unity that arises out of the un-brokenness of the love that gives itself away completely and by doing so manifests itself as the ground of all life and relationship.[30]

[30]To emphasize the utter self-givingness of God does not in any way mean that God is unreceptive to, or unaffected by our own love in return. Critiques of the residually patriarchal motifs in the notion of "unilateral" love need to be heeded. The idea of self-giving must be understood in a *relational* sense, in which case the self-emptying includes the act of making oneself "dependent" upon the love of others. As Schubert Ogden and other process theologians, following Charles Hartshorne, have convincingly shown, the "absoluteness" of God is not jeopardized by attributing to God the notes of relatedness, or vulnerability, to the "other." God's eminence or absoluteness consists precisely of God's being the *most related* of all realities. God's own relatedness is relative to nothing; that is to say, it is absolute. Viewed in this context, the self-humbling love of God is not intended to obliterate, but to render significant our own loving of God in return. See Ogden, *The Reality of God,* 47–70.

7

The Congregation of Hope

Jesus' life and death had a profoundly transforming effect on his followers. So moved were they by their encounter with him that they interpreted their subsequent existence together as a whole new "way" (the Greek word is 'hodos').[1] But while this "way" was in some sense a new departure, it still emanated from the context of Israel's ancient hope in God's promises. Out of the experience of renewed trust aroused by Jesus' life, death, and resurrection was born what has come to be known as the *ecclesia*. Literally, this word means the community of those who have been "called out." The *ecclesia* is the new congregation of hope.[2] This community of those who have been called to follow the new way toward the future is referred to as the "Church."

The Church may be defined as the community through which God's revelatory promise in Christ is received, celebrated, and communicated to the world. In word, sacrament, and mission, the Christian Church mediates to the world, of which it is a part, the promise received in Christ. Because of its promissory mission, the Church is continuous with "the people of God" first shaped into a community by events in the lives of Moses, the kings, and the prophets of Israel. The Church's distinctiveness within this tradition lies simply in the fact that it bears witness to the eternal promise especially (but certainly not exclusively) by reference to the life, death, and resurrection of Jesus. In essence, therefore, its mission is to convey Jesus' own proclamation of an inclusive reign of God, and to rehearse for each age the reasons we have for a sustained hope

---

[1]Originally they did not conceive of themselves as starting or belonging to a new religion, since this was not even a formal concept in their self-understanding, but as followers of the *hodos,* or the "way."

[2]Moltmann, *The Experiment Hope,* 58.

in God's encompassing vision of fulfillment for the entire world. By our belonging to such a community of hope and vision, we remain within the horizon of the paradigmatic biblical stories of promise and liberation that begin with Abraham and culminate in the resurrection of Jesus from the dead.

Although there is no evidence that Jesus self-consciously contemplated the institution of a new *ecclesia,* we may legitimately maintain that the Christian way, with its incipient ecclesial character, was founded by the revelatory promise that came to expression in him and his proclamation of the reign of God. In that sense, he is the Church's foundation. The Church's existence, then, remains essential to revelation as the sign or "sacrament" of God's fidelity to the promise first given to Abraham and ratified in Jesus' being raised up to new life. And our participation in the life of the Church provides a special (though not exclusive) access to revelation. Through participation in the life of the Church, its liturgy, sacraments, teachings, and praxis, we are enabled to situate ourselves within the revelatory vision of Christ with its promise for the liberation of the whole of history and creation.

Human nature is such that we exist and come to understand ourselves, our identities, and our destinies only in community with others. Existence alongside others who share our sense of life's meaning is not accidental but essential to our being human. Through participation in the rituals, actions, and stories of a common tradition, a people is molded into a fellowship of shared destiny. Every community with a tradition understands its existence and identity in terms of the narratives that recount the process of how it came into being and that tell where it is going. It is questionable whether any of us can live meaningfully without relation to such stories.

It is primarily through participation in shared stories about Jesus and the effects of what the New Testament and later Trinitarian theology call the "Spirit," felt by Jesus' contemporaries and poured out at Pentecost upon the early Christian community, that we experience even today the promise offered anew in his life. Our reception of specifically Christian revelation ordinarily requires therefore that we abide within a communal context guided by the Spirit and given expression through the Christian story in word and rite. Living inside this community of faith gives us an intimate access to revelation that we could not have if we remained disinterested and uncommitted observers outside. Sharing membership with a body of fellow believers allows the content of God's promise to insinuate itself into our lives with a depth of penetration that an external or detached standpoint would not allow.[3]

[3]In ways that we cannot examine here, it could be said that all of us, whether churched or unchurched, indwell in some degree the Christian story that has been so determina-

In his important book, *The Meaning of Revelation,* H. Richard Niebuhr writes that our knowledge of revelation is transmitted to the Church not so much through impersonal, external historical reporting as through a feeling-laden involvement with the community's internal historical memory of its founding events.[4] These events will probably have little more than academic interest to non-believers, and the latter will often cast doubt on the objective historicity of some occurrences such as the Exodus or the resurrection of Christ. But to the believer, only an affectionate, faithful involvement in the saving character of the events mediated to us through the inner history of the Church can put us deeply in touch with the reality of revelation.

An encounter with revelation's promise today can occur because of our immersion in the internal memory of the Church. Thus, those within the Church will speak of "our" fathers, "our" God, "our" Lord and savior. Niebuhr writes:

> When the evangelists of the New Testament and their successors pointed to history as the starting point of their faith and of their understanding of the world it was internal history that they indicated. They did not speak of events, as impersonally apprehended, but rather of what happened to them in their community. They recalled the critical events in their own life-time when they became aware of themselves in a new way as they came to know the self on whom they were dependent. They turned to a past which was not gone but which endured in them as their memory, making them what they were. So for the late church, history was always the story of "our fathers," of "our Lord," and of the actions of "our God."[5]

Niebuhr provides a helpful analogy illustrating how relation to a community's "internal history" can connect contemporary believers with the saving events that are often of little interest to those outside of the Christian faith tradition.[6] Consider, he says, the case of a man who has recovered his sight through a medical operation. As this former patient gives his enthusiastic and grateful account of the event of his recovery of sight, the quality or tone of his account will differ considerably from a purely clinical digest of the same event. The doctor who performed the operation will use a scientifically detached, personally uninvolved kind of discourse in order to describe what has happened. And the physician's words

---

tive in Western culture, even when this culture has become deeply secularized. For even the contours of modern secularity have been subtly molded by biblical motifs.

[4]See H. Richard Niebuhr, *The Meaning of Revelation,* 44–54.

[5]Niebuhr, 53.

[6]Ibid., 44.

are taken to be objectively true. But is the physician's report any more true to the reality of the event than the recovered patient's own emotionally involved account? Does the fact that the latter talks with such feeling and enthusiasm about his recovery constitute an obstacle to the truthfulness or objectivity of his report? Or is it not possible to say that the one who has been healed can give a no less truthful report of what happened than can the clinician?

Clearly we may view the two accounts as complementary rather than as inevitably conflicting. Likewise, what we are here calling internal and external history may be seen as mutually supportive ways of knowing events. It is not impossible that a faith community's enthusiastic, internal story of its own recovery of vision has the capacity to retrieve aspects of salvific occurrences that a more scientific account will leave out. Even in science, Michael Polanyi notes, the range of data that are visible to inquirers is determined in large measure by what is interesting to scientists as persons in community endowed with feelings and passions.[7] This element of interest will cause certain items to show up and others to remain in obscurity. Likewise, the specific focus of faith will highlight certain events of history and read them as interesting, whereas an inquiry devoid of this focus may scarcely notice them at all. The Church is a community held together in part by its shared internal historical interest in a specific set of events out of which it reads a special promise. And this interest is an essential part of a community's search for truth.

Of course there is always a need to be critical about accounts of events given by internal history, for sometimes they are distorted by the sheer force of enthusiasm. Even so, what appears as exaggeration from the point of view of external history is itself a way of calling attention to aspects of events that might otherwise pass us by. At times, our internal memories are subjective to the point of being unrelated to reality, and so they need the correction of a more clinical examination. But this does not mean that every place we find enthusiastic, emotionally tinged descriptions of events we should conclude that they lack objectivity or that they bear no relation to the real. For it may be that the interlocking of our lives with momentous events, and especially salvific ones, can occur in depth only by our sharing with others a life and language that evokes in us a certain *feeling* of involvement. We may need to look at the world through the eyes of the shared expectations of a tradition and community of faith and hope if we are to be grasped by the substance of revelation. And it is equally possible that the exclusive use of a completely external, scientifically historical method would leave us still stranded at a distance from the reality of saving events.

[7]Michael Polanyi, *Personal Knowledge,* (New York: Harper Torchbooks, 1964) 135.

Thus, the Church's language is primarily confessional, enthusiastic, and involved, rather than scientifically detached. But this does not mean that we need to be a priori suspicious of its authenticity. At the same time, however, it is important for us to add that scientifically historical study of the tradition is an important and necessary corrective to the possible excesses of a more passionate approach. In recent years, for example, the Church has learned much from a detached scientific study of the Bible and traditional teachings. Niebuhr says, "There is no continuous movement from an objective inquiry into the life of Jesus to a knowledge of him as the Christ who is our Lord."[8] Only a decision of faith can make this jump. But recent developments in biblical research using various kinds of scientific methods have added helpful corrections to our pictures of Jesus and other events that faith perceives as revelatory.

The heavy reliance on its own internal historical memory may seem to imply that Christianity is just another esoteric religion, accessible only to a group of insiders. There is, of course, a certain insider's perspective in any faith tradition, but it would be contrary to the inclusive character of Christianity to interpret our belonging to a Church community as though it were a position of privilege that separates us from those not so gifted. In the past, some forms of Christian faith have not escaped the tendency to close all doors to outsiders. It is clear that a one-sided reliance on what insiders think to be normative to faith can at times lead to an elitist gnosticism. If the content of a faith is not checked by some externally objective evaluations, it can easily become too esoteric. In recent years, the work of scientific historians, philosophers, sociologists, and psychologists of religion has built up an impressive roadblock to the evils of esotericism. The dangers of enthusiasm are present in all religions. But given the proviso just noted, the passion and joy that bond members of the Church to its founder and his message of hope need not necessarily be taken as interfering with the truthfulness and openness of faith in that promise. For without the feeling of excitement which belonging to a community of shared hope provides, it may be difficult for us to be grasped deeply by the reality of the mystery revealed in Jesus.

After emphasizing the advantages of such belonging, though, we should not push too far the necessity of formal membership in the Church as a condition for the reception of revelation. People who are unchurched may be touched deeply by the power of God's promise and even more specifically by Jesus' personality. In the latter case, this may happen by reading books about him, by immersing themselves in the history of Christian art and architecture, or by living alongside those who are explicitly members of the Churches. Portraits of Jesus abound in various media,

[8]Niebuhr, 61.

and the individual can derive much hope and inspiration from them without necessarily having formal association with a church. Today, for various reasons that we cannot explore here, many individuals have lost confidence in all formal ecclesiastical institutions. But they have not necessarily lost faith in Jesus and his teachings. And they find access to his personality—and even to his saving presence—through art, novels, films, academic studies of Christology, or private reading of the Gospels. The commanding authority of the figure of Jesus overflows the boundaries of purely ecclesiastical vigilance.

Still, in its fullest flowering, following in the footsteps of Christ requires in some sense or other the sharing of his promise and praxis with others. Christian faith pushes us beyond a purely private piety. A sense of promise can only be felt fully when it leads to a *shared* hope that leads to common action. Christian faith is essentially, and not just accidentally, ecclesial. This does not mean that the prevalent Church structures and practices of any particular age are inevitably ideal vehicles for the conveying of the substance of revelation's promise to the world or even its own members. *Ecclesia semper reformanda:* the Church is itself ever in need of conversion. But it is *normally* through shared life, prayer, and ritual activity with others, or through common reception of the Word, that we are brought into encounter with the Christ of promise. It is the function of the Church to facilitate this encounter. Where it fails to do so, it is to that extent unfaithful to revelation and in need of self-revision in order to execute its sacramentally representative mission.

According to the teaching of Jesus, what is asked of those who belong to his circle is a complete trust in God's love and fidelity to the covenantal promise, now renewed in the coming reign of God. However, the breadth and inclusiveness of God's promise and reign present an enormous challenge to us. They invite us to put into practice the acceptance and promotion of others that Jesus' God manifests toward us. Those officially enrolled in the Churches often show anything but this latitude. And so it is possible for us to remain in some sense outside the faith, even in the midst of our membership in the Church that proclaims the bold and inclusive message of God's reign. Moreover, many of those who have no formal membership in the Church are actually more inside the real circle of the tolerant faith that Jesus spoke of than those of us who have been baptized and participate bodily in the worship of the Church.

Nevertheless, a formal, sacramental community of believers shaped by an identifiable tradition built upon shared stories of origin and destiny is essential to the communication of revelation. The existence of a Church with a teaching tradition provides necessary informational boundaries for ensuring the reliable transmission of what the apostles received from their encounter with Jesus. To repeat what we stated earlier, such boundaries are necessary for any informational process. Without some doctrinal constraints, any message will sooner or later decay into a chaotic vagueness or indefiniteness and thereby lose its challenging and critical edge vis-à-vis the rest of culture. Reliable transmission of information—as we now know from science and cosmology, as well as from communications theory—requires information systems with clear boundaries. The establishment of a Church, together with a teaching officialdom and institutional structures, is not merely accidental to this informational requirement, though the specific features of these elements may (and should) vary considerably from one age to the next.[9] Any system, such as the Church, has to have what information theory calls "sets of constraints" in order to function as an informational medium. Yet, to repeat another point made earlier, if these constraints themselves become too rigid, as they often do in the unfolding of a religious tradition, then the communication flow becomes so burdened with redundancy that it loses any truly informational (in this case, revelatory) character and decays into the transmission of mere banality. An information process has to be bounded in some way by constraints, but it must also remain open to the influx of novelty if it is to be truly informative.

One of the functions of the Church is to protect the Christian story so as to ensure its faithful and undiluted transmission to the next generation of believers. Any religious community's desire to safeguard its sacred and saving information often leads it to be very solicitous, at times excessively so, about doctrinal orthodoxy. So, too, the Christian Church has sought to guard its borders against any blurring or rarefying of what it takes to be a specially revealed content. In its attempts to plot the requisite informational boundaries, however, it has experienced serious internal disagreements. One segment of the Christian Church lays out its borders in a manner inconsistent at times with others'. Thus we now have many churches within the Church. As in the case of the other religions of the world, Christianity has splintered into a variety of sectarian subsystems whose doctrinal boundaries have often hardened to the point of making conversation extremely difficult.

Yet from its very beginning the various elements of the Christian tradition, while always being concerned with doctrinal constraints, have also been open, at least to some degree, to novelty. From its Palestinian origins, the Church has reached out into alien cultural and linguistic settings for a conceptuality and imagery that would communicate to a continually wider circle of people the inclusive message its earliest disciples had experienced in Jesus. Our most venerable doctrinal formulations contain

[9]This, however, does not mean that the system has to be rigidly hierarchical and undemocratic. As we are learning from physics and other sciences today, systems come in many shapes.

elements derived not only from Judaism, but also from Gnosticism, Platonism, Stoicism, Aristotelianism, and other modes of thought, most of them unfamiliar to Jesus and his immediate disciples. Christian liturgies and feasts today are full of elements borrowed down through the centuries from what we have pejoratively called "paganism." The informational effectiveness of a tradition requires such continual borrowing. Periodically, the official guardians of Christian tradition become unsettled about theological attempts to communicate the content of revelation in a new idiom. Their reserve is partially understandable in that they implicitly see the need for boundaries and constraints in the informational processing of the content of faith. But if they seek to make the membranes surrounding the deposit of faith completely impermeable to the influx of alternative insights and modes of expression, this will inevitably lead to a serious inhibition of the transmission of the revelatory content of the faith.

The Christian story brings with it certain boundaries. But it also possesses a radical impulse toward inclusiveness. It is intrinsically opposed to boundaries even while remaining within them. In the life of the Church, these two biases often exist in serious tension with each other. At times destructive conflicts develop as a result, while at other times an enlivening synthesis of tradition and new ideas occurs. (An example of the latter may be the new evolutionary theologies that have emerged in this century.) Like many other religious traditions, the Christian story is open to being retold in diverse ways in new situations. Even in the New Testament, the many Christologies articulating the character and effectiveness of the one Savior are already evidence of the mingling of traditional constraints with the novelty required by ever changing circumstances. Subsequently, the Scriptures and tradition become the constraining informational sources on which members of the Church rely in order to situate themselves in the presence of the promising mystery that gave new life to the disciples after the death of Jesus.

Revelation, Past and Present

An essential condition for the Church's communication of revelation is that it have a deposit of faith that remains in some sense fixed or finished in order to remain a continually reliable source to draw on in new circumstances. But revelation is not *fundamentally* the normative deposit of accounts of saving events in the past. If revelation is to be real to us, it must be something that is occurring now in the concrete events, trivial and important, of our everyday lives. To encounter revelation is not primarily to look back, or to dig into a sacred book or a traditional set of teachings. These monuments of faith, of course, all carry with them essential constraints shaping the relevant information. But experiencing the self-revealing God is not simply a matter of looking at the scriptural and doctrinal boundaries laboriously established by the Church and its traditions. Such limits *do* give definiteness to the content of faith, but encountering revelation means, above all, being confronted by the inviting and challenging futurity of divine mystery in the immediate context of our own concrete situations. The content of revelation is a promise which, because it has never yet been completely fulfilled, can never be fixed or finished, but remains incalculable and to some extent mysteriously incomprehensible. And the reception of this revelation means that we experience a gracious, extravagant, and surprising future dawning at the frontiers of our own lives here and now. The Church's teaching tradition exists primarily to make it possible for us to look forward to God's promises in a new way every day. We make an idol of this tradition if we read it in any other way.

The content and substance of revelation is always mystery, and for biblical faith, this elusive but endlessly fulfilling mystery comes to us in the shape of an unfathomable future that promises complete liberation. Our being inserted into a community of fellow believers who have been gathered together on the basis of historical events in their past is an indispensable dimension of our encounter with this future. We "indwell" these past historical events not to make them absolutes, but in order to look *with* them into the mystery they anticipate. Living within a tradition is not so much a matter of looking *at* the past but rather *with* it toward a still unfulfilled promise latent within it.[10] Tradition invites us not to make an absolute of its constraints, but to focus our gaze toward the future in accordance with the coordinates it bequeaths to us. We continually recount our common past and seek to incorporate it ever more coherently within our memory, but we concretely experience revelation only by looking *forward* along with this past to the fulfillment of God's promise. To live within the horizon of Easter is not simply to look at an event that took place long ago but, even more, to look forward to the fulfillment that it promises for our future and that of the whole world.

If we do look back to the record of God's mighty deeds accomplished in the past, as indeed we must, it is not in order to restore something that is no longer, but to find the basis there for hope here and now. We dwell within our tradition in order to be more sensitive to the promise and futurity of God that are still on the way. Too often, theology and religious education have left us with the impression that everything important has already happened and that therefore faith's main posture is one of restoring

[10]See Niebuhr, 54.

the past. We are often instructed to look back into Israel's history or even into the New Testament times in order to find there the fullest appearance of God's revelation. But this is a way of "abolishing time" that finds no authority in the Bible. The Bible constantly invites us to look ahead into the future for the fullness of revelation. Repristinating the past, even if it is a glorious past, is asking for the impossible. And it contradicts the very nature of human existence with its essential orientation to the future.[11] The fact is, people are not looking only for a "salvation history" somewhere in the traces of historical events. Rather, they are fundamentally in search of the meaning, purpose, and renewal of their own lives as they exist in the here and now.

We look to the past, then, in order to find there some ways of orienting ourselves toward our future, but not in order to absolutize or romanticize a lost age. If the idea of revelation, is to have any relevance it must be essentially a *present* experience of God's coming to us from the future, and not simply a set of stories dragged out of the past. The deposit of revelation is said to be finished or fixed, but this can be a salvific teaching only if it means that there is sufficient evidence in our past history to convince us that we live within the horizon of a promise which by its nature always looks to the future for fulfillment. Revelation fundamentally means the arrival of that future and not a retrieval of the past.

Still, the ancient stories are obviously indispensable, for it is in their continual retelling that we find the informational constraints that give appropriate shape to our hope. The Church community, its normative writings, and its traditions are repositories and mediators of those stories of hope that we stand within as we reach forth toward the future. The Church is (ideally at least) a community in which hope is kept alive by the retelling of the mighty acts of God. In a sense, revelation is simply the unfolding of a great story of which we ourselves are a part, but which has its fulfillment only in the future. We need then to know the earlier chapters in order to have at least a dim sense of the story's more complete unfolding. We cannot look toward an ending of a story unless we know where we have been. In recounting the past acts of God, we are placed within the horizon of the hope awakened by those events.

Revelation as Salvation

The promising mystery of the future always seeks to carry us into itself. It does so by sacramentally concealing itself in the concrete objects of our human hopes. But we nevertheless resist the promise of that future

[11]See Wolfhart Pannenberg, *What Is Man?*, trans. by Duane A. Priebe (Philadelphia: Fortress, 1970) 41–53.

and its promises. This rejection of God's future, the refusal in other words to let God be God, a refusal to which the biblical stories are a constant reminder, is the fundamental meaning of sin. The fuller meaning of revelation can be understood, therefore, only if we take into account the fact of a human sinfulness that has continually resisted the freedom, extravagance, and surprisingness of the divine self-promise.

In the face of our resistance to God's promise, revelation assumes the character of *salvation*. Revelation is not just a take-it-or-leave-it disclosure of the future. It is the divine future's relentless quest to liberate us from any fixation on the past. Revelation is God's making the divine selfhood known to us, through the mode of promise, in such a way that we will perceive that there is no limit to what we may hope for. The mission of the Church, therefore, is to keep open the limitlessness of the horizon of God's future. This liberating open-endedness is the Good News that the Church must continually proclaim to the world. When it fails to do so, it is unfaithful to its calling.

Revelation can be called salvation because its visionary promise of an ever new future redeems us from the prison we build around ourselves out of our hopelessness and mistrust. In its saving character, there is also an inevitably judgmental aspect to revelation. The self-emptying God of the future seeks to break through our resistance to the fullness of what we can hope for. This is the meaning of divine judgment. And this is how we may interpret the many passages in the Bible that refer to God's anger:

> God's revelation is a saving activity because it penetrates the closed state of man, and thus it is also the revelation of divine wrath (Rom. 1:18ff.). The mystery of the "righteousness of God" (Rom. 1:17) could not be revealed (Rom. 1:17; 3:21) without simultaneously revealing God's "No" to man's godlessness and unrighteousness.[12]

But we must be careful to interpret the meaning of godlessness and unrighteousness in terms of how the Bible understands God, and not in accordance with the moralistic and despotic ideas of God that linger in ill-formed religious imaginations. God, as the giver of the future, is the limitless origin of promise. Godlessness or sin, therefore, is at bottom our refusal to let into our lives the fundamentally promising character of reality. What is subject to judgment, therefore, is the assumption that our own paltry visions of the future are ample enough to satisfy our deepest longings. Divine judgment is the shattering of those limiting projections of our future that arise from a consciousness not yet attuned to the breadth and inclusiveness of the divine vision of our future and the world's fu-

---

[12]Otto Weber, *Foundations of Dogmatics,* Vol, I. trans. by Darrell L. Guder (Grand Rapids: William B. Eerdmans, 1981) 175.

ture. Though such judgment initially seems to be negative and evokes our strong resistance, it is really a gift in favor of us rather than an interdiction opposed to us. Its concern is that we lift the lid on what is realistically possible for us as a human and cosmic community shaped by hope.

The Church, too, stands continually under the judgment of the divine promise. It constantly needs correction from the wider vision contained in the revelation to which it witnesses. It fails in its mission whenever it allows the promissory character of reality to sink under the weight of any past age of allegedly splendid "orthodoxy." The Church can glory in its past only to the extent that this past carries the seeds of a hope that can be sown anew in the present. And it remains a sinful Church particularly to the extent that it fails to represent in its own structures the inclusiveness that it proclaims in its word about the promise on which it is founded.

According to this understanding of revelation, sin means the obscuring of our true possibilities from ourselves, a circumscription that leaves us unfulfilled and enslaved. Divine judgment, therefore, is part of a process of liberation. If this judgment initially seems to be a contradiction, this is only because it conflicts with the restrictedness and pettiness of our own aspirations. It is a signal that we are not dreaming and hoping with sufficient breadth. We are not being open enough to the freedom, extravagance, and unexpectedness of our genuine future.

It is part of the Church's mission, therefore, to be critical of all political, cultural, and psychological constraints, including the ones imbedded in its own figure, that prevent the breaking in of the promise of God's future made manifest especially in Jesus the Christ. It is required to carry a judgment against the "world," understood as the product of our excessively narrow and non-inclusive efforts to secure our existence. In order to do so effectively, however, it must begin with a critique of its own non-inclusiveness. That this has not yet been accomplished is a major source of the Church's failure to move the world toward the promise given in revelation.

The Church's own failure in this respect is itself rooted in a refusal to be informed by the image of God's humility that lies at the center of Christian revelation. The Church can truly sacramentalize the mystery of promise, the person of Christ, and the reality of God only to the extent that it, too, exists as an embodiment of self-emptying humility and defenselessness. Through much of its history, though, the image of God resident in its ecclesiastical self-image and conveyed to its members has been one of power and might. Its "God" has often been understood after the model of political potentates instead of the humble shepherd of Nazareth who died on a cross. And it has often taken as its own a conventional conception of political force contradicted by the crucified Jesus' redefinition of power. Though some within the Church have taken seriously the kenotic character of the mystery it stands for, by and large the sense of God's self-emptying love has been obscured in its preaching, practice, and theology, as well as in its internal and external politics.

An understanding of revelation as the gift of an ever-more-inclusive future rooted in the kenotic love of God can help transform the Church's self-understanding in a way that would make it more closely related to the needs of our contemporary world. We would be deceiving ourselves if we pretended that the Church today is not largely ineffective in the world. Its inherent message of hope and comfort to those in need has not penetrated very far into the affairs of the planet. Its clinging to pre-revelational, pre-kenotic images of God fails to stir the hearts of people toward appropriate compassion. It often remains self-preoccupied in a manner utterly in contradiction to the self-abandoning God incarnate in the Christ.

Still, it is not helpful for us to be unforgiving toward this ambiguous community of sinful men and women that we call the Church. For it remains the indispensable bearer of the fullness of God's promise and the Good News of the divine self-gift to the world. If it is often unfaithful to the substance of its own *raison d'être,* it is nevertheless forever commissioned by the Spirit to proclaim the good news of revelation.

Revelation and Sacrament

Generally speaking, religions have a sacramental aspect through which they both receive and express their sense of mystery. As we have argued previously, the revelation of mystery occurs also in the mystical, silent, and active ways of religion. But it is through sacraments or symbols that we first and most explicitly encounter the sacred. In Christian tradition, Jesus is the primary sacrament, and the Church, both as the body of Christ and as the carrier of a set of sacraments, brings the reality of God bodily into the lives of its members. Along with attending to the Word, Christians have felt God's redemptive love quite palpably in such sacraments as baptism, Eucharist, and marriage.[13]

---

[13]Catholic Christianity has traditionally spoken of *seven* sacraments: baptism, reconciliation, confirmation, Eucharist, marriage, holy orders and anointing of the sick. We need not enter here into the controversies that have arisen among Christian denominations regarding this precise number and their relative importance. Rather, our concern is simply to situate the sacraments in the context of revelation as we have been portraying it in this work. In that respect baptism, Eucharist, and matrimony may be taken here as the primary ways of sacramentalizing the promissory aspect of revelation that we have been highlighting, but which has not always been sufficiently emphasized.

These sacraments are familiar enough to most Christians, but what is not always so obvious is their promissory character. How often is the sacrament of baptism celebrated in a spirit of genuine hope for the whole world's future liberation? Moreover, do we often see marriage fundamentally as the sacramentalization of God's fidelity to the promise, so that it is not just the present sacralization of human mating, but also one of the most powerful signals we are given in our human lives that the mystery of the future deserves our absolute trust? To a great extent, the dimension of hope or futurity has been lost sight of in sacramental theology, just as it has disappeared from our inherited notions of revelation. Until quite recently, for example, the Eucharist has rarely been seen by the majority of Christians as the radically eschatological celebration it is. Even though there is much in its traditional formulations that begs us to interpret it as a celebration of hope and a looking forward into the future, it is often felt to be little more than a reenactment of a past event. How often has it been experienced deeply as the anticipation of an eschatological banquet or as the sharing of life with the One who has risen and is still coming? How often is it experienced as an encounter with the Christ who himself *still has a future* precisely because the lives of those he loves, with whom he wills to remain in solidarity in the Eucharist, are still at a distance from completion? The powerful theme of promise has typically been subordinated to the sense of the Lord's presence in our midst.

Obviously, we have no wish here to soften the sense of the divine presence sacramentalized in the Eucharist. Instead, we need only to highlight the specific *mode* of that presence. If we follow the patterns of thought set forth in the Bible, it must be seen as a presence in the mode of promise and not an exhaustive presence that leaves no room for further manifestations of an incalculable future. Sacramental presence is not appropriately interpreted as a divine availability that would render any further hope for future fulfillment irrelevant. The Christ whose presence in our midst is sacramentalized in the Eucharist still has a future in communion with our own unfinished existence.

Likewise, in the Eucharist the important theme of *anamnesis* ("do this in memory of me") has sometimes edged out the theme of hope ("we hope to enjoy forever the vision of your glory"). Obviously, the sacraments are reenactments or memorializing rites as well. They are indispensable symbolic ways of making ourselves in some sense contemporary with the past events of salvation history. But in view of what we have been saying about the character of revelation, the purpose of this *anamnesis* is not to reconstruct the past for its own sake, as though it holds the fullness of salvation. Rather, it is to align our lives with the yet unfulfilled sense of promise that came to birth in a heightened way in those momentous events that are remembered in the sacraments. Revelation is fundamentally the arrival of the future.

Sacramentally speaking this means, for example, that we celebrate the new exodus of baptism not only to immerse ourselves in Christ's death and thus become purified of sin, but also in order to realize that we are the inheritors of God's yet-unfulfilled promise to Abraham and his off-spring. If being baptized means being raised here and now to new life, then this present sharing in Christ's resurrection cannot yet mean final fulfillment, but rather a life of hope which is cognizant of the inadequacy of the present state of things to contain the fullness of God's future. In our present state of existence, it is hope for fulfillment and not fulfillment itself that constitutes our life. And the Spirit poured out in our sacraments in order to make us experience the nearness of God is the Spirit of hope and not a conclusive presence.

The distaste for "presence" that we find in so much modern philosophy, art, and literary criticism is something we need to attend to if we think of the sacraments only as ways in which God becomes present to us. There is an apophatic, silent, or distancing impulse in these contemporary movements that, in spite of the nihilistic extremes to which they often tend, can be assimilated into the themes of hope and promise. By protesting our typical religious (including Christian) sacramentalizing of God's presence, they poignantly highlight the fact that fulfillment has not yet arrived. Their protests against our often shallow sacramentalizing of God's presence provide a needed antidote to our tendency toward an idolatrous closing ourselves off from the wider vision of revelation's promise arriving out of the inexhaustible future.

In general, the sacraments can be truly revelatory of God if they are interpreted in the spirit of promise rather than simply as theophanies. It is true of course that God is present in these sacraments in a special way, but in the light of revelation we are encouraged to see God's presence in the mode of the arrival of the future.[14] This means that we must learn to see the sacraments not as manifestations of the fullness of deity but

---

[14]In Bernard Cooke's learned book, *The Distancing of God* (Minneapolis: Augsburg Fortress, 1990), the author laments the way in which God has been gradually distanced from sacramental modes of mediation. Cooke is correct in chastizing much classical theology for making God too remote. And yet there is a certain sense in which God's not being fully present is what opens up the future to us. A self-renouncing God humbly withdraws, and in doing so paradoxically becomes more intimate with us, evoking the response of love, patience, and action. A full self-presentation of God would bring history to an end, and given its presently unfinished character, this would be a most unsatisfying experience to all who have hope in the infinite mystery of the future. For this reason we need to see the sacraments not only as the mediations of God's presence, but as tokens of a future which is not yet real. Thus there has to be in some paradoxical way a "distancing of God" in order to allow for the intimacy of a relation based on fidelity and trust.

as expressions through which God's future touches us without yet being fully actualized. The world remains unfinished, and it would be deadening to pretend that our hopes for this world have already been fulfilled. It is sufficient, and in fact more enlivening, for us simply to trust that the back of evil has been broken, and not to imagine that the final victory has been completely won. The disillusionment we sometimes experience during or after a sacramental celebration may in part be the result of our over-burdening the rites themselves with the task of bringing the fullness of mystery to presence. An excessive emphasis on the sacraments as making God present needs correction by the mystical, silent, and active aspects of hope. The world is yet in the making, filled with ambiguity, still at a great distance from the destiny it seeks. It is sufficient then that we see the Church's sacraments as promises, for it is in the mode of promise that God becomes most intimately present to us now.

Inspiration and The Scriptures

In the life of the Church, the notion of revelation has come to be closely associated, though not identified, with that of the inspiration of Scripture. The Church's doctrinal boundaries began to take on a more definite shape when, in response to the need to determine what falls within and what without the pale of authentic faith, it authorized a canon of Holy Books which it holds to be inspired by the Spirit of Jesus and his God. These books, in spite of their wide diversity of genre and style, have a certain guiding character essential for the shaping and transmission of Christian faith. Thus, they are said to be the product of divine inspiration.

In what sense, though, may we today understand the doctrine of inspiration? As in the case of the idea of revelation, it no longer appears fruitful or meaningful to understand it merely according to the propositional or illumination model. Theologians today have abandoned the simplistic theory which has the Holy Spirit dictating sentences to prophets and evangelists. Inspiration has to mean something much deeper than the infusion of holy truths into the minds of isolated biblical writers.

We may reach a deeper understanding of the Church's view of inspiration by reflecting on the remarkable and felicitous fact that in its determination of those books it holds to be inspired, it did not throw out, but instead enthusiastically embraced, the texts we have traditionally called the Old Testament.[15] Apparently, it was their promissory character that endeared these writings to the Church. The Church's reverence for these

---

[15]Today we have become conscious of the need to be somewhat reserved in our using the adjective "old" to refer to books which are not at all obsolete either for Jews or for Christians.

books, it is true, is due in great measure to the fact that they provide the essential background for appreciating the fulfillment of God's promises in Jesus. The momentousness of the Christ-event could never have been grasped except in terms of the highly charged atmosphere of expectation that received its written expression in the ancient books of the Israelites. Hence the books are taken by the Church to be inspired.

However, even independently of their bearing on the Church's interpretation of Jesus' life, death, and resurrection, these texts have been held holy for the simple reason that they give authoritative expression to the central themes of promise and hope that constitute the core of biblical faith. In the final analysis, then, the root of inspiration is the very same promising mystery that comes to faith's awareness through revelation. Those texts are held to be inspired which convey the sense of God's fidelity to the promises first given to Abraham. Some of these texts do so more explicitly than others, and occasionally the Bible includes works that seem to question whether God's promise is really going to be fulfilled. Ecclesiastes, Job, and some of the Psalms wonder at times whether we live in a universe that embodies God's promise and fidelity. And the Wisdom literature does not always focus very explicitly on the theme of promise. But even these texts still fall within the general horizon of a faith shaped by trust in God's fidelity. And when taken in the context of the whole of Scripture, they provide the dialectical nuance that gives even more substance to the central message of the holy books, namely, that God is one who makes and keeps promises.

In its choice of those books that comprise the New Testament, the Church has also been guided by criteria rooted in a balanced vision of God's promise. As we have seen several times before, the criterion of genuine hope in God's promise consists of a willingness to temper the sacramentalism of our dreams by a willingness to look mystically into the future symbolized by our images, by a steady posture of patience and silence, and by a transformative praxis that refuses to escape from the troubles of present history. Even though it had the opportunity to survey many gnostic texts in circulation at the time the canon became fixed, we may conjecture that the Church finally left these off the list because of their failure to embody the balanced kind of hope and deep sense of mystery's futurity that we find in the canonical books. Though full of titillating tales and occasional bits of edifying wisdom, the gnostic gospels lacked the balance of sacramentalism, mysticism, silence, and praxis that we find for example in the kerygmatic presentations of the Christ of Mark, Matthew, Luke, and John. They are examples of what happens to religion when the mystical component becomes disengaged from the sacramental, silent, and active elements. And when we turn to the epistolary texts of the New Testament, it is also tempting to conjecture that it was their balancing of these four ingredients that gave them depth and breadth of authority.

In conclusion, then, we may say that biblical inspiration is the effect of God's promise on individuals writing within the context of a community of faith brought into existence and sustained by a vision of promise emanating from the Spirit of hope.

PART THREE

8

Revelation and the Cosmos

Toward the end of his life, Albert Einstein is reported to have said that the most important question each of us has to ask is whether the universe we inhabit is friendly or unfriendly. The response we give to this question will, to a large extent, determine the shape of our lives and the degree of satisfaction and joy we find in living. It would seem then that if the notion of revelation is to be of any consequence, it must at the very least help us formulate some answer to this largest of all puzzles.

In the present chapter, we shall attempt to unfold something of what the universe might look like when interpreted in the light of revelation. We shall propose that when our consciousness is shaped by faith in the divine promise, as well as by a trust in the gift of God's self-limiting love, we will be able to see in the cosmos a depth and breadth otherwise obscured.

We know from modern science that the events of our lives occur within the story of a universe that is much vaster than our earthly history. Even in the Bible, the redemption of Israel and the establishment of the Church fall within the more encompassing chronicle of nature's own creation and liberation.[1] The cosmos itself, having come into being eons before the arrival of human history, is the more encompassing context of God's self-revelation. The divine vision for the world goes far beyond what takes place in the course of our own species' history or of events here on earth. Yet faith allows us to read cosmic events in the light of the revelatory promises of God that occur within our terrestrially bound human history.

[1]From one point of view the doctrine of creation seems to be subordinate to that of salvation history, but it is also possible, as Moltmann in particular has shown, to view salvation within the horizon of creation and cosmology. See *God in Creation,* 1–56.

In the light of Christian faith, we may even say that billions of years before biblical religion emerged on earth the universe had already been seeded
with promise. The reflections of the present chapter are rooted in the conviction that a faith-enabled consciousness can catch at least a glimpse of
this promise in the cosmos.

From revelation's perspective, the world presented to us by science appears to have been shaped by the same longing for future fulfillment that
came to light consciously, explicitly, and historically in Abraham, the
prophets, and Jesus. Science itself does not—nor should it be expected
to—discern this promise of fulfillment. It does not concern itself with teleological or "final causal" questions. Yet nothing that faith tells us about
the creation or about God's promise contradicts the findings of science.
In fact, as we shall see in Chapter 11, the perspective of biblical faith actually nourishes and supports the process of pure scientific inquiry.

This faith is rooted in a revelation that comes to us through the medium
of human history. But revelation is not simply a plan for God's people,
for humanity, or for history, as theology has usually put it. This way of
speaking, we are now beginning to see, is too narrowly earth-centered and
anthropocentric. It also fails to speak to our current environmental crisis. Revelation must now be interpreted as God's envisagement of the *whole
universe's* possibilities and ultimate destiny.[2] Obviously, we ourselves are
in no position to grasp what the fullness of this vision entails. From within
our human history God's vision of cosmic destiny can be grasped only
through the relatively limited and time-conditioned stories of promise that
serve as the foundation of our biblical tradition. And yet faith, aroused
by the images associated with revelation, may lead us to look for and see
things in the universe that would escape a kind of inquiry not so gifted.

Both the Bible and modern science place the cosmos within a narrative
setting. When surveyed from the point of view of current evolutionary
models, for example, our universe quite clearly has the character of a story.
And like all stories, it is revelatory. From its very beginning, the universe
seems to be the unfolding and disclosing of a mysterious secret potential
and inexhaustible depth, aspects of which are only now being brought to
light by science. The universe itself is, in a sense, an ongoing revelation.
In its immensities of time and space, as well as in its love of endless diversity, it sacramentalizes the generosity, extravagance, and unpredictability
of the creator known by biblical faith as the God of promise. Let us take
a brief look at the cosmic story so that we may eventually explore more
closely its relationship to the idea of revelation.

---

[2]This wider-than-human view of revelation is quite biblical. It is present in the creation story, the Wisdom literature, and the Psalms, not to mention the theology of
John and Paul.

The Cosmic Story

The outlines of the cosmic story began to appear as early as the seventeenth century during the period of the birth of modern science. But following the triumph of evolutionary theory in the past century, the narrative character of nature's unfolding has become ever more conspicuous.[3] Recently, astrophysics has brought us into more intimate proximity to the beginnings of the story. The current scientific consensus informs us that cosmic evolution began in a singular event, known today as the "big bang," occurring fifteen or so billion years ago. After that event, the universe continued to unfold in a series of transformations, none of which could have occurred the way they have unless the cosmic beginnings had already been configured in a very precise way.[4]

After the mysterious big bang the universe began to expand outward creating space, time, and the galaxies. For billions of years its free hydrogen gases labored through various phases, eventually giving rise to stars and constellations. At the heart of immense stellar bodies, lighter elements were compressed and heated to exceedingly high temperatures and gradually became the heavy chemical elements (carbon, oxygen, nitrogen, phosphorous, etc.) required for life. This process itself took several billion years of "cooking time" before supernovae explosions eventually dispersed them throughout space.

Some of these elements eventually began to assemble into planetary bodies like the earth. Chemicals and compounds that had been fashioned in the crucible of some remote burnt-out stars came together five billion years ago and formed our own planet. Then after another billion years or so, the earth's surface having cooled sufficiently, primitive forms of life began to appear. Biological evolution had begun, but like other cosmic episodes it was not in a hurry. It was patient, experimental, random, and extravagantly "wasteful." After tossing up and discarding millions of primitive species, it finally gave rise to elaborate arrays of more and more complex organisms, to plants, reptiles, birds, and mammals, most of which are now extinct. And then, perhaps two million years ago, our immediate pre-human ancestors came onto the scene, probably in what

[3]This is not to deny that in a subterranean way the biblical view of time has also prepared the way for the arrival of evolutionary thinking in the West.

[4]This perspective may seem compatible with the ideas associated these days with the anthropic principle. According to this principle, the physical constants and initial conditions of the universe at the time of its origins were fine-tuned so that eventually the cosmos would give birth to life and consciousness. Even if the specific theories of contemporary physicists concerning the anthropic principle turn out to be scientifically unacceptable, a theology of revelation is obliged nonetheless to emphasize that the universe is at least in some way open to such promise from its very inception.

we now know as East Africa. Finally, several hundred thousand years ago, our direct human ancestors appeared and began to spread out over the face of the earth.

We know that the unfolding of cosmic evolution has not always been progressive, but this does not detract from its narrative character. For in all great stories there are numerous dead ends and regressions. In the chronicle of any great struggle, there are long spans of waiting punctuated by brief but significant episodes of terror, victory, and defeat. Still, over the long haul, the evolutionary story clearly displays a trend toward the emergence of more and more elaborate entities. Matter does not remain lifeless and completely dispersed, but gradually converges upon itself and evolves in the direction of more complex life and eventually consciousness.[5] In spite of what some contemporary scientific skeptics have written about the aimlessness of evolution, it is hard to miss the generic sort of directionality (toward more intensely organized complexity) that the cosmic story has followed thus far.

It is obvious that life and consciousness have come into being out of elementary forms of matter. But after they came onto the cosmic landscape, evolution tended to complicate itself more and more, for reasons that scientists are still trying to unravel. Life was not content to remain stuck at a primitive level but instead advanced toward more sentient, conscious, and eventually self-conscious forms. And having produced the human species, the struggle for further complexity did not suddenly cease. Cultural evolution began to occur. After a long period of hunting and gathering, comprising by far the largest portion of our human history (from at least 100,000 to 10,000 B.C.), humans invented agriculture, civilization, and other aspects of culture such as art, music, poetry, politics, education, and science. These developments at the level of consciousness are additional evidence that our universe, as embodied in human life, is still impatient with monotony. It continually seeks more subtle shading, contrast and novelty. In other words, it has the character not just of a story but of an adventure. The adventure now persists, especially in our religious excursions into mystery.

This cosmic adventure seems to have had a definite temporal beginning, followed by chapter upon chapter of dramatic events. These narrative features make us wonder, as humans always wonder when they attend to a tale, where this immense story might be heading. Toward what sort of destiny does it possibly tend? The expansion of the universe, its experimentation with so many peculiar patterns, and above all its hospitality to the evolution of life and the birth of consciousness persuade us that it may

---

[5]See Teilhard de Chardin, *The Phenomenon of Man,* trans. Bernard Wall (New York: Harper Torchbooks, 1959).

be a story with great consequence. For this reason, it is more urgent than ever that we connect the story of the cosmos with that of revelation.

We have said that the story is more aptly called an adventure. Adventure may be defined as the search for ever more intense versions of ordered novelty.[6] Adventure is what moves a process beyond triviality and monotony toward more highly nuanced forms of order. Any process that seeks thus to complicate the arrangement of things may be called adventurous. A tendency toward becoming more intensely complex seems to be an intrinsic characteristic of our whole universe, including our own species. The restlessness that impelled matter toward complexity, beginning with the big bang, has not yet been stilled.[7] It continues now in our human inquiry and exploration. The cosmos reveals itself as an adventure of continual experimentation with novel forms of order. Hence, being part of this cosmos already means being a participant in a momentous adventure story.

Is this adventurous evolution of our universe already perhaps an aspect of what we call revelation? Thomas Berry, for one, argues that the universe is indeed not just vaguely revelatory but is instead the "primary revelation."[8] It is the fundamental self-manifestation of mystery, and our religions should be seen as further episodes in a continuous unfolding of the depths of the cosmos itself. Whether or not we wish to understand revelation in such broad terms, it is at least imperative, especially today, that we relate the Christian idea of revelation to the larger story of the evolution of the universe.

What Does It Mean?

One can hardly listen to the cosmic story without asking about the meaning of it all. Theology can no longer honestly ignore what science tells us about the universe, nor can it suppress the questions the new cosmology has raised. The largest of these questions has to do with whether there is any final meaning to the cosmic adventure to which we and our history belong. Is evolution going anywhere, and how do we fit into the process? Is there really anything to the universe? Was anything of significance going on prior to our emergence? What exactly is going on now? What is our cosmic future? Can revelation shed any light on these questions?

[6]For this understanding of adventure see Alfred North Whitehead, *Adventures of Ideas* (New York: The Free Press, 1967) esp. 252–96.

[7]See, for example, Louise B. Young, *The Unfinished Universe* (New York: Simon and Schuster, 1986).

[8]See Berry, *The Dream of the Earth,* (San Francisco: Sierra Club Books, 1988) 120.

We cannot begin to discuss such matters without first recognizing the fact that numerous modern scientific thinkers adopt a tragic interpretation of the universe which they take to be much more realistic than any theological vision. Basing their "cosmic pessimism" on materialist interpretations of science, they insist that there is no evidence of ultimate meaning to the universe. The universe is composed of mindless chunks of matter with no intelligible explanation, originating by chance, moving in no particular direction, and fulfilling no inherent purpose. There is really no story at all inscribed in the confused series of cosmic occurrences brought to light by modern science.

Though it originates in antiquity, this cosmic pessimism has become a serious option among modern intellectuals, always challenging any religious vision as unrealistic and unscientific. Even though to cosmic pessimism the universe outside of us appears to be devoid of any objective meaning, this is no cause for personal despair. It is still possible for the individual human person to gain at least some sense of significance. Even though the cosmic process is hopeless, the absurdity of the universe as a whole provides each of us with the opportunity to exercise a kind of courage to create our own meanings and values that would be impossible if we thought, with religion, that the universe were itself inherently purposeful. And so, by identifying our fate with that of an Atlas, a Sisyphus, or a Prometheus and other tragic heroes, we may discover in ourselves a hidden strength and sense of well-being that hope and eschatology cannot accord us. We do not need any overarching cosmic teleology to assure us that our personal project of existing is still important.

To many intellectuals today, this tragic view seems more truthful than any religious belief in cosmic purpose. It apparently accords better with empirical reason and logic. It does not require that we make imaginative projections about a future to hope in. In fact, it judges such "illusory" thinking as a symptom of weakness which the stout of heart will shun. It sees no promise in cosmic events, but instead reads natural history as a vacuous process leading only to eventual doom. And it proposes that by resignation to an absurd fate we can find an individual contentment unavailable to those who bury themselves in the shallow consolations of religion.

Sometimes those of us who live by hope and promise fail to appreciate how alluring such cosmic pessimism can be. For it often seems more rational to embrace an absurdist view of the universe than to remain steadfast in hope, especially when there are so many happenings within our evolving universe that, taken in isolation, seem to warrant a tragic interpretation. Even the biblical story contains several intriguing chapters where there is a strong flirtation with tragic thinking, for example, in Ecclesiastes, Job, and some of the Psalms. Sometimes it appears that accepting the present unintelligibility of the universe is a lot simpler than waiting for a revelatory word that might illuminate it and give us reason to hope in a surprising future that brings all of creation to a glorious fulfillment.

Yet it is not preposterous for us at least to ask whether the billions of years of cosmic evolution have transpired completely without any inner meaning. Is it really conceivable that no principle of care has ever nourished the process, or that the universe from its beginning has been completely untouched by promise? Whether pessimistic cosmologists would approve or not, we still cannot but wonder whether there is any sort of purpose to, or promise concealed within, the cosmic process.

Science itself cannot answer this question, for its method deliberately leaves out any consideration of purpose or meaning. By definition, science puts aside questions of final causation or teleology. Even so, however, contemporary science is now in the process of drastically altering the picture of the universe out of which cosmic pessimism arose. For example, developments in astrophysics indicate that the universe is not so alien to life as it was formerly thought to be. In some of its early modern formulations, science had almost convinced us that the universe of matter is fundamentally uninhabitable by living and conscious beings. It held that living and thinking beings had emerged only by the sheerest of evolutionary accidents. Now, however, the picture is changing, largely due to developments in physics and astrophysics. These sciences, which formerly laid before us a universe fundamentally inhospitable to life and consciousness, are now instructing us that our world is quite remarkably congenial to their eventual emergence. The realm of physics is naturally conformed to the appearance of life and mind in a manner that conventional scientific wisdom had obscured from view. Today's physics has observed that the universe's initial conditions and physical constants were configured in such a delicate way during the cosmic dawn that, if these conditions and constants had been only slightly different, the universe would never have permitted the evolution of life and mind. An immense number of physical coincidences had to have converged in the initial stages of the universe, as well as later on, if it were eventually to bear life. If the force of attraction between protons, for example, had been just infinitesimally different from what it actually is, there could never have been hydrogen atoms (which require free protons). If there had been no hydrogen there would have been no galaxies and no stars to convert the hydrogen into the heavy elements essential to life. In other words, without a careful fine tuning at the beginning, there would never have been a life-bearing universe.[9] From its birth, the physical constants and initial conditions have been such as eventually to allow for the origin and evolution of life and

[9]See Hawking, 124–27.

mind. There is no reason, from the point of view of physics, that these initial conditions and physical constants might not have been different and led to a universe incapable of such evolution. To an increasing number of scientists today, it is appearing more and more remarkable that the physical conditions in the universe were from the beginning configured in such a way as to make the eventual emergence of life and mind a relatively probable development.

A few scientists have even gone so far as to argue that the initial conditions and fundamental constants established at the time of the big bang were fine tuned in such a way because our own species would *inevitably* be forthcoming.[10] In some way, the beginnings of the cosmos were already oriented toward the eventual emergence of living and conscious beings who would be aware of the universe. The majority of scientists are uncomfortable with such an obviously teleological explanation. Likewise, theology would do well not to make too much of this so-called strong anthropic principle. But even if one does not wish to baptize this principle, it is now at least clear that there are many stunning, and as of yet not well-understood physical coincidences that needed to be present in order for life to evolve. Thus it is tempting, especially in the light of revelation by which we view the cosmos with the eyes of faith as well as science, to hold that the material dimension of our cosmos was shaped by the *promise* of life, consciousness, and faith from the time of its earliest formation. Indeed, from the point of view of revelation, if not from science, there can be no alternative to our looking for such promise in the cosmic dawn. Freeman Dyson, a well-known contemporary physicist, says, "It almost seems as if the universe must in some sense have known that we were coming."[11] And many other physicists now concur that the early phases of the universe have always held out much more promise for evolving into life, mind, and spirituality than earlier science had allowed. There is now an emerging suspicion that the universe is much more amicable toward life and consciousness than we would ever have thought before the advent of twentieth-century physics and astronomy.

But it also remains clear that science by itself is ill-equipped to answer the big questions about any possible purpose and meaning to the cosmic process. Science always leaves out such considerations, and it does so rightly. It is neutral on those questions that are most important to us as persons who seek a meaning to live by. It does, however, leave open the question of purpose and meaning, and this is why religion and revelation may be allowed to respond to the question of cosmic purpose without at

---

[10]Ibid.

[11]Freeman J. Dyson, "Energy in the Universe," *Scientific American* 225, no. 3 (September 1971) 59.

all intruding into the territory proper to science. Revelation must not contradict what science tells us about the cosmos. And a theology of revelation should be informed by science, so as to avoid making incoherent statements about the relation of God to the world. But there is nothing in the scientific picture of the cosmos that forbids our envisaging the story of the universe, in its modern scientifically established character, as simultaneously a story shaped by the same promise that becomes explicit in historical revelation. Indeed, recent developments in science even seem to encourage such a vision.

Christian faith believes that it is the role of revelation to address the question of universal meaning. Faith affirms that we have been addressed by a Word of promise that uncovers the meaning not only of our individual lives and of history, but also of the entire universe. In the midst of what we often take to be a cosmic darkness, faith discerns a light that has always been shining. It hearkens to a word telling us that the universe is not now, nor ever has been, completely alone. Even "in the beginning" there was the "Word" that gives meaning to the cosmos. At no time in its existence, then, has the universe as known by faith been devoid of meaning. Though the Word breaks out into the daylight of consciousness only with the birth of persons and human history, faith allows us to discern a great promise even in the very earliest moments of the cosmic adventure. And by dwelling within the stories of our faith, we are enabled by grace to look for and even to discern a pattern of promise in the evolving universe. If we came to the cosmos armed only with the useful but limited abstractions of science, we might miss this pattern altogether. Faith can complement science in our human search for the ultimate character of the universe.

Faith's Shaping of the Story

At the beginning of the story of our faith, Abraham experienced the promise of a deeply fulfilling future summoning him to leave his ancestral home behind and launch forth into the unknown. And his children, having the same hope in their own hearts, are instructed by faith to carry on the quest for what had been promised to their father. The names of Abraham, Isaac, Jacob, Joseph, Moses, Joshua, and the great judges and prophets of Israel all remind us that a word of promise has broken what we may have taken to be the silence and indifference of the universe. For Christian faith, the person of Jesus is the decisive breaking out into the open of the promise. The event of Jesus the Christ and especially the accounts of his having been raised up are fundamentally *promissory* realities. We must now learn to see them as inseparable from our concern about the destiny of the universe as a whole.

In his evolutionary Christology, Karl Rahner writes that Jesus Christ is God's gift of self to the *universe,* bestowed definitively and irreversibly.[12] The substance of the promise to Israel and the Church is, in the final analysis, nothing other than the very being of God. The same divine self-gift that planted hope in the hearts of our ancestors in faith had earlier aroused the cosmos into being and continually stirred it toward further evolution. Revelation is the self-gift of the promising God, not just to history but to the entire world of nature which includes us. From the moment of its creation nature, too, even apart from human existence, has felt the promise of God. This promissory divine self-donation to the cosmic totality is God's universal or general revelation. General revelation is the self-outpouring of God into the whole created world. Revelation in the broadest sense includes God's presentation of relevant new possibilities persuading the cosmos to reach for further and more intense modes of fulfillment. It is only by way of the revelation of such possibilities that the cosmos could ever evolve toward new kinds of ordered complexity.

The promise of God to Abraham, Israel, and the Church, therefore, may be viewed cosmologically (and not just historically) as a special instance of the general breaking in of God's promise to the entire emergent universe. Previously, we mentioned the problems that arise in a situation of religious plurality whenever one religion claims that it is founded by a special revelation withheld from others. The term "special" can easily smack of pretense and appear at times to bear the assumption of superiority. But from the point of view of an evolutionary cosmology, the special character of Abraham's calling or of Israel's election or of Jesus' unique status need not a priori be taken as an embarrassment for theology. For by the very nature of cosmic evolution, of which the birth and growth of religious traditions are a component, the introduction of unprecedented novelty inevitably has to be a unique and local event. At an earlier time in evolution, life itself came about at a particular place, as a unique and privileged event, and we do not object to the rather undemocratic style of its entrance. Within the cosmic process, novelty appears at very particular times and locales rather than all over the place all at once. Hence, if we situate the call of Abraham, as well as other special revelatory moments of the history of religion, within the wider context of cosmic evolution, this may help soften the "scandal of particularity" associated with any unique or distinctive summoning by God of a particular people to bear witness in a novel way to the divine promise and mystery that come to expression first in the very creation of the world.

[12]*Foundations of Christian Faith,* 178–203.

Thus we may interpret evolution as itself an aspect of revelation. The implication is that like revelation in general, evolution's meaning consists not only of its achievements (which are in themselves often ambiguous), but even more of its promise. We cannot evaluate evolution simply by looking at its past history, one which is often quite tumultuous, violent, and confusing. And we make a great mistake theologically if we look into the cosmos only for a finished design that would prove to us that God exists. Such a theological approach is possible only by placing the cosmos itself outside of the theme of promise. For the most part, modern theology has separated the natural world from the notions of subjectivity and history and has made the latter the locale of God's promise and revelation. However, today we are encouraged both by science and especially by faith to look at the cosmos from the point of view of the promise it contains in itself. Viewed in this light, we may see the birth and deaths of stars, the emergence of life, its moments of complexification, and the eventual rise of consciousness as sacramental evidence of revelation's promise no less significant than God's calling of Abraham and the prophets. The cosmos remains unfinished, and so we may look to its various evolutionary episodes for signals of its promise but not for any categorically diaphanous epiphany of God.[13]

However, many Christians in the last century have been paralyzed with fear about the whole idea of evolution. The so-called creationists even teach that revelation contradicts the theory of evolution. Both skeptics and believers have wondered why an omnipotent Creator would allow the universe to unfold so ponderously and in such a long, drawn-out evolutionary manner. If God is all powerful, why was not the universe created in its final, fixed state once and for all? Why fifteen billion years of struggle, randomness, and waste before our own species eventually materialized? What is the meaning of the apparently enormous waste of time before anything of such consequence (at least in our typically anthropocentric estimation) occurred?

Although none of us can give definitive answers to these questions, our central revelatory image of God as self-emptying love may be invoked here once again at least as an experimental hypothesis to make sense of this puzzle. If, along with the theme of promise, we interpret natural evolution in the light of the image of God's loving self-renunciation, then its long and arduous struggle takes on considerable significance. Cosmic evolution itself becomes a sacramental revelation of God's personality. It is

[13]See the parallel argument of Ted Peters, "Cosmos as Creation" in Ted Peters, ed. *Cosmos as Creation* (Nashville, Abingdon Press, 1989), pp. 86–102: "The call to faith is not a call to place our trust in the ordered cosmos but rather in the faithfulness of the Beyond which has committed itself to determine a future that is redemptive. In short, trust God, not nature!" (102).

the narrative representation of God's giving away the fullness of divinity to the cosmos.

The cosmos in its finitude is unable to receive the boundlessness of God's self-gift in any single instant. A finite reality, even if it has the dimensions of our seemingly unfathomable universe, is never sufficiently expansive to contain an infinite love. Hence in its response to the overflowing self-bestowal of a promising God, the cosmos would be subject to an incremental intensification of its own being in order to partake ever more fully of the divine life given over to it. In other words, it would be invited to evolve. The finite world would move and grow (undergo a kind of self-transcendence)[14] as a result of a continual impregnation by the self-giving mystery of God. Evolution, when interpreted by the revelatory images of God's love, is both the expression of God's gift of self to the world and at the same time the world's response to the non-coercive, defenseless divine self-bestowal. Karl Rahner interprets the Christ-event cosmically as the definitive and irreversible moment of God's self-communication to the evolving world and at the same time the climactic reception by the world of God's revelatory promise.[15]

The universe cannot contain the infinite in any single moment. Hence it is allowed, but not forced, to inch gradually forward by way of what science knows as evolution. Only over a period of time would it move toward fuller participation in the promise that comes to light historically in the faith associated with Abraham. Christians, however, may understand the decisiveness of Christ as the moment in evolution when God's promise and self-gift, which have been continually and creatively present to the cosmos from its birth, are embraced by a human being without reservation. In Christ, the vision of God for the universe is accepted fully, and the significance of cosmic process eternally guaranteed.

Out of the inexhaustible "futurity" of God, the revelatory promise is issued to the world and the world lured toward its fulfillment. To the eyes of faith, evolution—even in its pre-human episodes—is already a revelatory story of the world's movement into God's future. From the perspective of science alone, evolution has no meaning. It is simply the gradual appearance of more and more complex entities and societies. But from the perspective of revelation, cosmic evolution is the story of a self-humbling God's entering ever more intimately into the universe and drawing it toward a meaningful fulfillment.

It is especially in the crucified man, Jesus of Nazareth, that Christians have discerned the disclosure of God's humility. The conviction of a divine *kenosis* could scarcely have entered our consciousness apart from this

[14]Karl Rahner, *Foundations of Christian Faith,* 178-203.
[15]Ibid.

event.[16] It is in Jesus' death that faith discerns the complete outpouring of God's own selfhood into the world. And out of this faith, theological reflection is gradually learning to regard the divine self-emptying as an *eternal* characteristic of God. Such humble condescension, manifest historically in the cross, is of the everlasting essence of God, and not just an *ad hoc* historical occurrence only externally connected to God's inner life.

This divine humility is the foundation even of the creation of the universe. The coming into being of the cosmos already involves an act of self-humbling on God's part. Creation may be understood not so much as the consequence of God's self-expansion as of God's self-limitation. God's allowing the world to exist is made possible by a restraining of divine omnipotence. Divine power humbly "contracts" itself, surrendering any urge to manipulate events or persons. This humble retreat is what allows the world to stand forth as distinct from its creative ground. Creation is less the consequence of divine "force" than of God's self-withdrawal.[17] It is especially in the image of the crucified that Christian faith is given the key to this interpretation of creation. The cross reveals to faith the self-sacrificing of God out of whose limitless generosity the world is called, but never forced, into being.

This kenotic image once again brings a surprising intelligibility to our evolutionary universe. Evolutionary theory has two main features that have made it seemingly irreconcilable with traditional theism. In the first place,

[16]In the light of this event, however, it may be possible for Christians to see indications of the humility of God in other religions also.

[17]This kenotic view of creation is found also in kabbalistic Judaism. Likewise, it occurs occasionally in the writings of Simone Weil as described in detail in Geddes MacGregor's *He Who Lets Us Be*. It is even more prominent in the later writings of Jürgen Moltmann. See, for example, *God in Creation*, 88. A recent Jewish reaffirmation of the view that creation is grounded in God's self-withdrawal may be seen in Michael Wyschogrod, *The Body of Faith* (New York: Harper & Row, 1983) 9–10. What Wyschogrod says about God's creation of humans can also be adapted to the creation of the cosmos: "A world in which the divine light penetrates and fills all is a world in which there is nothing but God. In such a world no finitude and therefore no human existence [cosmos] is possible. . . . The creation of man [the cosmos] involves the necessity for God's protection of man [the cosmos] from the power of God's being. This protection involves a certain divine withdrawal, the *tsimtsum* of the kabbalists, who were also puzzled by how things other than God could exist in the light of the absolute being of God. To answer this question they invoked the notion of *tsimtsum*, by which they meant that the absolute God, whose being fills all being, withdraws from a certain region, which is thus left with the divine being thinned out in it, and in this thinned out region man [the cosmos] exists." Some such notion seems essential to resolve the theological difficulties, especially regarding human freedom, resulting from the traditional habit of modelling God's creativity on the rather deterministic idea of efficient causation.

it holds that chance or randomness is the raw material of evolution. If chance is real, then it apparently places God's omnipotence and omniscience in serious question. A universe that possesses such a degree of randomness seems to lack intelligibility. God, the alleged divine designer, is apparently not in control. In the second place, evolutionary theory insists that an impersonal and ruthless process known as *natural selection* is the sole and sufficient explanation for the survival of some species and the extinction of others. A process that selects mutant species only on the basis of their accidentally favorable traits seems incompatible with a beneficent and intelligent creator. Evolutionary theory seems to think of the creative process as a prolonged, impersonal lottery rather than the "mighty act" of an omnipotent God.

In the light of revelation we are provided with a way of addressing these objections. We must begin, though, with a confession that the idea of a designing and controlling deity whose existence is rightly denied by many skeptics is also problematic from the point of view of a kenotic theology. If God is all-powerful in the sense of being able to manipulate things at will, then the facts of evolution do indeed cast doubt on the plausibility of theism. However, revelation's image of a self-limiting creator, whose power is made manifest in a kind of defenselessness or vulnerability, is not only congruous with, but also possibly explanatory of the world that evolutionary theory presents to us. The randomness, struggle, and seemingly aimless meandering that the theory attributes to the universe are more or less what we should expect if creation is the product of the non-obtrusive love of a self-emptying God. The absence of strict determinism that recent physics has discovered at the most basic levels of matter, the chance mutations that biology finds at the level of life's evolution, and the freedom that comes forth with human existence—all of these are the expected features of any world we might claim to be distinct from the being of its creator. In order for the world to be independent of God and to possess its own existence, or to undergo a genuine *self*-transcendence in evolution, its creative ground would in some way make itself absent from that world instead of overwhelming it with divine presence. God would concede to the world its own autonomous principles of operation, such as the "law" of gravity or the "law" of natural selection. A self-limiting God, the humble God of revelation, makes more sense within an evolutionary framework than in any others that have been proposed so far by science.[18]

[18]A God who withdraws from the world in this kenotic sense, however, is nothing like, and should not be confused with, the useless God of deism. Paradoxically, it is out of love of relationship and dialogical intimacy with the world that God renounces any overwhelming, annihilating "presence" to the world. The retracting of annihilat-

We have been looking at how cosmic evolution may be interpreted in the light of revelation. But how does revelation appear when seen in terms of evolution? We may say that the revelation of God in Christ is the coming to a head of the entire evolutionary process. The intuition that Christ is the fulfillment of a cosmic promise, one that has a breadth that carries revelation beyond the sphere of human existence, is already present in Paul's letter to the Romans: "The creation waits with eager longing for the revealing of the sons of God. We know that the whole creation has been groaning in travail together until now. . . ." (Rom 8:19, 22) When viewed from the perspective of evolution, revelation is the flowering fulfillment of the universe itself.

Care for the Cosmos

A cosmic interpretation of revelation is important today not only because of our need to address the question of purpose in the universe, but also because our globe is now threatened by an environmental crisis of unprecedented proportions. Does revelation have anything to teach us about the worth of our natural environment that we cannot already find in the resources of science? Let us first examine the possible roots of the crisis itself and then look at how religion and revelation might be situated with respect to it.[19]

It has often been argued that an excessive anthropocentrism (overemphasis on the human dimension of our world) is the main source of our current environmental crisis. An exaggerated focus on human significance places value so heavily upon our own species that it thereby drains value away from the non-human aspects of nature. And this robbery leaves nature open to our own abuse. For this reason, our locating revelation as a cosmic and not just an historical reality already has salutary environmental implications, for it counters the excessive anthropocentrism that has misshapen so much Christian theology. God's gift of self is offered to the *whole* of the universe and not just to humans or terrestrial history.

It is environmentally important today that Christian theology sustain the critique of exaggerated anthropocentrism implied in this formulation. Anthropocentrism, however, is quite possibly secondary to and symptomatic of a more fundamental sense of our being "lost in the cosmos."

ing presence is, as we know even from interhuman experience, the very condition of dialogical presence.

[19]What follows is an adaptation of ideas developed at more length in my article "Religious and Cosmic Homelessness," in *Liberating Life,* edited by Charles Birch, et al. (Maryknoll, New York: Orbis Books, 1990) 159–81, and in my book, *The Promise of Nature* (New York: Paulist Press, 1993).

Exaggerating our human importance may be the consequence of a more basic assumption that we are exiles from any value-bestowing cosmos. When humans feel that they do not really "belong" somewhere, they feel ashamed. And sometimes they seek to counter this shame by way of self-inflation. In the case of *cosmic* homelessness this reaction has led to a domineering and destructive attitude toward the life-systems of our planet.

Therefore, a head-long attack on our anthropocentric tendencies may not be the appropriate way to begin building a theology that would promote an environmentally sensitive outlook. Even though it is by way of a relentless assault on anthropocentrism that most contemporary environmental criticism begins, such an approach may not be very effective in the long run. Instead, it may prove more fruitful to address the fundamental feeling of cosmic exile to which anthropocentrism is one important response. Why is it that we often do not feel truly at home in this universe?

Environmentalists hold that if we fail to experience deeply our own belongingness to the natural world we will not sufficiently care for it. They insist that only those ways of thinking that encourage us to make nature our "home" can be environmentally helpful. But this advice already raises a serious question about the environmental significance of the world's religions, including the Christian tradition. Religions and philosophies of the East and West, at least since the axial age, have at times made us feel alien to the natural world. They have convinced us that we are strangers in a foreign land to which we do not really belong. At times they have even led us to a hatred of the earth. They give us the impression that authentic existence involves a sense of being exiled from the cosmos. How can we reconcile the environmental imperative to respect the earth as our home with the important religious imperative to live as if we were homeless?

Religions clearly do invite us to an attitude of detachment, or to what we are calling homelessness. But does this religious injunction demand also that we learn to feel lost in the cosmos as though it were not a home that we should care for? Biblical religion tells of Abraham's being called to move from his ancestral home in response to God's promise. But is there not a danger that the dislocation required by fidelity to the revelatory promise will be interpreted as a call to *cosmic* homelessness? The theme of "the land" is glorified in the Old Testament, but the period of wandering homelessly in the desert is also emphasized by some of the prophets. In the New Testament, the natural world is an important basis for Jesus' sacramental representations of the kingdom, but "the Son of Man has nowhere to lay his head." And in most traditional Christian spirituality, we are said to be only pilgrims on earth. The theme of homelessness is so central to Christian revelation that we simply cannot dismiss it. But how can we reconcile it with today's environmental concerns?

In other great religions, some form of homelessness is also our predicament, and we are instructed to embrace it for the sake of our salvation. In Hinduism, for example, religious teaching idealizes the *sannyasin,* one who eventually forsakes home and hearth, and through this detachment reaches out for more intense union with the divine mystery. And in Buddhism, the story of Gautama's Great Renunciation—in which he abandoned home, wife, and child is presented as an exemplar of the kind of detachment essential for enlightenment. Unless we feel somewhat uncomfortable with "the world," or at least "this present age," religions tell us that we will not experience true fulfillment.

The biblical focus on history as the locus of redemption, as we shall see in the next chapter, seems at first sight to lessen the significance of the natural world. The prophets forbade the Israelites to seek refuge in nature. And biblical religion transformed "pagan" rites of spring and harvest into festivals celebrating historic events. The exilic motif is central to biblical religion, but it seems, especially in its Christian interpretation, to mean that we should move beyond the ensnarements of the physical cosmos. Thus, revelation may easily be interpreted as a justification for our sense of cosmic homelessness. And this raises the troubling question about the environmental value of biblical revelation (not to mention that of other religious traditions). How can we sincerely make the natural world our home if the theme of homelessness is so central to faith in God's promise? Or is it possible that the revelatory promise can bond us even more firmly to our planet and to the rest of nature?

To reiterate, there has traditionally been a tendency to interpret the biblical requirement of spiritual homelessness as though it also entails a *cosmic* homelessness. This translation, in turn, has seemingly made the natural world a victim of revelation's promise, a promise that invites us to live, like Abraham, as wanderers. But if this association of religious with cosmic homelessness is inevitable, then revelation will be taken as incompatible with environmental ethics. If spiritual journeying requires also that we feel lost in the natural world, then religion and revelation will remain cosmically problematic.

Dualistic deposits in Christian theology are themselves partly responsible for the feeling of cosmic homelessness that underlies our present environmental crisis. Traditionally, an exaggerated mysticism, having lost its connection to the sacramental, silent, and active aspects of religion, has turned our attention toward a spiritual world existing apart from the physical universe. Today, most theologians would deny that this withdrawal from the world is consonant with the biblical vision. They would argue that it stems more from Greek and gnostic influences than from the Bible itself. Yet a feeling of cosmic homelessness clings to Christian religious teachings, and to academic theology as well. Christianity, no less than our scientific culture, is still tied to dualism. And with some notable exceptions, its theologians have not yet given us an environmentally adequate theology of revelation.

Take for example the widespread use of existentialism by theology in this century. Theologians turned to existentialism in order to find a set of concepts in terms of which they could articulate the meaning of Christian faith for our times. They found in the existentialist emphasis on human freedom a point of contact with the message of the Gospels. Christianity, Rudolf Bultmann declared, is fundamentally about freedom, and existentialism can help us explain what Christian freedom means. Unfortunately, however, this theologian imported into his theology a fundamental flaw in existentialist philosophy, namely, its uncritical acceptance of a materialist-mechanistic conception of nature and the corresponding assumption that freedom can never be at home in the machine of the cosmos.

Existentialism is an understandable attempt to save human freedom from being snuffed out by mechanism and determinism. In order to complete this rescue operation, however, existentialists posited a distinct realm for humans, one radically discontinuous with nature. They located human reality in the arena of freedom and subjectivity. In making such an absolute distinction between freedom and nature, existentialism perpetuated the dualistic view of the world and the negative environmental consequences it entails. As long as materialism or mechanism seems to be the only plausible philosophy of nature, this existentialist maneuvering is an understandable and forgivable way of keeping us free from absorption into the world-machine. In this respect, existentialism has made noble and moving contributions to humanism, and we must not be excessively critical of it. But existentialism usually requires that we accept our existence as in some way alien to nature. And the theologies that employ existentialist concepts are therefore also likely to be uncritical of the negative environmental implications implied in this segregation of humans from the cosmos.

However, it is not enough for us to criticize existentialist and other kinds of theology that have neglected the environment. If we are to move toward an environmentally wholesome theology of nature, we must also reshape our inherited ways of understanding revelation. We must look at it not simply as a set of historical events, but even more fundamentally as a *cosmic* phenomenon. Revelation is at root an expression of the universe and not only of humans and their history. If we give the universe a larger role in our theologies of revelation, and at the same time decentralize (without diminishing) human history and existential selfhood, such a way of thinking might change our entire attitude toward nature.

Fortunately, because of our contemporary scientific knowledge of the cosmic story, we are now able to connect the promise of revelation to a wholesome environmentalism. And we need not forfeit the biblical requirement of homelessness in order to accept the cosmos as our proper habitat. The narrative developments in scientific knowledge referred to above help to make this adjustment intellectually and theologically plausible today. We cannot simply ignore the ideal of spiritual homelessness entailed by the divine promise. For if revelation has any consistent theme, it is that an exodus faith in the promise requires our not accommodating ourselves too comfortably to any present actuality. To do so would be idolatry. However, faith promotes homelessness not as an end in itself but as a necessary moment in the quest for our true home guaranteed by God's revelatory promise. It is not that faith is intrinsically opposed to our instinct for being "at home," but rather it resists our settling for something as home which is really not adequate domicile for our hope. According to the biblical vision, nothing less than the inexhaustible futurity of God can be the appropriate destiny of the human spirit. Such a promissory vision inevitably provokes a kind of restlessness in those who take it seriously.

But how can the hopeful restlessness required by faith prevent an escapism that carelessly leaves the cosmos behind? Can we keep together a feeling of fully belonging to nature, while at the same time embracing the insecurity required by faith in God's promise?

The sense that the universe is itself a story grounded in promise may be the key to such a reconciliation. This vision allows us to accept the disposition of being on an endless religious journey while at the same time allowing us to put our roots down deeply into nature. For if the cosmos is itself a revelatory adventure aroused by God's promise, then we may embrace both the natural world and the biblical ideal of homeless searching. We may thereby reconcile the biblical imperative to journey with Abraham into parts unknown, with the environmental requirement that we also feel completely at home in nature. For nature, too, as we now know from evolutionary science, is and always has been creatively restless. Its restlessness is also the consequence of the promise and self-gift of God. We need no longer idealize nature as though it were a haven apart from the perils of homeless historical existence. For the cosmos itself is homeless with respect to the fulfillment promised to it by God.

Because the universe is itself fundamentally a story of restless searching for novel forms of order, we do not have to segregate it from the history of salvation and the realm of freedom. We can now accommodate the entire universe to the revelatory theme of homeless wandering. If we are to be faithful to nature and our continuity with it, we may now accept the universe's own inherent instability as the precondition of the biblical, historical revelation. The cosmos is not merely a point of departure that we must leave behind us in our obedience to the promise. Rather, it is more akin to a fellow traveler that has begun the journey of responding to revelation's promise epochs before we ourselves arrived on the scene to join it. We may interpret the companionship of nature less as a paradisal refuge from history and more as the root system of our own response to revelation. We need to acknowledge its own inherent exploratory dynamics (rooted in the divine promise incarnate in it from the beginning) as the condition of our own faith and hope. This means that revelation and environmental ethics are not merely compatible, but that they are mutually complementary. If we could learn to see the universe as the story of the unfolding of God's promise we could then integrate our hope in the promise with the vigorous environmental concern that is needed today if life is to survive on this planet.

9

The Meaning of History

We have just observed that the universe of modern science presents itself to us in the form of a story. It appears to have a singular beginning
followed by a period of existence measurable in terms of enormous spans
of time leading up to the present, and it also apparently has a long future
ahead of it. Dramatic developments have taken place in the course of its
existence, even independently of our own species' recent emergence. We
can say therefore that the cosmos has a history of sorts. In the broadest
meaning of the term, "history" is the total series of events that have taken
place in the universe. And so, in a very general way, we may speak about
the history of the universe or the history of nature.

Usually, however, history has a stricter meaning. It refers to the sequence
of specifically human and social events that have taken place on the earth,
especially since the birth of civilization. We must now seek to relate the
notion of revelation to history in this narrower sense. We may do so by
raising once again the ageless question of whether the human story has
any meaning to it, and if so, what is it? Is there—anywhere in the course
of human events—a key to unlock the enigma of our social and historical
experience? If the notion of revelation is to be of any real consequence
to us, it must offer some response to our questions about the purpose of
human existence on this planet. Notwithstanding the fact that whatever
human meaning we may discover would be inseparable from the meaning
of the cosmos, it is still necessary for us to focus our quest for the meaning of revelation on the question of the significance of our own existence
as a distinctly historical species.

However, we cannot expect from revelation a vividly detailed picture
of the future direction our historical existence will take. Revelation is not

in the business of offering forecasts. It will speak to us of the meaning of history not in the mode of prediction, but in that of promise. And it is according to the logic of promise that we must seek this meaning out.

The Idea of History

When and under what circumstances did our sense of historical existence arise? Although the recording of significant events, especially those in the lives of monarchs, began to occur in the ancient kingdoms of Mesopotamia and Egypt, this was not yet history in the sense of understanding time as an irreversible sequence. Mythic consciousness, with its need to return periodically to the origins of the cosmos, cancelled out any inkling of time as an irrecoverable series of events. Throughout most of the ages in which our species has dwelt on this earth, its various tribal units have had no sense of historical time. It was probably not until the axial age, when the Israelites began to experience mystery more explicitly in the mode of future and promise, that humans began first to realize that we do not dwell in nature with the same instinctive ease that other species do.[1] It is true that in several other contemporary religious contexts there was also an emerging impression of the distinctness of human existence from nature. Around the eighth century b.c. in India, for example, the *Upanishads* began to point more explicitly to a transcendent realm of meaning known as *Brahman*. Conscious union with *Brahman* was said to provide final deliverance from *samsara,* the cycle of rebirths in nature. A couple of centuries later, Buddhism sought to release people from their suffering by opening consciousness to a world-transcending experience of enlightenment. In the Greek world, aspects of pre-Socratic philosophy, and later Socrates and Plato, located true reality in an ideal realm apart from nature's becoming and perishing. All of these developments signaled a new kind of human existence, one less tied to purely natural realities.[2] But most of these religious developments continued the older mythic habit of "abolishing time," to use Mircea Eliade's expression.[3] A full sense of

[1]In a sense, also, the writings of Hesiod and Thucydides in the Greek world are part of the rise of historical awareness, but their histories were primarily *chronicles* of events whereas the Hebrew historians were concerned more explicitly with the *meaning* of events.

[2]Another axial religion, Taoism, on the other hand, taught that our true being consists of conformity to the "Tao" from whose "natural" truth and humility we generally stray.

[3]Mircea Eliade, *Myth and Reality,* trans. by W. R. Trask (New York: Harper & Row, 1963) 75–91.

what we know as history was still not awakened in these religious situations. Probably only in biblical religion did there come into being a specifically "historical" way of understanding human existence. In its portraits of God's revelation in the mode of "promise," biblical religion gave rise to the experience of history as an opening of events to an always new future bearing a universal meaning for the events that take place in time.

In spite of the fact that the cosmos is truly our home (as we argued on scientific, biblical, and environmental grounds in the preceding chapter) our species nevertheless began (during the axial age) to feel gradually somewhat exiled from subhuman patterns of natural existence. And so people became restless to find exactly into what context they fit if nature does not itself suffice to locate the fullness of their being. Dualistic religion and philosophy sought this setting in a spiritual sphere completely beyond or above the temporal world. Biblical religion, however, refused to abolish time. It gave time a salvific importance and made history the basic horizon of human life.

In doing so, however, it exposed us to what Eliade refers to as a kind of "terror."[4] With the sense of history, there arose a new form of anxiety consisting of an unprecedented preoccupation with the irreversibility of time, a heightened sense of temporal becoming and perishing, along with a need to discern the significance of the transient events that make up human existence. The concern about meaning, which had been present even beneath the very earliest cosmological myths, was now considerably magnified by the emerging disquiet concerning the possible outcome of historical events. Today, we still stand within the purview of this concern for the meaning of history. Since this meaning is not presently available to us, some contemporary modes of thought have despaired of the possibility that history has any meaning to it. And it has become increasingly difficult for theology to present a portrait of the intelligibility of history that rings true to many people.

The biblical conviction that we have been exiled from any non-historical paradise has been one of the most adventurous developments in the unfolding of the story of humanity, of religion, and indeed of the entire cosmos.[5] But like all adventures, this movement out into history has been disturbing as well as exciting. Because it has been so agitating at times, we continue to feel the strong tug of non-human nature, or other ahistorical lures, beckoning us to return to a more secure and predictable kind of existence. The anxiety that always accompanies the sense of an unpre-

---

[4]Ibid., 68.

[5]It is important to emphasize once again that history is a movement of the cosmos, and not a movement away from it. It can only be interpreted as a movement away from the cosmos if nature is taken abstractly as itself devoid of historical features.

dictable historical process can be momentarily relieved by any number of efforts to put an end to history, to "abolish time." Taking refuge in nature's regularities seemingly offers one such haven from the turmoil of historical existence. In modern times, however, numerous efforts to turn history completely into a *science,* according to which we might calculate, predict, and control the future, has become another way to conquer our anxiety in the face of the unknown.[6] From Auguste Comte to Karl Marx, philosophers have made repeated efforts to eliminate any profound uncertainty about the future by placing it within some scheme of inevitability or determinism that might calm our vexation about its destiny.

Another way to escape from history is to follow the gnostic path of dreaming up some radically other world, to which we "essentially" belong by virtue of an esoteric knowledge or "gnosis," membership in which therefore keeps us from having to dwell fully within the messiness of historical existence. Not a few theologies of revelation have succumbed to this gnostic temptation.[7] Still another, more subtle, way of domesticating history's terror is simply to declare it and the universe, a priori, absolutely meaningless. If one adopts a nihilistic perspective from the very start, this will avert the kind of disappointment that utopians experience when their visions inevitably fail to become fully actual in history.

All such retreats, of course, violate revelation's pivotal injunction that we learn to live by promise rather than prediction or tragic resignation. An adequate Christian theology of history and revelation maintains that only by trusting in the promise of history, without either fleeing it or nullifying it, do we find a security proportionate to the incalculability of God's future, as well as to our deepest human aspirations.

The "flight into nature" has perhaps been the most prevalent way in which humans have extricated themselves from history. But as we saw in the preceding chapter, recent science itself has taught us, in a way that earlier generations of theologians were not in a position to see, that nature itself is historical. Therefore, any escape into nature cannot in any case be the flight from history that we might wish it to be. Even on scien-

---

[6] Jürgen Moltmann, *Theology of Hope,* 236.

[7] Both Karl Barth and Rudolf Bultmann have attempted to understand revelation in a way that would allow it to be critical of human culture and thus prevent any easy synthesis of Christianity with contemporary socio-political realities. But by locating revelation in the realm of transcendental subjectivity, or on a plane radically discontinuous with actual human events, they have removed it from a more challenging proximity to our historical existence. In this book we are following, with some modification, the approach of Jürgen Moltmann, namely, that of understanding revelation as a promise that makes history possible and that enters deeply into history while at the same time, in its partly unavailable futurity, exercising an ongoing critique of any contemporary culture.

tific grounds we can no longer allow an artificial separation of nature from human history. The cosmos itself is historical, from the point of view of both science and Christian faith. The birth of a sense of history removes us not from nature itself, but only from the frozen, abstract, and ahistorical conception of nature that we had for centuries projected onto the flux of cosmic events.

However, even though any separation of nature from history is both scientifically and theologically questionable, some sort of distinction of human history from natural history is necessary. For there is an emergent quality that makes our existence different, though certainly not separate, from other natural beings and from earlier phases of the cosmic story. This emergent quality is what we now know as human *freedom*. Today, many scientists allow that there is something analogous to freedom—a sort of indeterminacy—resident in all levels of nature. Even physics, which had formerly been the stronghold of determinism, has now abandoned the rigid notions of causation that Newtonian and Cartesian science had followed and upon which classical determinism was based. Nevertheless, practically speaking, sub-human dimensions of nature still present themselves as relatively more predictable and determined occurrences than we find at the human level. Nature would not be accessible at all to scientific understanding if it were not largely composed of many invariant routines. Human existence, on the other hand, brings with it an intensification of the indeterminacy that appears in a much less explicit manner in non-human nature. Human existence transcends non-human nature even while being continuous with it and constrained by it. This transcendence of other levels of natural reality consists of a personal freedom that lies outside the sweep of scientific comprehension. It is especially this quality of freedom that allows human existence to be "historical" in addition to being "natural." And it is the same freedom that makes it impossible for us to put an end to history and its terror by turning it into a science capable of exactly forecasting the outcome of events.

It is true, of course, that the social sciences go as far as they can toward formulating "laws" governing human activity. And these sciences are useful especially when dealing with the habits of large numbers of people, or with statistically predictable reactions of humans to certain events. Still, there is always a residue of individual freedom that eludes scientific prediction.[8] Thus, because of the fact of human freedom we may here think of history as an aspect of our general "situation," distinct, though not separate, from non-human nature. What then does revelation

---

[8] Philosophically speaking, we can only postulate the existence of freedom. We cannot prove that it exists. Any attempt to demonstrate scientifically, that is, in terms of causation, that freedom exists, would probably be self-contradictory.

mean in terms of this more restrictive notion of history and human freedom?[9]

History as a Gift

The specifically historical character of human existence may itself be understood as the first fruits of the divine promise of an ever-new future. God's promise to Abraham and to Israel sparks a unique kind of restlessness. A trust in God's promise leads away from earlier styles of human existence defined simply by the seasons. The promise of a new and uncontrollable future opens out into the insecurity, indefiniteness, and adventure of history. History is both a gift and a serious challenge rooted in the promissory nature of revelation. And from the biblical perspective at least, the meaning of history is found only in our pursuit of this promise.

Theology has become accustomed to speaking of God's revelation *in* history. But it is no less appropriate to speak of God's revelation *of* history. History, at least insofar as it is a consequence of God's promise, is itself the content, and not just the context of revelation. What is unveiled or revealed by the revelatory promise is precisely the historical character of reality.[10] God's revelation takes the form of a story evolving in a direction that no human planning, necessary though it is, can adequately divulge. This promissory and storied character of reality allows it to unfold in such a way that novelty and surprise can continually come into view and thus render the universe and history both more complex and more intelligible than we could ourselves imagine on the basis of previous patterns of occurrence. Revelation allows reality as a whole, and human life in particular, to take on the character of adventure.[11] Its promise allows reality and human history to embark on the pursuit of more intense beauty and enjoyment. Only a faith that perceives reality to be grounded in promise can activate and continually energize such a pursuit.

This promissory experience of reality reshapes our whole understanding of time. Time, in the light of promise, is what allows reality to unfold dramatically and meaningfully. Without this dramatic time, our world would be frozen into a repetitive triviality. Promise-laden time allows the universe and human existence to evolve in such a way that newness and freshness can continually enter into them. We seldom think about what

[9]Henceforth we shall be using the term "history" in the sense of human history rather than natural history.

[10]See Wolfhart Pannenberg, *Faith and Reality*, trans. by John Maxwell (Philadelphia: Westminster Press, 1977).

[11]Recall our Whiteheadian definition of adventure as the quest for more and more intense versions of ordered novelty.

a gift time is, but without it, reality would be stuck in an intolerable monotony. Or as Whitehead persuasively argues, the world would simply cease to exist. In a temporal universe, there can be nothing "at an instant." If time suddenly (and unimaginably) came to a stop, the world would simply no longer be actual. Time, we know now from physics and astronomy, is woven into the very texture of things. It allows novelty, nuance, unprecedented forms and patterns to come into the universe and into culture and civilization. It permits the world to be this particular world. It brings definiteness to what would otherwise be only an abstract possibility. Revelation identifies the origin of this usually taken-for-granted gift of time as the very promise of God's own self.

Yet we must not forget that the advent of historical existence brings challenge and suffering along with the promise of heightened beauty and enjoyment. It is clear from the biblical texts that the emergence of Hebrew religion was quite unsettling. The sense of history's promise required that Abraham abandon, we may assume with a good deal of pain, the home of his ancestors. It compelled Moses to lead his followers, many of them reluctantly, away from their preferred compliance to slavery. It aroused the prophets to risk their lives and reputations combating the nostalgic religious inclination to localize and naturalize the divine presence. The sense of promise undergirds a wide variety of biblical challenges, e.g. apocalyptic renunciations of the "present age," Jesus' sense of homelessness, the Gospels' message that turning our attention toward the Risen Lord requires a forfeiture of worldly security, and St. Paul's summons to realize our freedom by living without the comforts of legalism.

Because it constantly portrays mystery in the form of a gracious promise, the Bible forbids our searching for meaning, salvation, or fulfillment completely apart from historical existence. However, as we have already seen, Christian teaching and theology have obviously not always paid attention to this directive. They have avoided it by interpreting mystery in ways that overlook its fundamentally promissory character. Much traditional theology of revelation has almost completely suppressed the promissory nature of revelation and with it the value of historical existence.[12] Yet from a biblical point of view, the refusal to accept the promising character of mystery is the fundamental meaning of sin. Human life and conduct become twisted and begin to miss the mark whenever mystery is domesticated into a sanction of present or past patterns of existence instead of a stimulus to transcend them and move toward a new future. By shaping the experience of mystery in exaggerated mystical, Platonic, Stoic, and dualistic ways, rather than in terms of a promise that beckons

[12]In preparing this book, the author has seldom found the theme of promise to be prominent, or sometimes even mentioned, in traditional Catholic treatises on the subject of revelation.

us deeper into history and the future, theology has become innocuous and irrelevant. A theology of revelation consonant with the biblical vision now needs to address this failure and propose a suitable alternative.

Where theology has failed to take up the historical theme of promise, secular ways of thinking—such as Marxism or the dubious Western dream of indefinite economic progress—have often done so instead, thereby filling a need to which religion and theology have failed appropriately to respond. People cannot live without the prospect of a future, and so utopian musings, sometimes of the most unrealistic nature, have always attracted followers. The theme of promise, even in the form of secular eschatologies, speaks to something ineradicable in the human heart. By failing to acknowledge the natural human openness to promise, our theologies have sometimes lost touch with the actual lives and dreams of real people. They have substituted an other-worldly escapism for the biblical vision that sees promise even in the most impossible of historical situations. And when the other-worldly flight from history grows stale because of its failure to connect with present reality, dreamers are tempted to the opposite extreme of milking perfect fulfillment out of a purely secular environment.

Sooner or later such exclusively human efforts themselves also use up their energy and lead to disappointment and despair. The religious wisdom of the ages insists that any efforts to fulfill our hopes all by ourselves and with purely human resources will themselves inevitably become idolatrous. Peter Hawkins writes:

> Utopia forgets . . . that we do not have it of ourselves to help ourselves; it ignores our need for grace. . . . The heresy of utopia . . . is that it forestalls the human journey toward genuine fulfillment by reaching premature conclusions. It can make an idol of its own ideals, imprisoning us in the very structure that was meant to set us free.[13]

Mystery without promise can easily lead to religious escapism. But promise without mystery eventually ends up in the deadness of visions of the future too narrow to accommodate the inexhaustibility of our longings for fulfillment.

Biblical revelation speaks to this impasse through its perception of mystery as appearing to us precisely in the mode of promise. And it understands this promise not as an escape from the present but as new possibility *for* the present. It frustrates thereby our instincts for religious escapism. An awareness of promise often miraculously blossoms even amidst the most absurd circumstances: barrenness and infertility; conditions of oppression and slavery; exile from homeland; death by crucifixion. If promise is present even in these historical extremes, then it is present everywhere.

[13]Peter S. Hawkins, *Getting Nowhere* (Cambridge: Cowley Publications, 1985) 9.

It must therefore be the enveloping and sustaining context of all of reality. To those who object that happiness is impossible in a present that always looks to the future for fulfillment, revelation proposes that the kind of happiness most pertinent to the "now" is precisely the awareness of promise in every present situation. A happiness fully proportionate to the present moment is realized in the experience of hope. Hope *is* the happiness of the present.[14] Unhappiness then is not the result of present suffering, but of the absence of hope in the midst of either present suffering or present prosperity.

In the Bible, the truly virtuous, happy, or "blessed" are precisely those who perceive a promise in every present. In the Magnificat and the Beatitudes, the poor are presented as those most likely to be open to the fulfillment of God's promise. Abraham's trust in God is what makes him a just man. On the other hand, the Israelites become miserable whenever they lose sight of the promise during their difficult desert journeying. In Luke's infancy narrative, Zechariah expresses misgivings about God's promises, while Mary's "blessedness" consists of her spontaneous trust that the promises of God to her would be fulfilled. Luke's portrait of Mary as trusting in God's promise provides a vivid paradigm of the authentic human response to revelation. To a great extent our theological understanding of faith, virtue, and happiness has lost this emphasis on the primacy of openness to the surprise of promise.[15] We have substituted a whole list of other ethical attitudes as more fundamental to Christianity than trust in God's promises. We have often idealized virtue as a stoical asceticism which in the absence of hope can become intolerably burdensome. The consistent biblical position, however, is that only trust or hope can fully energize the ethical life. Even love is impossible unless the beloved's life is seen as having possibilities for future realization. It is only hope in the other's future that renders my concern effective. The promise of new possibility for oneself and others is the condition of any truly virtuous life. Only the horizon of promise allows human caring to thrive.

The Meaning of History

We would probably not be much interested in revelation unless it offered us answers to the big questions, such as the meaning of history. Obviously, those of us who trust in revelation cannot state in clear terms what the meaning of history is. Ultimately the future is God's, and it therefore remains somewhat cloudy to us. This is why Wolfhart Pannenberg con-

[14]Moltmann, *Theology of Hope*, 26–32.

[15]To a great extent, also, traditional Mariology has failed to highlight this most important aspect of the New Testament portraits of her character.

tinually speaks of God's revelation in history as "indirect." The meaning of history can only become clear at its end. Until then, revelation is provisional. In the Resurrection of Jesus, we have an anticipatory disclosure even now of the end of history.[16] But until the end, we must be content once again to say only that what has been revealed is not complete clarity but a promise that demands trust. It is the *promissory* nature of revelation that we must accentuate here once again. As of yet, historical process does not make complete sense to us. And yet, to Christian faith a simple hope in the promise of history is sufficient to imbue it with meaning. In the perspective of faith, it is God's promise that gives meaning to history.

Hope, as we have emphasized several times before, has an apophatic dimension that cleanses it of false optimism. It seeks a wider meaning for present events than can ever be stated in our words. In the face of the apparent absurdities that take place within human events, this hope renounces easy answers and opens itself to the surprise of unanticipated fulfillment. It requires a patience that liberates it from the trivializations of human expectation and premature utopian portraits of history's meaning. Impatience for fulfillment has led time and again to the establishment of merely provisional conceptions of social order as though they were the climactic outcome of all previous history. And those who set up such regimes have often resorted to unspeakable atrocities towards any who refuse to accept the finality of their visions of the golden age.

Hope's injunction of silence in the face of mystery's promise teaches us to wait for something more. At first sight, such waiting for deeper fulfillment seems unacceptable. And if it is not tempered by the ethical imperative to concrete action, it can indeed lead to passivity. Or if it attempts to thrive in the complete absence of present sacraments of promise, it will also wither. Still, Tillich is right in affirming that we are stronger when we wait in silence than when we possess:

> The condition of man's relation to God is first of all one of not having, not seeing, not knowing, and not grasping. A religion in which that is forgotten, no matter how ecstatic or active or reasonable, replaces God by its own creation of an image of God. . . . It is not easy to endure this not having God, this waiting for God. . . . For how can God be possessed? Is God a thing that can be grasped and known among other things? Is God less than a human person? We always have to wait for a human being. Even in the most intimate communion among human beings, there is an element of not having and not knowing, and of waiting. Therefore, since God is infinitely hidden, free, and incalculable, we must wait for Him in the most absolute and radical way. He is God for

---

[16]Pannenberg, ed., *Revelation as History,* 125-58.

us just in so far as we do not possess Him. . . . We have God through not having Him.[17]

Tillich is aware that such patience is often difficult. But he goes on to say that in the final analysis it is the most fulfilling attitude we could take toward the future:

> If we wait in hope and patience, the power of that for which we wait is already effective within us. He who waits in absolute seriousness is already grasped by that for which he waits. He who waits in patience has already received the power of that for which he waits. He who waits passionately is already an active power himself, the greatest power of transformation in personal and historical life. We are stronger when we wait than when we possess.[18]

It is important to observe, in this connection, that the sense of the breaking in of a revelatory promise has generally been most lively among the poor, that is, among those who are forced to wait and who are most removed from possessing. Because of their present destitution, they can only look toward the future. The future breaks into the lives of all of us most decisively at those times in which we find that the present and the past are unsatisfying. To the poor, however, the present and the past are always inadequate to sustain them. They can only live off the future. Thus, it is those most oppressed by present circumstances who usually awaken the rest of us to revelation's promise. Not those who hold the power, but the weak and dispossessed, bring us the promise, often clothed in the imagery of a seemingly inaccessible future. It is especially those compelled to wait for this future who open our present existence to the Good News of history's promise.

For that reason it is important also that we retrieve and hold in our memory the forgotten sufferings of the past. Recent theology has emphasized that any accounts of meaning we may see in history must, for the sake of honesty and integrity, not forget the human pain that has made up so much of our history. If we fail to recall the harsh episodes of the past, we will end up with a naively narrow sketch of history's meaning instead of a full picture. In this respect, too, our cosmological emphasis encourages us to include in our memory not only the suffering of our own species, but that of others as well. Our theologies have often forgotten this suffering, but an adequate theology of revelation must make a special place for the travail of natural evolution as well as of human history.

[17]Paul Tillich, *The Shaking of the Foundations* (New York: Charles Scribner's Sons, 1948) 55.

[18]Ibid., 151.

Reasons for Our Hope

Without the promise of a future to hope in, the move into history would be unbearable. But hope is impossible unless it is based on past and present events that provide the grounds for our trusting in a future fulfillment. The biblical authors were apparently aware of this need, and so they saturated their narratives with specific reasons to trust in the promise. As the author of 1 Peter says, we must be prepared to give a "reason for the hope" which is in us (3:15). The reason for our hope is depicted in stories, songs, and celebrations of how God has *already,* time and again, acted faithfully and effectively, how God's "word" has been effective, and how God may now be acting in our lives. Revelation is not a vague and empty stab at the future, but a way of interpreting reality grounded in actual events in our lives and those of our ancestors in faith. It points narratively to actual evidence that grace and redemption are operative in history. It even reaches back to the beginnings and interprets creation itself as the pledge of God's eternal power to keep promises. Only on the basis of actual creative and salvific events can we build our hope for history's ultimate fulfillment.

It is in relation to this need for a basis of hope in previous and current events that we may also speak of God's revelation *in* history. As we read the biblical texts, we note how often major strands of the tradition emphasize God's fidelity to the promise made to Abraham. This fidelity is made concrete especially in stories of a divine covenant. In the creation story, in the promise to Noah, in Yahweh's pledge to Moses at Sinai, in Jeremiah's prospects for a new covenant written on the heart, and in accounts of the life, death, and resurrection of Jesus, God is always portrayed as promising everlasting loyalty. As we mentioned earlier, the accounts of the resurrection appearances of Jesus can themselves best be understood as promissory, in the genre of the appearances and new pledges of fidelity by Yahweh narrated in the Hebrew Scriptures.[19]

God's fidelity to the promise is the Bible's dominant theme. But in order to be assured of its substantiality, we have to look into our own history as a people formed by the promise. We will find there numerous accounts of how God's fidelity has never failed and how it constantly overcomes our own infidelity. God's revelation in history takes the form of recurrent actions possessing the qualities of graciousness, extravagance, and unexpectedness that characterized the promise first made to Abraham. If we could learn to indwell the stories about these actions and allow them to sweep our own present lives into their schematizing of historical existence, then we too could more consciously become children of the prom-

---

[19]Moltmann, *Theology of Hope,* 139–229.

ise. By our surrender to the stories of promise we would become receivers and transmitters of God's revelation.

The revelation of God is experienced in connection with significant historical events that take place in the life of the faith community. But it is the "word of God" that interprets these events and allows us to see in them a promise of future fulfillment. In other words, it is God's word that gives meaning to history. In a certain sense, revelation *is* the word of God. René Latourelle writes:

> If the Old Testament lacks a technical term for the idea of revelation, the expression "Word of Yahweh" remains a favorite expression, the most frequent and the most significant to express the divine communication. In the theophanies, the visible manifestation is always subservient to the word. What is primary here is not the fact of seeing the divinity, but the fact of hearing His word.[20]

In the story of Abraham's calling it is God's speaking and not any appearance or vision of God that stands out. In Moses' intimate encounters with Yahweh, he could not see God's face but could only hear the word of God. And in the prophets, revelation occurs much more explicitly through the word than through theophanies.[21] Word or speaking is more natural to the act of promising than is vision, though the latter can be a vehicle of hope as well. In traditional theological discussions of revelation, the theme of God's Word as disclosure has often been emphasized, but its character as promise has not.

The word of God is both promise and creation. It not only tells us what our future is, but actually brings it about. In biblical times, the spoken word carried a power and effectiveness that it appears to have lost in more recent periods. It is through the word, however, that God creates the world out of chaos or nothingness. And it is through the power of the same word of God that we may anticipate the fulfillment of history's promise out of the nothingness of every apparently hopeless situation. It is important that we understand the creation story in Genesis in terms of the theme of promise. What this account delivers to us is not simply an interesting story about the beginnings, such as we find in all other myths of origins, but even more the basis for a confidence that God's word can create new hope and promise out of every impossibility. The ability of God's word to create the world gives faith the confidence that no matter how confusing and hopeless history seems at times to be, we may nevertheless continue to look for its meaning.

[20]René Latourelle, *Theology of Revelation* (Cork: Mercier Press, Ltd., 1968) 21.

[21]Ibid.

But it is not evident to everyone that there is a creative, gracious, and promising God at work in human history. It is not clear to most intellectuals today, for example, that history has any meaning at all. As they survey the past, they see no pattern of promise, no special events that would provide a clear basis for contemporary confidence and hope. How can history be read as pregnant with promise? There are so many horrors in our past and in the present that tempt us to give up on history. How are we to speak coherently of history's promise in the face of these facts?

This question anticipates a discussion concerning the justifiability of the truth-claims of revelation that we shall undertake more explicitly in Chapter 11. But even at this point, we must at least begin our response to it. Here again we may invoke the notions of internal and external history that we spoke about earlier. Discernment of the promissory character of historical events, especially those connected with the theme of covenant, requires that we belong, in some sense at least, to the inner life of a faith community that grounds itself in those events. Experiencing a certain belongingness to this inner history allows us to abstract a certain sector of coherent events from the welter of confusion that makes up history, and to employ this abstracted series of events as a kind of key to interpret the whole. That there will be a certain relativity and historically conditioned quality to our scheme cannot be denied. But our selection of promissory events from Abraham to Jesus and the early Church allows us to focus on the totality of events in a meaningful, if not comprehensive, way.

This confession of the limits to our faith perspective seems to place in question what has traditionally been held out as the universality of Christian revelation. But here we may invoke once again the concepts of information science that we discussed in Chapter 4. There, we showed that the transmission of information requires constraints without which the information becomes lost. Any information needs to be constrained if it is to be something definite, and revelation is no exception. It must be incarnated in the consciousness of a particular people with a specific history. It must in some way be "bounded" if it is to have a definite shape.

Dwelling within a community of faith shaped by the significant events in the life of Israel and the Church orients our perception and consciousness so as to be able to read in the larger context of history a pattern of promise and fulfillment. Those "outside" the reach of this story will obviously not have the same orientation, and so they may fail to discern the significance that believers perceive in the Exodus or in Jesus' death. But those who participate in the internal history of the covenant will see the call of Abraham, the Exodus from Egypt, the lives of the prophets, Israel and Judah's release from captivity, the disciples' missionary fervor after the death of Jesus, and the establishment of the Church as all having a promissory significance that a "scientific" historian might not appreciate at all. It is through our specially charged participation in the internal memory of a tradition that we are placed in touch with the promissory interpretation of what might otherwise appear only as a series of inconsequential occurrences. A purely external, detached, or "objective" account of historical events cannot by itself conjure up the significance we ourselves may attach to these events.

Our conviction that we belong to a meaningful and redemptive history could hardly take shape outside the life of a community whose very identity is based on hope in that promise. By indwelling a faith community that sees things in terms of certain paradigmatic events (such as the call of Abraham, the promise to Moses, the Exodus), we acquire the skill of discerning meanings that would otherwise completely elude us.[22] This is not entirely different from what goes on in a scientific community. For even there, certain non-scientific factors are operative, leading scientists to focus on particular sets of data. All sorts of extraneous cultural and personal factors determine what sort of data the scientist will find interesting enough to deserve consideration. The scientist no less than the believer dwells within a community that orients inquiry in a particular direction. Such social orientation is not an obstacle to, but a condition of understanding.

Science is not just objective reporting, but also the work of an authoritative community that has determined what is interesting to look into. And this means that things that are not interesting to it will not show up in scientific theses. Human cognition, whether scientific or religious, can work only by being selective. Scientific and religious envisagements of reality are all historically, culturally, and geographically bound, and this means that they cannot encompass everything. In the world of religions, for example, we would hardly expect a Buddhist from Sri Lanka to designate the same human experiences as salvific that a Muslim or a Christian would.

Thus, it is only from within a relative and limited framework that we can provide a justification of our hope. We do not stand on any Archimedean point from which we can, in a detached way, survey the totality of history. We can only testify to the trustworthiness of the promise on the basis of what we know from the stories of God's mighty deeds told to us in the context of our faith. But any complete verification of the validity of our trust awaits the fulfillment of God's promise. We shall develop this point in Chapter 11.

[22]For a discussion of how such skills are formed see Michael Polanyi, *Personal Knowledge* (Chicago: University of Chicago Press 1958).

History and God's Humility

Throughout this book we have understood the notion of revelation not only in terms of the theme of God's promise, but also of God's humility. In our inquiry into the meaning of history, we may once again see the intimacy of these two themes. To state it somewhat abruptly, it is the humility of God that serves to open up the historical future as the arena of promise and hope. It is only by virtue of God's humble self-absenting, by the kenotic withdrawal of any overwhelming divine presence or power, that the gift of history and its openness to the mystery of the future become possible. When we experience the mysterious abyss of an indefinitely open future, this *mysterium tremendum* which is in fact the gift of a self-renouncing deity, we are tempted and usually succumb to the tendency to cauterize it with our own narrow visions of the future or of the end of history. In doing so, we simultaneously invent our own petty deities, not recognizing them as our own projections. We create idols of oppressive power and presence, calling them "God" in order to sacralize them in their narrowness. And we substitute devotion to our utopian ideals for the posture of trust in an open future. This tragedy occurs time and again in our encounter with the promising mystery that beckons us into history.

Ernst Bloch, the great philosopher of the future, sensed our need for hope in an indefinite "forward dawning." But it seemed to him that the idea of God constituted an enormous obstacle to our need for an open-ended, limitless historical future. Only in the absence of any such limitation, he thought, can our hope thrive. Similarly Friedrich Nietzsche had earlier announced the death of any God who places a limit on the "innocence of becoming." Much modern atheism appears to be a protest against the God whose overwhelming power and presence serve to hem us in and suffocate our freedom and hope. We need a totally open future, and the existence of God seems to place limits on this openness. However, to Christian faith, the God of revelation who becomes manifest in the humiliation of the cross is disclosed as one who has from the beginning emptied the divine self of any claims to the kind of power and presence that might frustrate the openness of historical existence. The self-absenting of God opens history up to us in a radical way. This kenotic mystery removes the constraints on human becoming to which serious atheism is often rightly sensitive. Revelation challenges us to transform our history by submitting ourselves to no other constraints than those to which God has submitted, namely the self-limitation that allows others to be and that therefore permits the mutual relationships that constitute the stuff of history. Such a constraint is known as love. It is not the frustration, but the very condition of genuine historical fulfillment.

God has accepted the lowly limits of human existence, especially those imposed on human beings by the exercise of oppressive political power omnipresent in history. The God of revelation is not an ally or legitimation of this powerful suffocation of our being. Rather, God is one who suffers along with us in opposition to this power and presence. The self-renunciation of God is the condition of the possibility of our own and the atheists' protests against oppressive power and presence. The self-emptying God does not stand over against us closing off the historical future to us, but in abandoning such a dictatorial posture, comes over to our side and leaves the future open to indefinite surprise. The meaning of history is its openness to this surprise. The meaning of history, in other words, is the reign of God.

10

Revelation and the Self

Does my own life have any significance? If revelation is to make any difference to *me,* I rightly expect that it will respond to this undying question. In the previous two chapters, we portrayed revelation in terms of the universe and history. Here we ask, more explicitly than before, what it may mean for us as individual persons concerned with meaning and, perhaps above all, with freedom. Such preoccupation with individuality would probably not have occurred to Abraham, Moses, and most of the prophets. Their emphasis was on the meaning of God's promises for the family, the tribe, the people, or the nation. They did not formally ask, "what does it all mean for *me?*" Concern for the distinct self in our modern sense had not yet arisen. Perhaps for that reason, even the question of subjective survival beyond death was not a major preoccupation. The Israelites understood God's promise in terms of the survival and status of a whole people. Israel's sense of divine revelation responded primordially to a communal hope in the future rather than to private aspirations.

Up until the time of Jeremiah, Israel's emphasis on collective responsibility and guilt at times obscured any clear apprehension of singular selfhood. But Hebraic thought had long contained the seeds of a sharper sense of individual existence, and it occasionally showed signs of a quest for personal significance alongside that of the entire people. Even in some of the earliest psalms, for example, we are presented with prayers that express a deep feeling of aloneness and existential anguish, and an intense preoccupation with Yahweh's significance for the suffering individual. The prophets themselves could not but lament their own personal ostracism. Out of the inevitable loneliness to which rigorous fidelity to the promises of God often leads one, there quite naturally arises the need for clarification of what it means to be a self in relation to God. In the literature of Israel, the Book of Job is perhaps the most obvious expression of this demand. This work makes it clear that revelation must respond to our personal suffering as well as to the more global demands of history and the universe.

In the Gospels, the question of human destiny is still largely framed in collective terms. God has visited the *people,* Israel. The Annunciation is understood by Luke as a climactic moment in a long series of divine promises intended not simply for an individual but for the whole people. The meaning of revelation is seldom if ever expressed in purely individualistic terms. Even when Jesus is raised up, he is still understood as the firstborn of the *many* who are destined for resurrection. Resurrection is primarily a collective event to which Jesus' personal exaltation provides access for all those devoted to the definitive coming of God's reign. Even in the writings of Paul, who relates revelation more immediately to the individual, it is inappropriate for Christians to think of their redemption in exclusively individualist terms. Fundamentally, the revelation of God is a cosmic and historical occurrence in which the individual is invited to participate. In fact, the individual's consciousness of salvation occurs only in those moments where there is a sense of *belonging* to a larger body comprised of others and the entire universe as they are collectively being brought into unity by God. There can be no purely individual salvation.

On the other hand, in the Bible the promise of deliverance is mediated to a group primarily through the consciousness and responsiveness of exceptional individuals. This is the case from Abraham through Jesus, Paul, and other personal vehicles of the biblical promise. The immediate context for the reception of revelation is the partly incommunicable consciousness of individual persons. Thus, the font of any specifically Christian revelation is, in some sense at least, Jesus' own consciousness.[1] We have previously pondered what seems to have occurred in the privacy of Jesus' own heart as he contemplated the divine promise in the light of his 'abba' experience. It is ultimately from this deeply interior and never fully communicable experience of Jesus' relation to God that Christian revelation has its specific origin.

Moreover, it is doubtful that we would be very concerned about revelation apart from its fortifying our own *personal* existence as well. Revelation must speak to our own deepest natural longing to be regarded as intrinsically valuable. That we all crave for such valuation does not need lengthy argumentation. It seems self-evident. Along with common human experience, the behavioral sciences provide much data that can only be

[1]This is the conclusion of Gabriel Moran's study, *Theology of Revelation* (New York: Herder and Herder, 1966).

explained in terms of the individual's fundamental desire to be valued. Even the pain experienced in our self-rejection stems from the fact that it is so deep in our nature to want to be valued and accepted.

Another way of putting this point is to say that we seek to live without shame. Shame is the feeling that takes us over when we begin to become aware of an aspect of our being that seems unacceptable both to us and to those in our social environment. Shame is a universal human phenomenon, and in a certain sense it is a necessary response to the facts of social existence. The most intimate aspects of our lives, in particular our sexual and religious feelings, need to be shielded from the objectifying and trivializing gaze of the public, and so shame can provide a sort of protective function.[2] But shame may also lead us into self-deception. It may push completely out of consciousness that which we take to be unacceptable in ourselves. Thus we may completely forget essential chapters of our own life stories and repress obvious facets of our personalities for the sake of wanting to fit into some social or even religious habitat. Shame holds us back therefore from full self-knowledge, freedom, and the fulfillment of our personal lives.[3]

According to the insights of depth psychology, our denial of any shameful aspect of our character may lead us to project it outside of ourselves onto those in our social surroundings where it will be interpreted as something alien to ourselves, and as deserving of our antipathy. We may easily displace the disowned portions of our self onto others whose existence then becomes interpreted as inimical to our own. The sense of shame may then have disastrous social and political consequences if we decide to harm or destroy those who have become the imagined or real carriers of our own despised features.

Hence, the specter of anything approaching a wholesome life or integral society requires that we eventually learn to live with and accept as part of our own constitution those experiences and those features of our character which at present put us to shame. Revelation, if it is to be of significance to us as persons, and through us to society, must somehow address this nearly universal situation of shame.

The Bible is clearly aware of the human condition of shame. The well-known third chapter of the book of *Genesis* tells of the embarrassment of nakedness that led the man and woman to hide from God. The aborigi-

[2]See Victor Frankl, *The Unconscious God* (New York: Simon and Schuster, 1975) 46–51.

[3]We must distinguish what we are calling shame from the healthier and essential feeling of true guilt or sinfulness, for the latter may itself be concealed beneath shame. The awareness of sin actually becomes most vivid in the experience of grace, an experience in which shame is removed and by which we are enabled to acknowledge our failings without trying to hide from them.

nal consequence of sin is shame. The historical books of the Bible, the Prophets, Job, and the Psalms make numerous allusions to the feeling of shame: "All day long my disgrace is before me, and shame has covered my face. . . ." (Ps 44:15) Indeed, shame could be said to be one of the dominant themes in the biblical description of the human condition. In Israel's experience, it was considered shameful to be barren, to be sick or menstruating, to be subject to the authority of an alien nation, and to be dying or dead. Such experiences were commonly interpreted as evidence of divine disfavor, of being cut off from healthy relationship to others and the world, as reasons to hang one's head or to seek refuge from the living God.

And shame still remains as a major facet of our own experience today, thus linking our situation very closely to that of the Bible. This aspect of our existence opens up a common context (a hermeneutical circle) allowing the Bible to speak directly to us in our concrete individual lives. Because of its dominating concern with this common human experience, it is difficult to support the notion that the Bible is too foreign for us to understand it. Shame continues to shade the lives of all of us to some extent, including those who call themselves followers of Jesus. In the case of many individuals, shame is especially crippling. It may not be an exaggeration to say that the anguish of shame is the main problem each human being has to face. And the fact of shame also still has enormous social repercussions. How many evils and horrors in our social and historical life can be accounted for simply as the result of attempts by powerful individuals to conquer or cover up their own private disgrace? By overcompensating for some unaccepted weakness in themselves, potentates and tyrants unleash their demand for significance in ways that end up destroying the lives of other people as well as their own subjects.

Erich Neumann, among others, has shown how those who think of themselves as strong and self-sufficient may at times project their inner sense of inferiority onto the more vulnerable ethnic, economic, and religious groups in their social environment. This is how he interprets the phenomenon of Nazism. Like all the rest of us, the Nazi has a "shadow side" consisting of disowned weakness, cowardice, moral ineptitude, and general vulnerability. And when this shadow side is not integrated into self-consciousness, it is easily projected outward onto others, or onto social minorities. This leads to an obsession with eliminating Jews and other groups who seem to embody those features that one hates in oneself. Ideal human development, on the other hand, consists of a conscious and often painful appropriation of this shadow side.[4]

---

[4]Erich Neumann, *Depth Psychology and a New Ethic,* trans. by Eugene Rolfe (New York: Harper Torchbooks, 1973).

One does not have to be a follower of C. G. Jung, though, to realize that we all have something like a "shadow side," a complex of feelings and character traits that we have perhaps unconsciously disowned. We usually first encounter this shameful side of ourselves as it is reflected back to us from other people who seem to carry our own despised features. The inability or refusal to acknowledge our own weaknesses leads us then to reject other people who appear to us to embody these traits. It would follow therefore that whatever propels us toward reintegrating the lost or shameful aspects of ourselves could also facilitate reconciliation between ourselves and other individuals or groups. Does revelation contribute to such integration? And if so, how might we articulate its effectiveness?

The Dynamics of Shame

The Bible commonly presents the prospect of salvation in terms of the removal of shame. The promise of God to the people of Israel is constantly one that in effect says: "I will take their shame away from them." "Look to him, and be radiant; so your faces shall never be ashamed" (Ps 34:5). According to the Scriptures, a human life shaped by the promise of divine justice is one in which we are liberated to walk boldly with our heads held high, with no need to look back, and with confident expectation of a glorious future. God's word, power, and revelation become evident in the life of the individual particularly through the experience of the removal of shame. The remarkable happiness Jesus brought to his friends and followers is due in large measure to their experience of the abolition of shame as they lived in his forgiving presence.

The feeling of shame stands in the way of any adequate satisfaction of the very wholesome human need for a sense of freedom and significance. A theology of revelation must ask, then, how it is that life in the presence of Jesus conquers the sense of shame and restores a cognizance of one's inner worth. In order to gain some insight into this remarkable possibility we need to examine the phenomenon of shame more closely than we have up to this point.

Shame can be defined only by contrasting it with the feeling that the self in its totality is significant. The need to be valued and esteemed is universal among humans.[5] We generally seek to fulfill our longing for esteem by carrying out our lives in the eyes of *another* or of *others* who regard us as significant. Sociologist Ernest Becker thinks that human existence is largely a performance we put on in order to gain a feeling of

---

[5]See, for example, Ernest Becker, *The Denial of Death* (New York: The Free Press, 1973); and Sebastian Moore, *The Inner Loneliness* (New York: Crossroad, 1982).

value in the eyes of others, or perhaps just one other.[6] And when our performance turns out to be a failure, we are beset by feelings of worthlessness. For example, a college student's relentless pursuit of academic excellence in order to become a very successful professional may, in considerable part, be an unconscious performance before his or her parents, teachers, or others who embody an important cultural ideal. In order to feel consequential in the eyes of such important persons, a successful performance seems to be absolutely necessary. Anything short of perfection may lead to a deep sense of being held in disfavor, and this can lead to various degrees of self-rejection. Such a student may at times suffer considerable torment under either the real or simply imagined expectations of esteemed others. The performance may become a terrible burden, especially when one fails to fulfill the intended ideals. A sense of shame is the inevitable result. More than one student has been tempted even to suicide in the wake of real or imagined failure.

One can think of many other ways in which shame follows from our failure to measure up to familial, societal, academic, ethical, psychological, and perhaps especially, "religious" standards of performance. Everyone's life story contains some threads of shame resulting from deficiencies of one kind or another. A particular cultural or religious community, for example, can lay out excessively rigorous criteria of personal self-worth systematically designed to make entire groups of individuals who fail the test of belonging feel ashamed and unacceptable. Africans, Hispanics, Asians, women, homosexuals, homeless, religious minorities, agnostics, doubters, uneducated, intellectuals, poor, and almost any other category of social life can, under certain conditions, be regarded as failing the appropriate tests of true membership in a society. Any society obviously requires some criteria for belonging. Hence, informational boundaries are erected and often fortified to make sure that distinctions among groups, including especially religions, remain clearly defined. Otherwise there might be no significance attached to membership. A society without at least some criteria of belonging could not be sustained for very long. But the other side of this requirement is that some individuals and groups will inevitably feel that they do not belong.[7] Then, in their interaction with the society at large, they will be reluctant to advertise the "unsocialized" com-

---

[6]Becker, 3–8 and *passim.*

[7]We may wonder whether any of us ever belong completely to a societal situation. It is the assumption and hope of religions that we do not belong in every sense to such a restrictive context. For if we do feel completely at home, then we quite likely have little taste for transcendence or for a wider and more inclusive future. For this reason, the longing for a radically new future, especially in the Biblical narratives, seems to originate in the awareness of those who feel they have been excluded and that they do not really belong (the poor, the marginalized, the untouchables).

ponents of their being. In shame they will conceal these aspects from others, and quite likely from themselves as well.

The establishment of social criteria of acceptability are closely connected to our basic human need for significance, and in a sense, they may be said to have their origin therein. The need to be esteemed requires an informational *context* within which to carry on the performance that will potentially prove one's significance in the eyes of others and oneself. And one of the functions of a culture or sub-culture is to provide this context. In Becker's helpful terminology, the life of performing before others is something like a quest for heroism. Our craving for significance requires that we experience our lives as heroic in a way that will fill us with self-esteem. We typically act out this urge within a system of heroics prefabricated by human culture.[8] And although human culture is not reducible to being a mere system of heroics designed to grade our individual performances, nevertheless it clearly includes such an ingredient.

It is always a startling discovery to have our culture or subculture's system of heroics exposed for what it is. And it would be most illuminating, Becker says, if we would each just admit our longing to be heroic, that is, our need to be held significant in terms of some system of heroics. "The urge to heroism is natural, and to admit it honest. For everyone to admit it would probably release such pent-up force as to be devastating to societies as they now are."[9] Such an admission might be the first step in our conquering of shame and placing our sense of self-worth on a less unstable foundation than we are accustomed to doing. This admission would also have repercussions for social existence as well.

Some understanding of what it is that causes us to feel shame might begin to emerge if we simply asked ourselves: "Whom am I trying to please and why am I doing so?" An honest answer usually reveals that we have been carrying out our performances in front of those whose positive regard we value deeply, but who may also be incapable of accepting or appreciating some hidden dimensions of our being. We may not even be aware of these aspects of our lives because we have been so intent on establishing our significance in terms of a clearly defined informational context. Often it is only after we have satisfied such requirements that a previously unacknowledged darkness within us begins to surface. Then we realize the limiting effect our performance has had on us. We recognize that a part of us does not belong at all to the circle of heroics in which we had become engaged. At such times, there often occurs a keen awareness of the deep loneliness of our existence. And it is often at such times that we begin to embark, perhaps for the first time, on the quest for a

[8] Becker, 82.
[9] Becker, 4.

context in which *all* aspects of our being can be included. It is in terms of such a search that we may understand the individual's quest for revelation.

Jesus and Shame

As far as the individual is concerned, the illuminative power and novelty of Jesus' person and gospel consist, at least in part, of their bringing to light the ways in which a cultural or religious system of heroics can lead us toward needless shame. Simultaneously, this same gospel's implicit announcement of God's self-emptying love enables us as individuals to move toward the "devastating release of truth" of which Becker speaks.

In Chapter 5, we observed that the novelty of Jesus' consciousness of God comes to light in an especially shocking way in his critique of the alternative proposals for holiness set forth by several religious movements prevalent at the time he lived and proclaimed the Good News. We may recall that Jesus' Jewish contemporaries were an oppressed minority within the huge Roman Empire. Given this circumstance, it would have been most difficult for many of them to build their sense of personal significance on any participation in power politics. This possibility was simply not open to them. In terms of the empire itself, they were utterly insignificant. However, in place of any opportunity to glory in Roman citizenship, their culture offered them several alternative systems of *religious* heroics as potential frameworks within which they might fulfill their need for esteem. The Essenes, for example, held forth ideals of righteousness that demanded the fulfillment of exacting ritual and other requirements as a condition for belonging. If one could fulfill these requirements, it might be possible to partake of a unique kind of heroism through which one could feel worthwhile. Likewise, the Pharisees and Sadducees set forth rigorous paths toward religious salvation that some could trod in order to discover and measure their self-worth. The problem, however, was that these religious ways involved stipulations that guaranteed the exclusion of all who were not strong enough or holy enough to adhere to them. And without any prefabricated religious systems of heroics into which they might fit their lives, many had little opportunity to discover and feel deeply the sense of significance they needed in order simply to exist as persons.

It was especially to those who felt left out and devoid of heroism that Jesus addressed the Good News and for whom he himself eventually took on the stature of hero or champion. But instead of imposing an alternative religious system of heroics on these poor, he spoke to them about a reign of God wherein one is not required to conform to *any* cultural or religious heroics as a condition of belonging to the divine fellowship. This reign of God lacks the severe informational boundaries that segregate people into those who belong and those who do not. The revelatory nature of Jesus' teaching consists of the disclosure of a loving God, abba, in whose realm we are not required to perform any heroics at all in order to feel significant.

This boundary-less situation is depicted vividly in such parables as that of the good Samaritan (Luke 10:29-37), given in response to the question: who is my neighbor? Who belongs, and who does not, to the circle of those about whose welfare I should be concerned? The answer Jesus gives frustrates the implicit boundary-drawing expected by the question. The Samaritan, who has been excluded from "right" religious communion, is the very one who proves to be unconcerned about religious boundaries.[10] Jesus' parable shows that belonging to the right religious sect is inconsequential in terms of what really matters. The point is that love of neighbor for neighbor, the praxis of the reign of God, may occur irrespective of cultic credentials. Love makes boundaries insignificant.

Likewise, the love of God for us occurs irrespective of our religious and ethical rectitude. The parable of the so-called prodigal son exhibits Jesus' revolutionary disregard for the walls that we normally build in order to guarantee our own favorable status in the eyes of God. The elder son represents our typical religious and ethical establishment of barriers between those who are "just" and those who are not. The younger son, on the other hand, stands outside the circle of those whose ethical and religious performance has apparently sealed their righteous heroism in the eyes of God. But the father's generosity overflows these boundaries and accepts the one who does not belong, even while "he was yet at a distance" (Luke 15:20). Even when standing outside the confines of right ethical and religious performance, he is fully embraced by the father's love. And the father in the parable, by adorning the lost son in the regalia of royalty, removes any need for shame. He restores the lost son's self-esteem even though it has not been earned by any performance.

In the Gospel of Matthew, the parable about the laborers who came late to the vineyard makes the same point (20:1-16). Namely, from the point of view of God's reign, our usual boundaries are nullified. Those who have labored the whole day long preferred, on the basis of their performance, to draw a clear line between themselves and the laggards. Jesus teaches that the reign of God does not work according to our own standards of heroism. Rather, it is the situation in which absolute generosity rules. And this means that performance counts for nought as far as our

---

[10]In this respect, Jesus himself is eventually shown by the Gospels to be the "good Samaritan," that is, the one who is indifferent to criteria of religious belonging. In giving this parable, he gives the key to his own self-understanding.

intrinsic worth is concerned. Children of the kingdom, those whose faith is pure, can rejoice in this subversion of our typical economic, cultural, or religious criteria of worth. The inclusive character of God's reign is revelation's response to our quest for individual significance at the same time that, in principle, it wrecks our normal social systems of heroics.

The subversion of our customary heroics is evident in Jesus' actions as well as in his words. This is especially true of his practice of table fellowship with sinners and social outcasts, a habit for which he was severely criticized by those whose religious heroism was implicitly put in question by such inclusive praxis. The simple gesture of gathering at table with tax-collectors and prostitutes overturned an entire system of heroics. In doing so, it subverted any effort to establish a human sense of belonging to God's reign on the basis of anything we have done. In the parable of the tax collector who admits his sin and the pharisee who recounts his religious heroics, it is the former and not the latter who is truly right before the God who looks not to performance as a basis for valuing humans (Luke 18:9-14).

There is unquestionably something deeply disturbing, even revolutionary, about Jesus' inclusive actions and teachings. For they entail, in principle at least, the overthrowing—the complete abolition—of any system of heroics that would lead us to experience shame about ourselves. Were we able through faith in Jesus' revelation to come to a more accepting posture toward our own shameful side, we would likewise be delivered of the compulsion to project it out onto others. And by appropriating our own darkness, we might also undercut the compulsion toward hatred and violence that occurs whenever we disown that part of ourselves.

The Humility of God and the Quest for Significance

The portrait of God as self-giving love, capable of sharing in our suffering, can have a very destabilizing effect on society and its history. We may now observe how this same image interrupts the "ordinary" life and self-consciousness of the individual. Those who have truly been conquered by this image have undergone a dramatic, inward transformation. They have found in the image of God's own self-effacement a refuge from the compulsion to persist in a life based on shame. This revelatory image of ultimate reality as self-emptying love liberates them from the anxiety of never having done quite enough to please the other. Let us look more closely at how this may be so.

So powerfully internalized are societal and religious criteria of personal worth, that often we cannot conjure up any other images of God than those modelled on significant persons before whom our societal performance is ordinarily executed. Thus, our "God" is likely to be in large measure a projection onto mystery of those very authorities before whom we experience shame whenever our performance is deficient. Hence, by its challenge to our favored images of God, especially those that present God as one whose favor we must win by our religious or ethical performances, the subversive, revelatory image of a God who participates in our own shame pulls the rug out from under a society that seeks by way of religion to legitimate its exclusivism. Simultaneously, it also undermines the individual's compulsion to "perform" in order to prove his or her significance.

In Jesus' teaching about God, our childish projection of a deity who scrutinizes our performance and keeps a record of it as a basis for accepting or rejecting us is shattered. And in Christian faith's never fully cherished identification of God with the crucified Christ, the projection is radically dismantled. Death by crucifixion was quite probably the most shameful situation imaginable for an individual at the time of Jesus. And Christian revelation, along with subsequent theological reflection, announces to us that God was fully present in this Jesus, in this most shameful of conditions. The corresponding image of God as one who embraces this depth of human shame as an aspect of the divine life amounts to nothing less than a metaphysical abolition of all the alternative ideas of God, most of which lend sanction to our exclusivist heroics. By identifying with the outcast Jesus, the man slain through the most shameful form of execution, God is disclosed as one who includes all that we normally exclude. And this means not only others that we may have rejected. It also includes our own weakness and shame.

Thus, devotion to the kenotic God can be altogether disruptive of our "normal" social arrangements, all of which have some degree of exclusivism. And the possibility of such suspension of normality helps us understand why so few societies and religions (including most forms of Christianity and Christian theology) have taken this image seriously. On the whole, they have been much more comfortable with the dictatorial image of God, an image that legitimates and preserves the status quo with all the built-in exclusivity that this implies. They have eschewed the defenseless deity revealed on the cross and have preferred instead one whose central function is to keep a record of our ethical and religious achievement. This works-oriented deity legitimates the comfortable, informational boundaries that keep us segregated from one another in our social and religious worlds, as well as from the suppressed dimensions of our own selves.

Any revolution at the social level cannot be effective in a lasting way apart from a radical change in our personal self-understanding. It is doubtful whether social transformations that might open us to the otherness within society could really become actual unless individual persons within that society simultaneously learn to accept the "shameful" otherness within themselves.[11] The individual's own partialized sense of selfhood is inseparable from and reflective of the exclusivist social situations in which we learn how not to be whole. A society that avoids the alien elements within itself teaches us as individuals to accept only those aspects of our own private existence that correspond favorably to the system of heroics that shapes our performance. For that reason, someone whose personal character becomes clearly manifest in its willingness to accept compassionately the excluded and forgotten, those whose lives are burdened with shame, will be exceptionally disruptive both to society and the individuals within that society.

By virtue of our personal avoidance of the shameful side of ourselves, we become accomplices of society's neglect of those elements that do not fit into its requirements of worth. Our self-definition in terms of a society's restrictive standards, as existentialist philosophers have taught us, is rooted in our own free decisions. We choose freely to shape our private lives by making concrete selections from the list of criteria of self-worth already available in society's inventory of values. Of course, for the most part we have not made these choices consciously, but it is important nevertheless to acknowledge our responsibility for them. Otherwise we will become paralyzed by the illusion that we can do nothing to help change things in a fundamental way.

In summary, how then does revelation confront this situation? By our faith in the God who identifies with Jesus, the God who is inseparable from the man forsaken and abandoned on the cross, we announce not only a revolution in our fundamental image of mystery, but also a drastic revision of our self-understanding. This inner revolution involves the conquering of shame and of the need for self-deception. It opens access to the otherness within ourselves even while it embraces the others without.

The Self, Freedom and the Future

When we reflect on selfhood and its deepest longings, including the need to live without shame, we are, underneath it all, thinking about the possibility of freedom. Today, we often speak of the individual's quest for

---

[11]See Erich Neumann, *Depth Psychology and a New Ethic*. At the same time, as we have been arguing, the revolution within the self cannot take place independently of a social revolution that dismantles those external informational boundaries that we internalize in such a way as to cause shame. It is not a question of the priority of self-transformation over systemic societal change. Rather, both can occur only in an ecology that involves an ongoing dynamic and reciprocity between individual and society.

meaning or the search for identity, but above all we think of personal freedom. Without freedom there is no self, no distinctive identity, no personality, no meaning, no real life. The experience of freedom is what the individual needs more than anything else in order to be a self.

And yet the actual situation of human existence is one in which the self is not really free, one in which people often do not have a clear sense of who they are, and one in which true personality is lost in various forms of enslavement to convention or mass-mindedness. Freedom is either taken away by force or it is willingly surrendered. As the Bible itself was aware, and as existentialist philosophers have recently accentuated, freedom is something we would often rather live without. To accept our freedom means to live with a certain kind of anxiety, and this requires a courage that we do not always have. Accepting freedom means accepting the future as open and full of unknown possibilities. This, as we have seen, can be quite unsettling, even while it is also enlivening. It means living without security in the present.

Hoping, on the other hand, means being open to surprise rather than living with a calculated certitude that would prevent a truly novel future from ever really happening. In the biblical vision, openness to promise coincides with true human freedom. In hope, we open ourselves to yet undreamed of possibilities, and this frees us from the settled past or a hopeless present, setting us forth to adventure and even to get lost in the indefinite mystery of the future which through revelation seeks us out. We may say then that our freedom too is a gift of revelation in that the latter opens the future to us as a realm of infinite trustworthiness. In the ambience of God's promise, a sense of personal freedom begins to blossom. Historically, freedom too is born out of promise. And by surrendering to the mystery of fidelity that faith perceives in the promised future, we are thereby given the courage to conquer the anxiety that goes with all true freedom.

But it is only when we reflect on the self-emptying love that lies in the depths of this mystery (or that constitutes the mystery itself) that we discover the true ground of human freedom. Readers familiar with the history of Western theology may recall that one of its most troublesome problems has been that of how to reconcile the fact of human freedom with the existence of God. For if God is omniscient and omnipotent, as theism teaches, then how can anything else exist autonomously? It is well known that some of the most significant atheism in the modern intellectual world has been aroused because of the apparent impossibility of reconciling the idea of God with the fact of human freedom and creativity. What can we create, says Nietzsche, if a Creator God has already done all the work for us? And in our own century, Jean-Paul Sartre has expressed the parallel conviction that God and human freedom are incompatible notions. Thus, he and many other atheists sense an antagonism between God and full human self-realization. And if no resolution seems possible, some courageous individuals will opt for human freedom and reject the idea of God as a form of enslavement. Then, in response to such a radical severance of freedom from any relation to God, theists will typically accuse the unbelievers of demonic arrogance or of an adolescent refusal of obedience to the Almighty.

It is of course undeniable that the atheistic rejection of theism is often accompanied by a certain kind of arrogance, but this does not fully account for the modern "revolt against God." Rather, as our best theologians in this century have increasingly confessed, the roots of much serious atheism can be found in long-revered ideas of God that have not yet been shaped either by the promissory aspects of revelation (especially in the case of the kind of atheism associated with Marx) or by the revelatory image of the kenotic God (especially in the case of the atheism associated with existentialism). For too long now, theology and religious education have presented us with a God who is the very contradiction of our freedom rather than being its ontological foundation. And even where there has been progress toward a more humanizing view of the absolute, alienating elements still cling to our God-images. It would seem then that the only way to purify our concepts of God of the false authoritarianism which can only sanction a suppression of our natural love of personal freedom, is to accept without reservation the image of the defenseless (but by virtue of that quality, radically powerful and creative) God who withdraws any intrusive presence and thereby opens up the future in which alone human freedom can dwell and find nourishment. The truly intimate God of revelation wishes dialogue with persons, and abhors a religious slavery that in turn invokes the accusation against the divine that we can observe, for example, in the writings of Nietzsche and Sartre. In order to guarantee the true otherness and autonomy of the dialogue partner, the humble God of revelation restricts the divine selfhood so as to give the other room for being. Thus our freedom is rooted in the loving "letting-be" which is God's creative style. It is not contradicted, but grounded and affirmed by this God's self-renunciation.

We should emphasize, though, that the self-kenosis of God is not a negative occurrence in the Godhead but a positive movement whose purpose is that of bringing about relationship to God's other. The theology of the Trinity discloses to us that God's own internal life consists essentially of relationship, and the theology of revelation shows that God wishes to extend this relationship of infinite love to the world and to the individual beings and persons who make up this world. In order to be absolutely related in love to the other, however, a willingness to share in the mode of being, including the sufferings, of that other is required. Therefore, revelation is in essence the self-gift of God to the other, a gift that holds nothing in reserve that might make that other feel slighted or resentful. And so what we have been calling the humility or self-abandonment of God is by no means intended as a model of masochism, but as a condition of God's loving relationship to the world.

In its kenosis, of course, the divine self becomes utterly vulnerable to the freedom of the other. Thus, its surrendering any control over that other will be interpreted, by those who understand genuine power to be a form of coercion, as the utter absence or even the "death" of God. But by those who have become sensitive to the fact that their freedom is a gift of God's self-absenting, a new and invigorating relationship of love and gratitude, and one of deep, mature dependency as well, may take over their lives and shape them into the new creation of which St. Paul speaks. Then they will understand that God is a powerful creator after all, but that God's kind of power or creativity is not opposed to human freedom. They will then see the reality of God as the very ground of freedom.

11

Reason and Revelation

Even though it presupposes the idea of revelation, the Bible does not make it an explicit topic of discussion. There is no self-conscious theology of revelation in the Scriptures, and the topic receives little formal attention even in the history of doctrine up until about the time of the Enlightenment. But we need not be surprised at this apparent neglect. Precisely because everything in the Bible presupposes something like what we are calling "revelation," it did not need to be an independently justified theme during most of the Christian centuries. The pervasive notion of God's word is already, in substance, equivalent to what we have been calling revelation. The tendency to establish on rational grounds the plausibility of revelation, or even to set it apart as a distinct subject of theological discussion, did not arise very explicitly until the birth of modern skepticism. The highly critical consciousness of modernity began to question the existence of God and therefore also the possibility of revelation. And so the formal concept of revelation became a major preoccupation of fundamental theology only in modern times.[1] The problem of revelation coincides (though it is not coextensive) with what might be called the "God-question." And deliberate theological defense of revelation occurs only in an age that has come to doubt the reality of any divine transcendence at all.

The modern situation of skepticism, however, has led to an overburdening of the notion of revelation in much contemporary theology. Since mystery often fails to show up palpably in ordinary experience or in the investigations of science and academic life, many Christian theologians

[1]See Otto Weber, *Foundations of Dogmatics,* Vol, I., 172.

have argued that it is the task of special divine revelation to give us our first awareness of the dimension of transcendence essential to religious experience.[2] Mystery, they imply, touches our lives only in our contact with the Christian Gospel. Evangelically inclined theologians, for example, generally insist that a special Christian revelation is our only authentic access to the sacred. Thus, for them mystagogy no longer precedes a theology of revelation but is a consequence thereof. Revelation provides the answer not only to the question about what God is like or who God is, but also to *whether* there is any divine mystery at all.

This approach, which makes the event of revelation also do the work of fundamental theology, is not always helpful for Christian faith's encounter with the modern world. First, it displays an unwarranted distrust of human nature and of the created order inasmuch as it denies our native capacity to know something of sacred mystery apart from our being specifically Christianized. Second, it undermines the possibility of our learning anything about God from an encounter with other religions. And third, it ignores the legitimate demands by sincere critics that a theology of revelation, though it cannot be derived from reason and science, must at least show itself to be consonant with them.

A theology of revelation that ignores these three objections collapses into an esotericism, releasing Christians from their obligation to participate in the realm of public discourse. Thereby, it renders their faith of little consequence to communal human life and at times also allows it to retreat into political and social irrelevance. Earlier, we supported the first objection by arguing that a theology of revelation must be prefaced with a mystagogical opening to the silent dimension of mystery from which any revelatory word or vision might come forth to us and thus be experienced as disclosed or "unconcealed." The very notion of revelation cannot make sense without some pre-apprehension of mystery.[3] And we articulated the second objection by insisting that a Christian theology of revelation must not be isolated from the revelation of mystery as it occurs in the sacramental, mystical, silent, and active features of other religions as well.

Having already addressed these first two issues, in the present chapter we shall focus on the questions raised by modern critics about the con-

[2]This is implicit, for example, in Ronald F. Thiemann's important book, cited earlier, *Revelation and Theology*. It is the approach taken by Karl Barth and many other, mostly Protestant, theologians.

[3]Wolfhart Pannenberg rightly states: "It is not true that the revelation, the self-disclosure of God, falls from heaven ready-made. Nor must it be the starting point of all knowledge of God, as if one could not otherwise know anything about him." "The Revelation of God in History," in *Theology as History*, edited by James M. Robinson and John B. Cobb, Jr. (New York, Harper & Row, 1967) 118.

sonance of rational and scientific discourse with the idea of revelation. Though it is not possible to establish that revelation is a fact on rational or scientific grounds alone, can we at least show that our trust in revelation bears the mark of truthfulness, especially in the face of so much contemporary skepticism rooted in the enlightenment and the scientific revolution? Is trust in revelation a "truthful" posture for human consciousness to assume?

Truth as Disclosure

Traditionally, truth means the *correspondence* of the mind with reality. In this sense, truth is formally an aspect of propositions or judgments. But there are other ways in which the word "truth" can be understood. One of these is the *pragmatic* model of truth, according to which the truth of something is assessed in terms of its functional value or its usefulness. Another is the *disclosure* model of truth, according to which truth is that which manifests or "unconceals" itself. For example, a great work of art or literature can have such a profound effect on us that we are immediately certain that a new depth of reality, previously unknown, has now been revealed to us. This experience of truth as disclosure is most naturally congenial to the idea of religious revelation, though in a limited sense the correspondence and pragmatic models may also be used in our assessment of its truth status.

If there is truth in religion or in revelation it would fall, primarily at least, in the category of "manifestation" or "disclosure." In this case, it would be inappropriate to employ the notion of truth as correspondence of mind and reality, since by definition the content of revelation far surpasses the adequacy of our own minds. As in art, music, and poetry, the truth of revelation is not something that we might arrive at in the same way as scientific or logical truth. It is, instead, a truth that grasps us by its disclosive power. We could hardly subject it to our verificational control, but would instead be required humbly to surrender ourselves to it in order to encounter its content.

Still, after acknowledging this obvious fact, we are nonetheless obliged to determine whether there is a positive relationship between revelation and scientifically enlightened reason which employs the correspondence notion of truth. If these are in conflict, as indeed they seem to many critics to be, then the notion of revelation will not be taken seriously by intelligent people. We must at the very least establish that revelation does not contradict science and reason. And if we could go further, and demonstrate that a trust in revelation actually *supports* the work of science and reason, we would have taken a further step in responding to the skeptics.

Skepticism approaches the question of revelation's truth-status by asking whether its content can be independently verified by science or reason. However, it seems that the very character of revelation places it beyond the scope of any procedure that might demonstrate, here and now, its congeniality to rational or scientific inquiry. For, as we have been emphasizing, revelation comes to us in the form of promise. If this is the case, then it would seem that in the present we are simply not in a position to verify it. We can do so only if and when the promise comes to fulfillment. As Ronald Thiemann argues, any justification of truth-claims about revelation "has an inevitable eschatological or prospective dimension. The justifiability of one's trust in the truthfulness of a promise is never fully confirmed (or disconfirmed) until the promiser actually fulfills (or fails to fulfill) his/her promise." And then he adds: "Until the time of fulfillment the promisee must justify trust on the basis of a judgment concerning the character of the promiser."[4] It is only in relation to what we can discern from our faith story about the character of God that we can make any defense of revelation in the face of critical objections to its validity.

How such discernment itself takes place, though, is itself not entirely clear. It would seem that once again we have to resort to something like Niebuhr's distinction between internal and external history, at least as a point of departure. It is not unreasonable to insist that an adequate discernment of God's character as "faithful to promise" could take place only from within the framework of our involvement in a faith community built up around the narration of *previous* instances of God's fidelity. To attempt a justification of revelation from a foundational standpoint completely detached from an involvement with the stories about God would be futile. Such an approach would amount to something like an attempt to prove logically or scientifically that someone has fallen in love with you even though you have never met that person or experienced his or her love. The experience of revelation occurs only in the concrete context of attending to the accounts of God's fidelity as they are told to us (or in some alternative way brought home to us) by others who have actually, according to their own testimony at least, been touched by God's fidelity in their own lives. And it is especially in our experience of the ways these others themselves sacramentally embody and live out the character of God's faithfulness in their own lives that we become convinced of the fact of a transcendent fidelity. The justification of revelation requires that we ourselves first risk involvement in a community that promotes a life of promise-keeping.[5] It seems fruitless to attempt any adequate justifica-

---

[4]Thiemann, 94.

[5]It is especially for this reason that a lifetime marriage commitment is such a powerful sacrament of God's own character as promise-keeper. Without sacraments of prom-

tion of Christian revelatory truth claims if at the same time we make only optional the requirement of belonging to a sacramental community.[6]

Nevertheless, it is not entirely without value for theology to attempt at the same time, in a subordinate and supportive manner, some kind of rational "justification" of the central claims of revelation. Such an effort is a necessary component of any sort of engagement of theology with those who live outside the context of the faith community. If we fail to make such an effort, we risk isolating Christian faith from cultural and academic life. It might even be arrogant (and "gnostic") for us to refrain altogether from such a dialogical enterprise. The recent trend of much Christian theology toward a so-called non-foundational approach runs the risk of such esotericism. Its a priori ruling out the possibility that there are shared cognitional characteristics between the members of the Christian tradition on the one hand and the kind of critical thinking that goes on outside of it on the other is defeating to both faith and thought. Only a joint faith in the possibility of finding some common ground can bring about genuine conversation between believers and non-believers, or between and among representatives of various faith traditions.

Chastened by our new awareness of the historicity, relativity, and linguistic constraints that shape all modes of human experience and consciousness, we may nonetheless attempt here to demonstrate that there already exists, even in the consciousness of skeptics and critics of revelation, a natural and ineradicable experience of the fact that reality at its core has the character of consistency and "fidelity" that emerges explicitly in the self-revelation of a promising God. It is possible to argue that without an implicit conviction that reality in its depths is faithful and not capricious, even doubt and criticism are inconceivable. The reflective discovery (by what is called transcendental inquiry) that reality is grounded in that most faithful bedrock, namely, "truth itself," is not incidental to a justification of Christian revelation's central truth-claim that reality at its core is forever faithful. While such assurance emerges in an adequate way only in the sacramentality of religious existence, it can be argued that it is also implicit even in criticism, doubting, and suspicion.

The Roots of Critical Consciousness

We live in what Paul Ricoeur calls an "age of criticism." Criticism thrives especially in our universities, but to an extent it has infiltrated popu-

---

ise, we might well wonder how we could ever be led to the belief that fidelity to promise is also the nature of ultimate reality. Such sacraments (and not necessarily in the formal sense) are our most powerful media of revelation.

[6]But see the qualifications regarding formal ecclesial membership made in Chapter 6.

lar culture as well. Criticism is the spirit of the intellectual component in our culture. Critical consciousness is at heart nothing less than a noble passion for objectivity and truth. It is suspicious of any ideas that seem to come only from authority, common sense, or faith rather than from reason, direct experience, or scientific inquiry. It is uncommonly aware of how easily the human mind is seduced by ideological biases and childish wishes. Thus, criticism seeks a method for discovering truth independently of human feelings and preferences. Understandably, then, it latches on especially to the procedures of science, for it sees there a detached, impersonal, or disinterested method of gaining access to the real. Scientific method allegedly keeps our fickle subjectivity as far out of the knowing process as possible. By suppressing personal biases, our minds seemingly have a better chance of approximating "reality" than a more passionately involved approach—such as we find in religious "faith"—would allow.

Critical consciousness maintains that our insights and judgments are meaningful and true only if they can be verified by publicly available methods. Criticism distrusts ideas and fantasies that individuals construct merely out of the privacy of their own imaginations. The methods of logical deduction and induction, and especially of scientific method, seem to possess a neutrality and public accessibility that renders them adequate standards for determining the veracity of all of our notions. The impersonal character of these cognitional methods rules out the subjective desires or involvements that might lead us away from reality. So if we can remove the subjective component from knowledge altogether, we have a better chance of getting in touch with the "real" world "out there."

This is not the place to dispute modern criticism's epistemological assumption that only impersonal cognitional methods are fully trustworthy. In fact, such a view appears excessively reductionistic in that it overlooks the ineradicably personal character of all knowing.[7] But here we shall be content only to show how even the possibility of mobilizing such critical consciousness requires beliefs or assumptions that correlate well with faith's claim that reality in its depths has the character of absolute trustworthiness. And we shall go even further, for it is not sufficient simply to argue that there is no contradiction between revelation and critical consciousness. We may also be able to show that a genuine trust in the substance of revelation actively promotes the process of critical inquiry and is in no way its enemy.

Let us recall that the goal of all critical inquiry is to put ourselves in touch with reality. The quest for the real is what motivates reason, science, and critical consciousness. That part of us which seeks reality may be called

[7]See Michael Polanyi, *Personal Knowledge*.

our "desire to know." Bernard Lonergan has argued at considerable length that human consciousness is rooted in an unrestricted desire to know. This desire is satisfied only with the truth, and so it is constantly concerned with distinguishing illusion from reality. In fact, we may best define reality as "the objective or goal of our desire to know." Put otherwise, reality (or being) is that which is intended by our unrestricted desire to know.[8]

The root of our rationality is this desire to know. And the fundamental standard of truthfulness is fidelity to the desire to know. Thus, if we are interested in being rational and honest, we must do everything we can to allow our desire to know to pursue its objective—being or truth—unimpeded. We must seek to remove all obstacles from its path. Being rational and realistic means that we must learn to cherish and nurture our desire to know. We must let this instinct for the truth assume the position of being the primary striving of our being. But we can begin to do so only by distinguishing it carefully from any other cravings that motivate us.

We do in fact have many other desires, some of which are at times in conflict with our desire to know. For example, we long for pleasure, for power, or for security. We seek to be admired, loved, and accepted. All of these desires are an essential part of our make-up, and it is always honest to acknowledge their powerful persuasion. But if they are not linked up with our more fundamental longing for truth, they can easily lead us into the world of illusion. The will to power, the need for pleasure, the longing for security, when detached from our desire to know, will inevitably lead us away from the real and toward the illusory. At times we allow our lives to be dominated by one or more of these other desires. And it is possible to live, sometimes for long periods of time, without any strong inclination to "face reality." But buried in the depths of our consciousness there is an often somewhat repressed, though nonetheless ineradicable, desire to know. If the reader is questioning this last statement, it is only because of the desire to know that underlies his or her own questioning. The simple fact that we spontaneously ask questions is evidence enough that a desire to know is present within us. How it will be released to pursue its own interest in truth, however, is another matter.

This discussion of the distinctiveness of the desire to know is applicable to our quest to know the truth-status of revelation. For it can be argued that trust in the content of revelation, an opening of ourselves to the fidelity of a promising and self-humbling God, can transform our consciousness in such a way that the desire to know is supported, strengthened, and liberated. By surrendering to and immersing itself in the images and stories of a faithful God revealed as self-emptying love, the desire

[8]Bernard Lonergan, S.J. *Insight: A Study of Human Understanding,* 3rd. ed. (New York: Philosophical Library, 1970) xviii, 4, 9, 271-347 and *passim.*

to know is set free to seek reality or truth. Indeed, a faith in revelation may release our desire to know and reinforce the spirit of criticism in a much more radical fashion than rationalism, scientism, or adherence to other ideologies would by themselves allow. If trust in revelation can thus liberate our desire to know, then we may conclude that it is a truthful posture for human consciousness to assume, and that the substance of revelation which evokes such trust may be called true also. But how is all of this so?

In the preceding chapter, while we were relating Christian revelation to the existence of the individual, we noted how the content of revelation has the capacity to erode our customary self-deception. The image of a self-humbling God who identifies with the broken, the lost, and the unaccepted has the power to remove the stigma of shame that leads us to self-deception. By restoring to us the sense of our intrinsic value, revelation frees us from the need to justify our existence and therefore from the accompanying inclination to evade the truth about ourselves. We saw that self-deception arises in the process of our seeking significance in terms of a restrictive system of heroics. But the revelatory image of a God who identifies with social outcasts, who embraces those sectors of human life that do not seem to "belong," has the existential implication of retrieving also those portions of our private selfhood that may have become lost to our explicit consciousness. The revelatory image allows us to accept without embarrassment our imperfections and our failures to fulfill all the criteria of worth that our familial, academic, social, or religious environments expect of us. As we have been maintaining from the beginning, there is an enormous heuristic power contained in the image of God's self-limitation as manifest in Jesus the Christ. This is a power to bring forgotten or marginalized elements, whether of society or of our selfhood, into a fresh and continually wider scheme of coherence. In the case of our own identities, this heuristic power consists of the fact that it encourages us to integrate into the concept of our self those aspects that we usually exclude because we fear that they render us unlovable or unacceptable. Thus our surrender in faith to the paradoxical image of God's own proximity to the lost and repressed aspects of the world (and therefore to the excluded aspects of our own selves, which are also a part of that same lost world) can bring a new intelligibility and truthfulness into the understanding of our own lives.

Still, how does this integration liberate and promote the interests of our rationality which is itself rooted in our desire to know? In response to this question we must first set forth the truism that our desire to know is fully unchained only if it can first get past the barrier of our self-deception. Self-deception is the major obstacle our desire to know has to overcome if it is to reach its objective, reality. It is self-evident that if we cannot be truthful about ourselves, we can hardly be truthful in our understanding of others and of the real world around us. We may be able to reach mathematical and scientific truth since these require less personal involvement. But in our relation to others, to ourselves, to the totality of the world and the mystery that embraces it, the fact of self-deception certainly frustrates our desire to know.

Self-deception, as we saw in the previous chapter, happens because our natural longing for significance often leads us into spurious kinds of "performances" before others whose esteem we regard as essential to our own sense of self-worth. In order to gain their positive regard for us, we are inclined at times to deny both to others and ourselves that there are aspects of our existence that simply cannot measure up to others' real or imagined demands upon us. But because we want so desperately to be heroic in their eyes, we hide our inadequacies, sometimes in great shame, in order to gain their acceptance. And in denying ourselves, we distort the rest of reality as well. Thus, truthfulness about the world requires that we begin to emerge from self-deception, at least to the imperfect degree that this is humanly possible. But this emergence from self-deception entails a critical look at those social criteria of worth that may have led us to self-deception in the first place. All of this would amount to a release of our desire to know, and thus to the liberation of the core of our rationality.

To summarize, if the desire to know is ever to be satisfied in its quest to encounter the reality of the world around us, it must first be set free from the restraints of self-deception. If our rationality is to become authentic, then we need to find a way to counter our self-deception and to relativize those criteria of worth that have led us to deny substantial portions of our being. Most of our own efforts to do so will probably prove unsuccessful. Even setting for ourselves the goal of removing self-deception can lead us to deeper self-rejection in the wake of our many failures to do so. However, the startlingly revelatory character of the image of God's identifying with the lost, at least as it relates to the repressed aspects of our selfhood, interrupts our frustrating attempts at self-justification. Because it so abruptly overturns our "normal" way of looking at ourselves in terms of our socially limited systems of heroics, it deserves the name "revelation." Indeed, revelation shows itself as interruptive not only in its judgment upon the narrowness and exclusiveness of history's social arrangements, but just as dramatically in its overturning our individual tendency to push out of consciousness the undesirable or shameful aspects of our own selves. By our indwelling the image of a God who identifies with the lost, we are—at least in principle—delivered of the need to exaggerate our performances or to lie to ourselves about our shortcomings. We are allowed to include in our self-concept those items that had previously been submerged in the sub-regions of awareness.

In other words, a trust in the revelatory disclosure of an ultimate environment of self-humbling love is capable of breaking through the contexts in which self-deception thrives. If we trusted deeply that the ultimate environment of our lives had the essential character of self-giving love, would we any longer feel the obligation to cling as tenaciously as we usually do to the more proximate, and confining, social criteria of worth in order to find the approval we legitimately seek? Trusting in such an ultimate horizon is capable of liberating us from the futile tendency to demand an impossible approval from those who make up our immediate environment. The love and care bestowed on us by others can then be seen as symbols or sacraments of an ultimate fidelity. They need not be taken as ultimate themselves and thus be overburdened with our unrealistic expectations. Likewise, revelation's gift to us of an image of ultimate fidelity delivers us from the need to "perform" to the point of self-exhaustion for finite others in order to gain their approval.

Sincere trust in the God whom revelation understands as absolute self-gift and unconditional outpouring of love could not help but promote the innate interests of our desire to know. By satisfying our deep and ineradicable longing for approval from a font of infinite love, this trust would deliver us of the need for self-deception before finite others. Hence, faith in revelation could be called truthful in the fundamental sense of liberating the core of our rationality.

The fundamental criterion of truth, following Lonergan's thought, is fidelity to one's desire to know. The conclusion to which the above argument leads is that any transformation in our self-understanding that eliminates the need to deceive ourselves also supports the interests of our desire to know. By definition, our desire to know is intolerant of deceptions and illusions. And so any mode of existence or consciousness that assists us toward truthfulness about ourselves must be functioning in the interests of that desire and of the truth it seeks. Revelatory knowledge provides the basis for such truthfulness. Therefore, trust in revelation could legitimately be called truthful.

This is not a justification of revelation in the scientific or foundational sense of independently verifying the "object" of faith. Such a detached mode of justification would be inappropriate for a subject matter that arouses the highly involved stance of religious devotion. Rather, it is an *indirect* justification of revelation's truth-value inasmuch as it allows the believer to examine the effect of faith on the desire to know, which is the source of all critical consciousness. Without first being caught up in the circle of faith in revelation, we would not be in a position to undertake the above exercise of justification. We cannot decide the question of revelation's truth-value from a completely neutral perspective. However, this does not mean that we have to fall back into a purely fideist posture whereby we would simply refuse to be interested in the question of faith's compatibility with reason. Only after the fact of having been grasped by the substance of revelation are we in a position to inquire into its truth status. But insofar as we find that our faith in revelation supports the desire to know we may conclude also that it satisfies what we have called the fundamental rational criterion of truth.

In light of the above argument, the kenotic image of God may be said to be especially truthful. For by its power to remove fear of retribution and anxiety about looking into ourselves, it arouses in us an unprecedented trust that counters our normal tendency to self-deception. It shatters every image of God that rests upon tyrannical notions of power or omnipotence which typically suppress our desire to know. Our ordinary, pre-revelational images of God are often little more than expressions and legitimations of those powers before whom we act out our heroic performances in an effort to gain the significance for which we crave. These are the images of a god that supports our self-deception and thus frustrates our desire to know.

Because our sense of God is usually overlaid with some aspect of those powers that we attempt to please in our ordinary heroics, we may acknowledge that there is a good deal of illusion in concrete theistic religion. In the interest of truth, we must open the illusory aspects of our God-consciousness to the purification of critical consciousness. Once we do so, Christian faith can begin to make some sense of the phenomenon of modern atheism. The most powerful forms of this atheism appear to have grown up in opposition to the kind of theism that has suppressed the kenotic God of revelation. As such, they are themselves perhaps expressive of a longing for a way out of the self-deception sacralized by God-images that merely reflect or magnify our limiting systems of heroics.

The "Odd" Logic of Promise

We have been looking into the question of the rational justifiability of faith's trusting in God's self-humbling love. But the other aspect of revelation that we have been highlighting throughout this book is its promissory character. In the biblical experience of revelation, mystery has the character of promise. Ontologically speaking, revelation is the self-gift of God, but historically and linguistically speaking, this gift takes the shape of a promissory utterance. Apparently, within our finite temporal context, the infinite mystery we call God can be received only indirectly as promise, rather than directly as knowledge.[9] Finite reality, in any case, could not assimilate the fullness of infinity in any single receptive mo-

[9]See Ronald Thiemann, 151–56.

210 Reason and Revelation

ment. Hence, God's revelatory self-gift could hardly become fully manifest in any particular present. In its superabundance it conceals itself, according to the nature of promise and hope, in the mysterious and inexhaustible realm of the future.

For this reason, Wolfhart Pannenberg rightly refers to revelation as the "arrival of the future."[10] The divine futurity reveals itself to us in our present history only in the mode of promise. The God of the Bible constantly "goes before" us and speaks to us out of an always new future. In order to receive this revelation, the addressees of promise must in turn assume a posture of radical openness to the future. This is the posture known as *hope*.

Our question then is whether such hope can in any sense be taken as a realistic attitude, one that could withstand the objections raised by those who consider revelation to be a groundless notion. To return to an issue raised earlier, how can we be certain that such so-called "hope" is anything more than wishful thinking? Can we distinguish the images of hope that biblical religion suggests to us, from the frothy fantasies that arise all too easily out of what Freud called the "pleasure principle?" How can we plausibly argue for the truth of revelation in the face of modern, and now post-modern, types of criticism? How can we say that trust in a divine promise is reasonable? Specifically, what response can theology make to critical consciousness as the latter voices its suspicion concerning our hope for resurrection and the constant biblical aspirations for new life?

There is a kind of logic operative in promise and hope that seems to resist critical consciousness as we usually understand it. Influenced by scientific method as it is, criticism takes its bearing from what seems plausible and expected on the basis of common sense, reason, and empirical investigation. If something lies in principle outside the domain of predictability, in the open future or in the arena of what Ernst Bloch calls the Not-Yet-Conscious,[11] it will likely be ignored. If there is any aspect of reality which by definition is surprising, extravagant, and purely gracious, the three notes we have observed in revelation, it would understandably elude the net of critical thinking. Criticism, after all, is generally conditioned to embrace only those ideas for which there are already analogies and precedents accessible to "objective" scientific verification. Scientific reason operates only by generalizing from large numbers of similar occurrences. If no analogies from past or present experience are available by which

[10]According to Pannenberg it is especially in Jesus' resurrection that we are met by our ultimate future. "By contemplating Jesus' resurrection, we perceive our own ultimate future." And he adds: "The incomprehensibility of God precisely in his revelation, means that for the Christian the future is still open and full of possibilities." *Faith and Reality,* 58–59.

[11]Ernst Bloch, *The Principle of Hope,* Vol. I, 114–78.

to interpret new data, critical consciousness is often inclined to discard, or completely overlook, any true novelty. As the history of science shows, it is often only reluctantly that one scientific generation abandons its pet paradigms for interpreting the world and opens itself to the revision that would render coherent the influx of new data. Though in theory scientific method is always open to revision, in practice this transformation does not take place easily.

Faith in revelation, however, is much more concerned than science is with the influx of the *Novum,* the New. If a completely novel, unpredictable, or unique occurrence took place, such an event would not be suitable subject matter for the kinds of generalization that scientific method or critical consciousness seeks. Only large numbers of similarly repeated happenings can provide the basis for an acceptable scientific law or theory. Hence, a conceivably unique reality or utterly surprising occurrence would fall outside the sweep of our typical critical inquiry. Scientific method is ill-equipped for dealing with the radically incalculable. And since biblical revelation always has the character of unpredictability, in that its arrival transcends our anticipations, its justification would strain critical thinking beyond its usual limits. Furthermore, revelation is usually experienced in the context of circumstances that seem to our normal and critical consciousness to be impossible, devoid of all promise. The experience of God's promises typically occurs, according to the biblical stories, in moments that would ordinarily generate despair. And so to those for whom scientific criticism is the only legitimate norm of truth, revelation will inevitably appear unrealistic. Its signals will not be picked up by a receiver wired only to accommodate that for which there are clear precedents. As we have emphasized, there is an element of informational surprise resident in revelation's promise. And it is experienced most decisively in those situations that we would normally characterize as hopeless since there appears to be no precedent, outside the stories of God's marvelous deeds of deliverance, on the basis of which one could predict deliverance. The real challenge of revelation to normal human reason consists of its defiance of the outcomes we would customarily expect to occur.

We must emphasize once again that what we are calling critical consciousness is shaped primarily by what it can clearly determine to have happened in the past. Scientific method relies on present data deposited by the past. For example, evolutionary theory needs the present fossil record, left over by past cosmic happenings, in order to arrive at appropriate judgments about the emergence of the various forms of life. The situation is quite different, though, when it comes to revelation. Here, the data from which the hypothesis of revelation is construed by faith have their proper origin in the domain of the promised future. It is from out of the future that the divine reality discloses itself. And since the future lies beyond what can be made empirically available, there is a sense in which we must conclude that it is impossible for us to justify revelation according to critical methods. If we had complete access to or possession of revelation, moreover, it would no longer hold out any promise to us. Hope would fade in the face of the total presence of what had been concealed but now has become perfectly clear. Life would lose its depth and there would be no more future to look forward to.[12]

We must, of course, agree with criticism's demand that we remain faithful to our desire to know and its requirement that we avoid all illusions. It would therefore be inappropriate for us to hope in something we suspect may not be grounded in reality. To this end, we must accept criticism's demand that we test our private aspirations by bringing them before the tribunal of a community shaped by a common interest. Our ideas must in some sense be publicly acceptable, as modern scientific criticism necessitates. This does not mean that the content of revelation needs to pass the specific tests devised by academically critical methods which generally accept only those ideas that pass muster with scientists. Such methods of testing ideas are certainly pertinent to a limited range of data. But when it comes to revelation's setting forth of the ways in which God acts to bring about the seemingly impossible, such methods would be strained beyond their proper capacity. To admit that our ideas require public verification does not mean that the scientific forum, or any academic context for that matter, is the best one in which to test the truth of revelation's substance. An ecclesial community would be more appropriate.

However, if we suggest instead that the ecclesial community is the only one qualified to pass such judgment, we are inevitably going to be presented with the charge that group bias or some such collective illusions can seize this particular public and blind it to the truth, perhaps even more readily than private caprice can cloud the consciousness of the individual. At least the scientific community employs detached and objective standards that undermine our efforts to take refuge in the slanted judgments of shared faith. Can theology point to anything comparably rigorous and objective as a context for testing the truth of faith's trust in the self-emptying mystery of God and the promises given to us in revelation?

This question seems to presuppose that science and criticism are themselves activities of the mind completely unconnected to a deep personal or communal trust. Such an assumption, however, is no longer acceptable in many contemporary philosophical discussions of science and reason. All kinds of knowing, Michael Polanyi, among others, has demonstrated,

---

[12]It is questionable, therefore, whether even an eschatological fulfillment for finite beings could be one in which the divine presence completely obliterates the futurity (mystery) of God.

have a "fiduciary" aspect, that is, a coefficient of personal faith or trust. Moreover, this personal faith is not unrelated to the community in which the individual's trust is nurtured. The entire project of scientific inquiry and criticism, for example, is not self-justifying, but is instead built up out of an undeniable trust.[13]

The fact that the enterprise of science is grounded in trust is brought home to us if we reflect upon the limit-questions that scientists occasionally find themselves spontaneously asking. These limit-questions, to which we referred in Chapter 3 in our attempt to show the place of mystery in relation to academic disciplines, include the following: Why should I be scientific at all? Why should I seek truth through science? Why should I remain faithful to the scientific method? Why not distort the data in order to promote an ingenious hypothesis and thus ignite my career? Why do I have this insatiable desire to know the truth and the need to avoid illusions? Why should I be faithful to the spirit of criticism when it would be so much easier to be less rigorous in my methods? Why should I sacrifice my own interests for the sake of the progress of truth? One could think of many other similar examples of limit-questions. What is notable about them is that they lead us to acknowledge that scientific work is energized throughout by a *faith or trust that truth is worth pursuing,* by a faith that it is worthwhile joining with others in an effort to uncover the facts about the world, and by the belief that it is wrong to deviate from a method that brings us to the truth. These are assumptions that we cannot have arrived at by way of science itself since they are necessary to get science off the ground in the first place. Rather, they are a priori assumptions akin to faith. We have *believed* in their self-evident truth as a condition for doing science, and we have entrusted or committed ourselves to them as we follow the spirit of criticism.

This commitment is of a deeply personal nature. We have risked something of ourselves in our allowing these beliefs (such as the belief that the pursuit of truth is worthwhile) to grasp hold of our lives. And without taking this "risk of faith," we would be utterly unable to dedicate ourselves to the scientific pursuit of truth. It is clear then that science and its offspring, critical consciousness, are not as innocent of trusting or believing as skeptics often think. Such trusting is obviously not identical with the faith that believers may have in revelation, but the presence of the unverifiable assumption that reality is intelligible and that truth is worth pursuing is highly consistent with and supported by revelation's claim that reality is at heart faithful, that God is truthful, and that the appropriate life of human persons is one of bringing our lives into conformity with the fidelity made manifest in revelation's promise.

[13]Polanyi, *Personal Knowledge.*

Our thesis then is that revelation as we have understood its substance throughout this book, though it is not verifiable by science, is fully supportive and nurturing of the faith assumptions that undergird reason and science. In the context of a university, for example, revelational knowledge does not conflict with but can properly be understood as assisting the autonomous search for truth undertaken by the various disciplines. We may recall (as stated in Chapter 3) how our limit-questions place all the disciplines in question and demand a justification that lies outside the boundaries of the disciplines themselves. Why bother with science? Why be concerned about the ethical life? Why seek beauty? What started out in this chapter as a question concerning the rational and scientific justifiability of revelation has at this point turned into a question about the justifiability of the enormous amount of trust that underlies the scientific, critical enterprise itself. That there is such trust beneath reason and science now seems undeniable. And this trust is no less in need of justification than is faith in the word of promise that we find at the heart of revelation.

It seems therefore that critical consciousness itself cannot find a point outside of trust, or devoid of trust, whereby it could settle the issue of the justifiability of the trust that motivates science and reason. Trust is a condition that makes critical consciousness possible in the first place, and it would also be a factor in all critical efforts we might undertake to justify any beliefs. The validity of trust in truth, goodness, and beauty, therefore, is incapable of being scientifically grounded, for it would have to be already present in every such grounding activity. Hence, faith in revelation's word about the ultimately trustworthy character of reality is no less rational than is the trust in truth, goodness, and beauty that makes all academic pursuits possible. It is a companion to, and not an opponent of, the trust without which there simply can be no rational and scientific inquiry. Hence, it seems inappropriate for criticism to demand a scientific justification of faith in revelation when it cannot do the same with respect to the trust in which it is itself rooted. In the case of both faith and criticism, human consciousness seems to be related at some level to what we can only call trustworthiness or—in terms of revelation—fidelity.

We started out by asking whether the claims of revelation are in conflict with the desire to know. The fundamental test of the truthfulness of any content of consciousness is whether our holding onto it promotes the interests of our desire to know. We have argued that faith in the promise of divine fidelity given through revelation liberates our desire to know from the self-deception that stands between it and reality. By allowing our lives to be informed by trust in God's fidelity, our desire to know can flow more freely toward its objective than could a life in which such trust is absent. Therefore, reason, science, and criticism are not in conflict with, but are actually supported by, the trust evoked by the promises of revelation.

Conclusion

Jesus spoke about, and he prayed in complete confidence to, the promising mystery that encompasses the world. He experienced this mystery as most intimately personal, and so he addressed it as *abba*. Christians are instructed to relate to this same mystery while simultaneously thinking of the man Jesus, his life, his parables about God's reign, his healing compassion, his words of encouragement, his fidelity, his death and resurrection to new life. For it is especially through these that the mystery of the world is revealed to faith.

Yet the God that Christian faith associates with Jesus is the same one who spoke in promise to Abraham, Moses, and the prophets. It is the same God who pledged fidelity to Israel at Sinai and later to David and his progeny. This God is revealed as one who makes and keeps promises, as one who is always coming and the fullness of whose presence always eludes us. It is the God who in everlasting self-emptying love gives away the divine self unreservedly to the world. This God is revealed as one who in the most intimate self-withdrawing humility opens up the future in which God's other, the world, can have its own being.

Revelation is God's word of promise. The world's reception of the promise and love of God requires that at all levels of its evolution it undergo creative transformation. If it is truly responsive to God's self-revelation, it cannot simply remain the same. It has to be a somewhat restless world since the promise on which it is founded, and which continually beckons it forward, has not yet attained its fulfillment.

The world has the enduring character of not-yet-being. Our awareness of the "not-yet" at the level of human history leads us to invest our hopes in dreams of ideal social orders. But because our sketches of a future for humanity and the cosmos are usually too small and insufficiently inclusive, God's own vision of the future bursts them asunder and invites us continually to widen our sense of what is possible. God's revelatory promise invites us to imagine beyond narrowness, evil, and injustice, beyond poverty and oppression, and beyond even death.

The reception of revelation, then, is not a quietistic or passive acknowledgement of what God has done in the past moments of our history. Its reception entails our present transformation in order to allow God's future to penetrate more fully and deeply into our world. Revelation does not require our transformation as a priori condition of its coming. For it is always gratuitous, surprising, and extravagant. But it does imply, as a consequence of these characteristics, that we surrender in obedience to its demand for inclusiveness and breadth. In this sense, it judges us. It challenges our narrowness—for the purpose of uplifting and ennobling us. And not only us human beings, but the entirety of the cosmos in which we are rooted and to which we are inextricably connected.

Revelation, we have said repeatedly, is the arrival of the future. We open ourselves to its coming by way of hope, and we are accounted blessed if we trust that the Lord's promises to us will be fulfilled (see Luke 1:45). Moved by this hope, we become servants of God's vision for history and the entire creation. Our service takes the form of working, praying, and playing in a spirit of ever-widening inclusiveness. This posture seeks through the praxis of faith to overcome seemingly insurmountable barriers between races, sexes, classes, rich and poor, oppressors and oppressed, humans and the natural world, Christian faith and other religions. Without wiping out differences, it seeks the beauty of a harmony of contrasts. It does not despair when this harmony fails to materialize. Instead, it renews its hope that even our failures will not be an obstacle to the opening up of unprecedented possibilities.

Faith attaches itself to the promise of revelation through the attitude of hope. This hope, in turn, has sacramental, mystical, silent, and active aspects. It is sacramental in the sense that it is not abstract but seeks concrete ways in which the future can become present and tangible. In other words, hope discerns the humble incarnation of an absolute and infinite future hidden in the medium of finite realities, in healthy human communities, and in an integral environment. At the same time, hope looks mystically beyond the sheer finitude of all our sacraments of the future. It perceives the reality of a transcendent Promiser beyond the finitude of specific promises. Hope eventually allows itself to be consumed completely by the desire for union with the self-revealing Promiser. In order to arrive at this status, however, it passes through the asceticism of silence. It learns to wait, sometimes in darkness and emptiness, for the fullness of the ripening promise to reveal itself. Without silent waiting, hope turns into infatuation with visions of the future that are too small. Or else it tries by force to bring the fullness of the largely unavailable future into the confines of a restrictive present. Finally, if hope is to open us fully to the promise of the future, it also becomes active in the affairs of the world and human history. It yields to a praxis that actively transforms the present so that it will correspond more closely to the breadth and inclusiveness of God's vision, a vision in which nothing or no one is finally left out of the picture. It prays with patience, but also without passivity: "We hope to enjoy forever the vision of Your Glory."

It is useful to keep these several modulations of hope in mind in order to avoid a one-sided emphasis on the notion of revelation as symbolic communication. For revelation also occurs in the mystical, active, and silent modes of religious life and hope. In recent years sacramentally oriented theology, stimulated by theologies of symbol, may have caused us to overlook the disclosive capacity of the non-sacramental aspects of religion. Thus, in this book we have proposed that revelation comes not only through sacraments of hope, although this is the indispensable entry point of God's promise; it also enters into our awareness by way of the mystical, silent, and active sides of hope.

The mystical aspect reveals the infinite *depth* of mystery beyond the finite symbol. The apophatic return to silence, whereby we distance ourselves from the inevitable narrowness of particular symbols, allows mystery's *breadth* to become more prominent. And finally, the praxis of the prophetic message also becomes a vehicle of revelation. Only through the doing of justice can we be said to know the God of Moses, the prophets, and Jesus. This does not mean that the doing of justice is a condition of God's revelatory self-gift. There are no such conditions. But what it does mean is that the manifestation of God's being in our world cannot occur apart from situations of social and economic inclusiveness. The glory of God is obscured and remains unrevealed to the extent that poverty, division, and oppression still reign. Where justice, unity, and love prevail, there God is revealed.

Index